SOMEBODY Loves ME

SOMEBODY Loves ME

2nd Edition

CITI OF BOOKS

Lilyana M. Srnoguy

With technical support from

Pamela Aklestad Bussi

CITIOFBOOKS, INC.
3736 Eubank NE Suite A1
Albuquerque, NM 87111-3579
www.citiofbooks.com
Hotline: 1 (877) 389-2759
Fax: 1 (505) 930-7244

Ordering Information:
Quantity sales. Special discounts are available on quantity purchases by corporations, associations, and others. For details, contact the publisher at the address above.

Printed in the United States of America.
ISBN-13:   Paperback   979-8-89391-067-4
                eBook   979-8-89391-068-1

Library of Congress Control Number: 2024908124

Contents

CHAPTER 1
SOMEONE LOVES ME

Patricia was losing her mind.

Driving through mid-day traffic was demanding and tedious as ever. Patricia would usually entertain her rambling mind with something nice that happened lately, the book she just read, or last Sunday's theater performance of - She frowned. This was not only the worst traffic ever, but also some pre-Armageddonish preview of the end of civilization or just the end of her sanity! Her galloping frustration rose with the realization that she is hostage in the middle of this annoying pace, along with the unbelievable rudeness of the other drivers around her. To make things worse, the heat mounted to an frustrating ninety-four-degrees, which felt more like 104 or worse. The car's air conditioner, working to its maximum, was not giving any desired relieve, and now she felt a tiny droplets of sweat rolling down her spine and under her arms. Patricia glanced into the review mirror. *Darn, I am not very pretty, nor exactly young any more – do I have, on top of that, to perspire like a construction worker?* The red light vengefully refused to turn green. Patricia glanced at her image again, and in desperate attempt to fix at least something, she ran fingers through her hair. It was damp, and now it looked worse than before. Several horns pierced straight through her ears and down to her toes, which make her press the gas pedal a little too fast and hard. The car lurched forward and almost smashed into the car in front of her, whose driver suddenly braked as did all the others down the line. Her nerves were shattered.

If I'm not careful I'll be responsible for some stupidity in the middle of this madness, and even the police will not be able to reach us. She rolled her eyes in destitute. *All of us will still be right here tomorrow morning.* That reminded her why she had to battle this hideous traffic. *Darn! I'll be late again to pick up my niece and nephew.*

Her watch showed that school would be out in five minutes, but at this pace she could not get there for at least a quarter of an hour. Miss Hutchinson, the children's teacher, will be mad as hell, as always. "Miss Patricia!" She will say in that sharp cold voice of hers, "Responsibility, Miss Patricia, is something all of us should learn sooner or later. Think about it! It is never too late to adopt good manners!" *She detests me for some unknown reason, but then, I am positive that the rest of the world does not enchants her more.*

It took the longest twenty minutes of her life to reach Summer Sunshine Private School. As Patricia expected, the school's parking lot was empty when she, in the manner of race driver velocity, surged through the main gate. The moment she hit the brakes her eyes caught Miss Hutchinson's stone chiseled face. The sharp screech of the brakes raised the teacher's eyebrows and her facial expression changed from icy indignation to disgust and contempt. *"Oh my! She is convinced that I am a complete idiot!"* Patricia mattered under her breath.

"Good afternoon, Miss Hutchinson!" She began cheerfully, getting out of her car. The idea was to prevent the teacher scolding her in front of the children. Knowing that her chances were slim to nothing, she continued in the same manner, "The traffic is awful this time of day as you very well know, Miss Hutchinson, I hope I didn't inconvenience you too much. Come on Timmy! Come on Puppet! We are in a big hurry! Get in the car as fast as you can, or we'll be late to Timmy's violin lesson!" While talking she shoved the children into the car, keeping her eyes off that iceberg poised on the top steps in front of the school door. She almost managed to slide behind the car's steering wheel, when the low, but piercing voice froze her in place.

"Miss Patricia! Do you remember how many times this month you've been late? No? I'll remind you! Four including today! This time

I will call your sister. She will have to make some other arrangement for her children. I have more important things to do than to be waiting here for you. Frankly, I don't think you are competent enough to be trusted with children. In addition, Miss Patricia, the children's names are Timothy and Samantha. They are not babies any more, and I would prefer it if you wouldn't treat them as such. Give my regards to your brother-in-low." Miss Hutchinson abruptly turned on her heals and marched decidedly toward the big school door.

Patricia politely stood by her car not concentrating on the older woman's so familiar sermon. *She looked at me as if I was some undeveloped worm. I don't know why I let her do this to me? I am not a child! Half of the city was late today – half of the city is late every day.* Miss Hutchinson graced Patrisha with one last cold disgusted look before disappearing behind dark heavy door. Patricia slid in the car with more dignity than she had left and thrust herself back into the stream of traffic with determination to go with the flow and if she is late again, so be it! *Who is she to tell me what to call my niece and nephew? Patricia turned toward the kids.*

Patricia turned toward the kids. "Hey Timmy, would you like me to call you Timothy? Do you think you are too big to be called Timmy?"

"No, Aunt Patty! You can call me Timmy... but not Miss. Hutchinson! I would never let *her* call me Timmy!" He was peeking between the two front seats, smiling widely at his aunt. "And, I am sure that Puppet don't like to be called Samantha, do you?" He turned to his sister who was playing with a little dog Beany Baby, which was waiting for her on the back seat of her aunt's car. Miss Hutchinson banned her beloved toy on the first day of school, and Puppet knew that if she brought it again it would end up in the garbage can.

"I like Puppet! I do! I don't like Miss Hutchinson, but Mommy said we have to deal with all sorts of people. She said we'll like some and not so much others. I think that Miss Hutchinson is the only person I dislike. I do! "Puppet was sliding the dog down Timmy's violin case.

I will be late for Timmy's lesson. Patricia was in haste again, but fortunately, Mrs. Burton was nothing like Miss. Hutchinson. *She won't even notice that we are late. I think the kids like her much more than their schoolteacher, just as I do.*

While Timmy had his violin lesson Patricia and Puppet picked up kids' father's shirts from the dry cleaners and then dashed through the grocery store. Dinner will probably be late too, but she was not upset any more. Patricia's natural good disposition took over and she started to look at today's events with amusement. Rushing through the store with a little chatty girl raised her spirits, and she was ready to take even Miss Hutchinson on the light side, not that Miss Hutchinson will accept being taken in any other way but death serious. Patricia smiled, answering Puppet's numerous questions, thinking not only what she needed for dinner, but also more what would be suitable for tomorrow evening. Her sister and brother-in-low, Timmy and Puppet's parents, entertained quite often and usually that was not her concern. Flora, the family's housekeeper, took great pride in her culinary creations; and Patricia's engagement, only from time to time if more guests were invited, was as a kitchen help. An accidental fall, last month when Flora attempted to dust kitchen cabinets, put her in the hospital. The chair she stood upon gave under her and poor Flora fractured her hip. The sixty-three-yea- old woman was recuperating amazingly fast, but the doctor grounded her for at least four months before she could get a green light to take over her normal duties. Naturally, it was completely expected, and nobody bothered to ask Patricia what she thought about it before she found herself taking over housekeeping duties just until things were back on track.

Patricia moved into her relative's house, deep into her new responsibilities before she realized what hit her. Annoyance by her sister's presumptions passed as fast as it came and she was happy to help. Patricia loved her older sister Francesca without any reservations. She was aware of Francesca's faults, but she could forgive her anything. Francesca was the most adorable child and the most beautiful girl in their neighborhood. Actually, she was the most beautiful girl in their little town of Church Hill, and everybody thought Francesca was going places in her life. As a child, Patricia did not understand what "going places" meant exactly. In her mind, she saw her sister as a famous movie star or model with the world under her feet. She was sure Francesca would marry a prince and rule the world with the graciousness of real royalty. From Church Hill's viewpoint, that is exactly what happened – Francesca married Timothy Baths – the only son of the richest and most powerful man in Church Hill.

Although they lived in the same city all their lives, went to the same and only high school, Francesca and Timothy didn't belong to the same social circle because of their parents' different backgrounds. The Baths were one of the oldest families in the area, rich and respected. On the other hand, the Johansson family was a newcomer, and there was no one to recommend them respectability-wise. Mr. Johansson bought the big farmhouse on the edge of town, although he never meant to farm or to take any other job. In spite of that, they lived quite well, and that became one of the biggest puzzles in town. Where Mr. Johansson's money came from was a big question of not small importance for the inhabitants of the town where everybody knew everything about one another. All the clever little tricks to extract that information from the members of Johansson family failed a long time ago and many speculations since then entertained people and kept this quandary on the level of a mystery. After all attempts to find out the source of his money failed, wild stories started to circulate, from the simple possibility of an inheritance to dark suspicions of embezzlement, extortion and even murder.

Mr. Johansson did not mingle with the people of Church Hill, and no one remembered him ever exchanging any friendly or causal words with anybody. People did not like him, considering him harsh and cold. But, everybody liked and admired his wife Lucie. She transformed an ordinary farm into a beautiful and exotic garden. Lucie used to spend whole days tending to variety of plants and the most unusual flowers, happy and content as a bird with the quiet and invaluable help from farmhand Freddy. Very soon after their arrival, some thirty years ago, even the people who were not interested in gardening started to seek her advice about plants, treatments, asking for seedlings, and bringing her some of theirs. Lucie was nice and very beautiful. Her gentile nature was completely opposite from her husband's, and that popped as another big puzzle. What was the attraction between them? Why he married her nobody questioned, but why would such a beautiful and nice woman want that brute who was not even slightly handsome. Maybe there was another dark secret? Maybe it was a blackmail, under the threat of hurting her loved ones, or maybe her family was so poor that he bought her as a slave bride, or he raped her, after which her disgusted family forced her to marry the assaulter, as it was all her faul. Whatever it was they did not want to believe that poor woman married him of her own free will.

The girls grew up in that odd environment. They, of course, heard most of the stories but heeded them differently. Patricia was mostly amused, not taking them seriously because her optimistic nature accepted it as affection toward her mother, while Francesca on the other hand hated it. Sometimes she was devastated after hearing some harsh remark about her father and would cry in Patricia's arms for a long time, consoling herself that one day she will show them all. She would do something so great that everybody would envy her. She would become an Oscar-winning star, or marry the most handsome, no, even better - the one of, no, absolutely *the* richest man in the world. Then she will come back and make them pay, make them suffer, make them take every single word back; and then she will destroy everything, every single house and street, then chase them all away. This evil town will produce only weeds, and nobody will want to live here. Patricia would enjoy these little sobbing outbursts as an interesting way to cope with a not-so-easy situation.

In reality, Mr. Johansson was just an extremely private man. He was not harsh or cold. Having a hard time showing his feelings even to his own family, he would never allow anyone to pry into his life. His wife and daughters could sense his affection because they loved him as much as he loved them. He adored his beautiful wife and she definitely loved him back with equal strength and devotion. Francesca, their firstborn became the center of his life. He loved her as a rare and beautiful piece of artwork, and he could never tire watching her or listening her ramblings. They used to spend endless hours together reading, discussing things, and laughing.

These were the only times Patricia saw her father laugh or relax. She was born three years after her sister and her father was not too happy about that. The pregnancy was hard on Lucie and during that time he almost lost his sanity just by the thought that he could lose her. He knew he would not be able to live without his wife. Patricia was born with some difficulties. Fortunately, Lucie recovered in full shortly afterwards. Nevertheless, Mr. Johansson never warmed up to Patricia as a baby and while she was growing up it was obvious that she lacked all the physical attributes of his wife and older daughter. Patricia looked more like him. Her features were much softer and gentler, but he could not say that she is beautiful, especially not when he had in mind Lucie and Francesca's extreme beauty. Others did consider her pretty in some calm and reassuring way. Her big blue eyes were always ready to see everything from an enthusiastic viewpoint, and people had a feeling that she could set everything right and many times much better.

When Francesca started Church Hill High School., Timothy was a senior and everything a young man wanted to be. Definitely a great student, the school's football team star, very handsome, and of course the sole beneficiary to the biggest wealth in town. His father had very precise plans for him, and Timothy, Tim as everybody called him, went along with these plans. After graduation, he planned to attend a Boston law school and one day take over his father's estates and business.

Francesca was just a freshman and the last to awake an interest in a blooming senior. She was very aware of her beauty and overwhelming admiration by all. Always the center of attention, esteemed solemnly for her looks, which she took as righteous and natural phenomenon. Never entered her mind that she should give any consideration to others or even like someone else in return. *She* was the object of love and adulation, not the other way around. All the freshmen and sophomores were infatuated with her. Being in love with Francesca was part of growing up in Church Hill. Why, even Francesca was in love with Francesca. The girls, of course, hated her, but for Francesca that was a bigger compliment then the glorification from all the male population in school.

Four years later Tim started to work in the east branch of his father's firm, as young lawyer, to gain some experience before taking over the family business. In the same time Francesca was in California trying to launch a career in the movie industry, while Patricia thrived as a young sophomore. For the first time in Patricia's life, her sister was not around and things were quite different. Her father missed his older daughter tremendously, and he was not happy with her obsession of becoming a movie star. Naturally that notion did not improve his disposition, and people found him even more cold and annoying.

After graduating, Patricia decided to go to Chicago to study English literature, but she continued to keep close tabs on the events and life in Church Hill's life. According her mother's letters, that same year, Tim came home to take his rightful place on the town's social milieu. The citizens' expectations were huge, but something was very wrong.

The town had new mystery to talk about, and boy, did they ever!

Like every rich and powerful family, the Bathes were afraid of scandals, and by trying to hide whatever happened with Tim resulted only in stirring up the town's enormous hunger for gossip. Different stories circulated, than rumors reached Church Hill straight from Boston. A dispute between Tim and his father was over a girl. No one ever found out what really happened, but it seemed very serious. Tim looked and acted as if the world was at its end. Although, he went regularly to his father's corporate building, but it was obvious that big office and important position in such successful company did not impress Tim at the least. His mother tried everything to pull her son out of his distressful state of mind. She organized numbers of lavish parties and forced Tim to be the reluctant co-host. Suitable debutantes popped-up every time, even so far away as Atlanta, but Tim never showed the slightest interest in any of them. During one of their ongoing fights, the employees in the front of Mr. Baths' office, overheard him to be afraid that he would never be a grandfather. This juicy piece of information stormed through the town propelling again all array of new gossip. Speculations that he is not able to function as a man to the suspicion he might be a gay nurtured the public's fever for months. Mr. Baths' reaction was on the level of a volcanic eruption. The family life turned into a never-ending confrontation and the result was Mr. Baths' mild heart attack.

All the pressure made Tim rebellious. The next stage, after his father came home from the hospital, was an all-so-easy-partygoing-animal Tim. He stopped going into the office, nor did he speak to his parents. Every girl in town and then the girls in all neighboring towns were parading through Tim's life, one after another. His reputation as a playboy kept girls on guard, but who could ignore the attentions from the handsome, popular, and most eligible bachelor in seven counties. His mother was devastated. None of these girls were blue-blooded enough to be her daughter-in-law. It seemed that this particular disadvantage were their major attraction for Tim. He made it his purpose in life to oppose his father and torment his mother.

For Patricia, these colorful little reports through her mother's letters were the spice of her life. Obviously, the life in a small town is far juicier than in a big one such as Chicago. Unfortunately, several years of such a life left its traces on Tim's health as well as on his soul. He became cynical, promiscuous and he drank excessively. Finally, his parents gave up on him, believing that he would never pull himself together. Even always-so-gossip-hungry Church Hill lost interest in his new girlfriends and drinking sprees.

That summer Patricia graduated from college with honors, she was looking forward to returning to Church Hill. Francesca decided that it was time for her to come home, too. For several years now, she knew that she would never become anything in the film industry. She stayed in L.A. out of pride because she could not face that wretched town defeated and just come home as an ordinary person without the possibility of showing them that she is "Francesca the Goddess." In reality, she was just a worn down wannabe actress like a thousand other girls from all over the country, who came to Hollywood in search of fame and glory. What she learned first in Hollywood was that there were too may gorgeous girls wanting the same thing she did. She was nothing special there, just another pretty face to be used. She did it all – modeling, starring in small roles on TV (usually half-dressed and nobody to single you out) starving, waiting tables, singing lessons, acting lessons, auditions, dancing lessons, more auditions, starving in a meantime, auditions for night clubs, unwanted male attentions, more starving. She could not take it any longer.

Francesca reached the decision - she will go home to her mom and dad.

However, being Francesca she would not allow herself to "just be coming home". She was *coming back*, which meant in grand style. If she lost her dreams it's something nobody needed to know. With a precision of a sniper, she planned her homecoming for weeks. Her father send her a large check and the money was spend on expensive clothing and accessories. Picking the date was the mastery of a good show director – the same day when the high school football team will return home after their last game of the season. Victorious or not, plenty of people will gather at the airport, and there she will be, a big show-stopper! With the sleekness of a fox and greed of a child, she knew that she had to be first out of the plane. Therefore, she bought a first-class ticket, closest to the exit. Francesca could not have planned it any better. The day was beautiful, Church Hill's team won, and almost half the town was there to greet the victors.

She was ready!

When the corridor from the airplane to the lounge opened, thousands of unsuspecting football fans were startled by a beautiful woman, gliding slowly toward them with a seductive smile on her perfect lips. The dress, hair, expression on her stunning face, slow oscillation of her hips mesmerized the crowd. Noise and all movement stopped while thousands of pairs of eyes forgot for a moment what they were doing here. Silently they were staring at this vision in front of them.

"Hey, Francesca! Welcome home!" A sudden loud voice pulled the people out of their stupefied state. Then most of them recognized her, moved forward to greet her, asking questions, trying to touch her. She, like a queen, graciously flashed smiles all around, shake hands with old acquaintances, and waving here and there. For them she was a vision, a big star who came down from the sky to shine on them.

Francesca knew that she was a success, and nobody will ever question her failure as a movie star.

Tim was there as well with two women hanging on his arms. He was not drunk yet but when he saw Francesca strolling down the corridor, his head suddenly felt like after half a bottle of gin. Tim instantly knew who she was, remembering her faintly from his high school days.

So, that was that. She was home and nothing to do. In feverish preparations for the perfect homecoming, not once did it cross her mind what she going to do when she was finally back home. For the next several weeks, Francesca still did not know what to do with herself. She was not ready for just any job, in fear of ruining her carefully created reputation and jeopardize that image.

Tim, meanwhile, could not get her out of his head. He wanted her more than any girl in town. Tim made his decision - she will be his next conquest. Every day Francesca found some reason to go into town. She would dress carefully and strolling down the Main street like she was on the runway modeling, which she did successfully – modeling not the dress, but herself of course. It was inevitable for the two of them to meet on one of those excursions.

He was not drunk, and she was on her best when they literally ran into each other's arms. He was charming and she was so gracious and sweet that he took her to dinner but not to his bed. On the way home that evening, Francesca made up her mind to marry him. The next day she started her research on Timothy Baths. First, from her mother, she heard all the gossip circling around since his return from college. From her father, she found out all about Baths' wealth, and Patricia informed her that Tim would probably never marry out of spite for his father. Well, Francesca could care less about his lost love and string of lovers, but she definitely respected the money and it's potential. Therefore, she devised a foolproof plan to make him marry her.

They regularly went out together. People would see them everywhere. The town was on its toes again. Francesca lasted longer than any girl before. The question was, how she managed to keep him interested for so long? She was the prettiest of all, but somehow the townspeople were sensing that was not the reason. Francesca was carefully following her plan and it seemed to be working. Refusing to go in bed with him, playing the virtuous girl, was a smart strategy. Tim, naturally, tried every trick in the book with no success. Time was passing. His mother started to worry again. Maybe her son is serious about this one! That dreadful thought created a petrifying fear that she would end up with a very improper daughter-in-law. It was time for a very serious conversation with her son, which only produced exactly the opposite reaction from Tim than the old Lady had hoped.

Tim, for the first time, began thinking about marriage. Why not? She was beautiful, very sweet, and probably would never be a demanding wife. On the other hand, it would be an appropriate punishment for his parents. He grinned with pleasure visualizing his mother's everyday torment inflicted by the presence of an unwanted daughter-in-law.

The next day he bought the engagement ring - big and flashy – for his mother's sake, and proposed that evening in the most expensive restaurant in town, making sure that everybody knew what he was doing. His mother found out about the engagement five minutes later by the prompt call from an anonymous Good Samaritan. Her parents guessed what happened when she flashed her new prize in front of their noses the next morning.

As much as his parents opposed his choice, he with more determination was preparing for the wedding. Tim wanted a big and lavish celebration knowing that his mother would not create another scandal for their family by not showing up and participating in it, just as a good mother of the groom would do. The bonus was that his father would have to pay for it "chewing his liver" in helpless anger.

The wedding was everything that Tim planned, Francesca wanted and his parents dreaded – big, lavish and vulgarly expensive. He moved his wife theatrically into his parent's mansion under the watchful eyes of Church Hill's citizens. To say that they lived in torment ever after, as everybody expected, would be farthest from the truth. It turned out that Francesca's acting lessons finally paid off. She was so gracious, so elegant in appearance and manners that her mother-in-law was sure that the most carefully bred debutante could never be a match to Francesca. Her father-in-law, as any man, was enamored with her beauty. Moreover, he just could not resist her charming and gentile way of addressing him. She treated Tim with her *adoring wife* routine so that after a while, he fell I love with her and obediently started to go to his forgotten office stopping his heaping revenge on his parents.

Within a year Timmy and Puppet were born. One of each, even Francesca could not plan it better. She was satisfied; she got what she wanted, her rightful position in society. Francesca was a queen, not a queen of the world, but being a queen of this small town was better than having nothing at all.

Patricia came home several weeks after her sister. Only her parents and a few curious neighbors noticed her arrival. Several days, after her return, she called upon some of her friends from school. Most of them were already married and had children. Regardless, she visited them all, admired the babies, listen to stories about their husbands, jobs, house payments, better future, and of course endless speculations about her sister and Tim. She would patiently listened to all the little episodes in her friend's lives, while all of them had *just one* question for her – what will she do now that she is finally back from college? Patricia asked herself the same question every day as well. Mom and dad, naturally, expected her to stay with them, and she did not have the heart to disappoint them knowing that Francesca is most likely to marry very soon, and what an acute heart ache that will inflict upon their father.

Life has its own way to move people as chess pieces – unexpectedly one of Tim's friends (a member Church Hill's school board) mentioned that the middle school had an opening for an English teacher, suggesting she should apply for it. The prospect of teaching seventh graders English appealed to Patricia. The next day she called to find out what were her chances for a job, not hopping for too much. To her big surprise, she got it in a matter of days. First, she was the only applicant, and second, living in a small town has its advantages - everybody knows everybody and everything about each other. Always regarded as a reliable quiet girl, and until now, it was common knowledge that she graduated with honors was big plus. Therefore, the school board was happy to resolve their problem on such satisfying and fast manner. What she liked, in addition, was that she would stay close to her parents in these trying times for her father.

Summer was blazing with all its usual heat, sunshine and dryness. Patricia amused herself by studying Francesca's clever game to get Tim to commit. She did not doubt her sister's success for a moment. Tim's public proposal swept through town faster than light, raising the heat to a boiling point. Nevertheless, deep down, nobody was very surprised by the outcome of Tim's and Francesca's affair. It looked so right and proper that the most beautiful girl would marry the most eligible bachelor - everybody, that is, except Mr. and Mrs. Baths. When the fever of wedding preparations, and then the actual event was over, Patricia discovered that nothing changed in her parent's house neither in their lives. Mr. Johansson missed Francesca, of course. On the other hand, she had been away from home for a long time so he did not mourn for more than a couple of days. Tim, naturally, did not deserve Francesca, but then no man on earth deserved his precious daughter. His new son-in-law, at least, had lots of money, so Francesca will have all she ever wanted and deserved.

CHAPTER 2

With Francesca on her honeymoon and Patricia at home to take care of the house and garden, Mr. Johansson decided that it was time for him and his wife to go on a little vacation. Truth was, he had been contemplating, for a long time, to visit the town where his beloved wife and he met, the place where he grew-up, met Lucie and married her there. A smidgen of bad conscience, from time to time, about the way he left everything behind, so long ago, would disturb his sleep.

*****

His mother's family, the O'Brien's, was one of the oldest and most respectable in the coastal part of Northern Maine, owning one of the first and biggest fleet of fishing boats. His father, Olaf Johansson, came from Europe in the early 1930s, poor and with no education, but determined to make himself rich and powerful. He started as help on one of the O'Brien fishing boats. Hard work and intellect soon singled him out from amongst the rest of the crew. It was not long before Mr. O'Brien put him in charge of dispatching the boats and handling the distribution of the fish. In his spare time, he read everything he could put his hands on, wishing for education and better social skills. Although, his work was the envy of the other shipping lines. New elegant clothes that nicely fit his tall Nordic figure, and pleasing manners, which charmed people, never resulted in an invitation into the society of the rich and powerful. They kept to themselves and nobody could penetrate the bubble. Olaf's frustration pushed him toward the bottle. Consequently, he was on his way to stagnation and most likely ruin. Then, a miracle happened.

After five years being away at school in London, Mr. O'Brien's daughter Margaret returned home. While abroad, she bloomed into a beautiful young girl, and the expensive school turned her into a sophisticated woman, with impeccable manners. As often happens, destiny turned everything upside down and changed people's lives forever.

On her second day back, a beautiful Margaret visited her father at his office. Her tiny figure clothed in, an out-of-this-world, white lace dress enchanted the townspeople. She walked as if her feet did not touch the ground, while the pleasant smile on her face turned the head of every man who beheld her. When Margaret turned to enter her father's office building, Olaf was exiting at the same time and smash, they bumped into each other. He grabbed her arms to prevent her from falling. She clutched his jacket's lapels to steady herself, their eyes met, and she was lost forever. Olaf did not see her at all, not really. He was mad. Mr. O'Brien had spent half an hour talking about his daughter and the big party he was preparing for her homecoming. While talking about what kind of fish he wants Olaf to get for the party, he was rambling about the guests he invited, and never crossed his mind to extend an invitation to Olaf

"*Bastard!*" Olaf was furious! *Not even after negotiating a great business transaction for him which, by the way, will make him nice lump of money, he will not invite me. I am making him richer than he has ever dreamt he could be, and still to him, I am just another dirty fisherman.* Now, to top it all, that stupid little girl chooses to get in his way. When he was content that she was firmly on her feet, he marched away continuing to contemplate his anger toward the old man and unfairness of it all.

During the next couple of weeks, it looked like he would meet her everywhere he went. Margaret found a way to be in places where she would most likely meet Olaf. It did not take her a long to find out everything about him. She knew that her father's anger would be awful, if he would found out that she had desperately fallen in love with one of his employees, especially with someone her father considered a nobody. But, she could not help it. His tall figure, rough but handsome face, wavy blond hair would not depart from her thoughts for a moment.

When Olaf finally figured out who she was, he wished he had reacted differently. Next time he saw her he looked at her carefully for the first time. What he saw make his blood pump faster through his veins, not because she was beautiful. Actually, he did not notice her appearance neither did he fall in love, but what he *did* notice caused him to instantly formulate a plan of action. She looked at him with admiration and love, and that was something he knew he can use to his advantage. Olaf spent that whole night perfecting his plan. The grand scheme was born.

For months that followed he courted her. Both of them knew that secrecy was essential. They did not want to think about what Mr. O'Brien would do if he found out about them. Olaf was sure that they could not keep it a secret for a long time. He had to work fast. Elopement was the only answer, but Margaret hesitated. She wanted everything to be proper, with approval of her parents, a big wedding, knowing perfectly well that her wish would never go through. Finally, they eloped. Olaf's big triumphant return did not turn out as he expected. He was sure that Mr. O'Brian would be mad for a while, but what did happen never crossed his mind.

Mr. O'Brien disinherited his daughter, threw her out of the house and, of course, fired Olaf from his company. Mrs. O'Brien - who was regarded in general as a disinterested woman, very quiet, never imposing her opinions - did not share her husband's position on the matter. Deep down in her heart of a hearts, she understood her daughter. As a young girl, she had a similar love affair, but she never dared to do what Margaret had done. Instead, she did what every good obedient girl in her position would do – she married Mr. O'Brien and lived unhappily ever after. The note she received on the day the young couple eloped rushed back all repressed memories from her past. When her daughter and new son-in-law returned, she decided, for the first time in her life, to do what she thought was right. Not openly, of course. She helped them whenever was possible financially and in any other way.

Mr. O'Brien, from his side, tried to force his friends promise not to employ Olaf, although all of them secretly envied the Old man having Olaf and wanted many times before to take him over. Mrs.

O'Brien was not idle either. She persuaded Patrick Wolf, her husband biggest business rival and her secret admirer, to employ Olaf. The job was his but the position remained the same. He had the same type of job, working even more diligently, but his social standing aspirations failed again. Within a year, Margaret gave birth to a son. They named him Robert after Mr. O'Brien. Having a grandson was something Olaf believed the old man would not be able to resist. Nonetheless, once again, he was wrong. Nothing could move that old ice-burg. He refused even to hear a word about his daughter and her son.

Margaret was devastated and hurt beyond consolation, and wanted them to move elsewhere and begin a fresh life far from influence of her father. Olaf couldn't and wouldn't give up. One day, he was certain, the old man's company would be his, especially with old lady on his side.

Young Robert grew up in that bizarre environment. From his earliest age, he knew that he was different from the kids in his neighborhood. Soon as he could comprehend, some *good soul* told him all about his family disputes. Sometimes he would see Mr. O'Brien on the street, but his grandfather never acknowledged him, although it was obvious that he knew who Robert was. That hurt him at first, but his natural pride made him hide it. In the years which came, Robert ignored his grandfather in like manner, nor spoke of him with a living soul. His grandmother would come occasionally to visit them, bringing money and to talk to him. As a boy, he liked her, but later as a teenager, he blamed her for not being brave enough to stand up to her husband and declare her approval of Margaret's choice of a husband. At the same time he recognized that his father never loved his wife and had married her just for what she was the daughter of a rich and powerful man. In time Margaret, realized it too, loving Olaf the same and pretending that it did not bother her.

Knowledge that the sick ambition of one man could ruin lives of so many, and made people around him miserable turned Robert into a silent unhappy teenager.

Around that time, he met Lucie, beautiful, sweet and very optimistic. Never seeing anything bad in other people, everybody loved and admired her. Her mother came to town couple of years before with a teenage daughter, to replace the old librarian at the public library. She claimed to be a widow, but most believed that she was never married. Robert was smitten at first site and tried hard not to fall in love with her, knowing it was losing battle right from the beginning. In his senior year of high school, they became a couple with total disapproval from his father. The history was respiting itself all over again. He wanted his son to marry a girl from the ranks of high society and take his rightful place in life.

Finally, what Olaf secretly craved for so long happened. Old Mr. O'Brien died of heart attack and left everything to his wife. It was clear that old Lady, who knew nothing about business, will appoint him executor of the company, and eventually Margaret will inherit it all, which meant he would finally own all that he craved for decades.

They moved into the O'Brien mansion. Robert got strict instruction to stop socializing with his childhood friends, especially Lucie. Fortunately, in a few short months Robert was to leave for college. His choice was Los Angeles, which was the furthers possible place from Maine and his father. Lucie will follow shortly and stayed with her grandmother to attend the same college as Robert.

Five of the happiest years of Robert's live were coming to its end. Now that he had his diploma, his father's expectation of him to return home and participate in the family business, heavily laid on his shoulders. All these years Olaf existed solely for his company and almost lived in his office. In the same time the patriarchal society of the past loosened up and opened their doors to mingle more or less with people of all social standings. The Johansson's received invitations from all social classes, equally from rich and poor. Margaret and her mother would happily attend whatever event they had time for, without worrying who the host or hostess was. Mr. Johansson never accepted any of them. Somehow, *his desire* burned upon its own flame.

Olaf did not care any longer, that his son was seeing Lucie upon their return from L.A. When Robert announced during the family dinner that he had proposed marriage to Lucie, Olaf just nodded his head and paid for everything. Robert's grandmother and mother outdid themselves with the wedding preparations. Old Mrs. O'Brien hated hers, and Margaret never had one. So, both of them looked upon Robert's wedding as a fulfillment of their own dreams. They adored Lucie because Robert loved her and she made him happy.

Finally, after so many years of turmoil and unhappiness it seemed that the O'Brien-Johansson family would finally sail into a peaceful harbor, but not for long. A couple of weeks after the wedding Olaf died in his office of a stroke. His wife, still loving him deeply followed him in a short order, passing away in her sleep.

Robert have done what was expected from him, immediately conscripted into a family business, which he knew nothing about, nor did he like it. Lucie watched for months her husband slowly turning into a bitter stranger. Something had to be done, so she summoned Mrs. O'Brien in an attempt to save her marriage, her beloved Robert and put an end to the O'Brien and Johansson curse.

Two women talked the whole afternoon about old O'Brien, Olaf and Margaret, Robert and his hatred of the fishing business, and about the two of them. Mrs. O'Brien, that afternoon, understood why her grandson loved Lucie so much, how clever she was and how much she loved him back. Besides that, for the first time in her live, she was free and ready to do exactly what she wanted. To be more exact, she knew what she *did not* want any more. She did not want to live in this town, nor in this house where she was never happy, and especially, she did not want this smelly business any more, which had brought more grief upon her family than anything else.

Her final decision was that the company should to be sold, money put into trust so, they all could live off the interest, however they want. Robert did not say much, but Lucie knew he agreed with his grandmother's plan. Mrs. O'Brien chose to move to Florida where her two sisters and some of her childhood friends lived.

A smaller town would be a much better place to raise teenagers. Shortly after that, while standing in line in a coffee shop, Robert overheard a couple of men talking about Church Hill and how much they missed its serenity and beauty. The next week Robert took Lucie to see the little town themselves. He liked the town on first sight and Lucie Loved it. While driving around they spotted an old farm for sale. The house was not much at first glance, but Lucie fell in love with everything about the farm, especially with the grounds. She wanted it and Robert could never refuse her anything so, they bought the farm.

*****

While her parents were on the trip through their past, Patricia minded the house, the garden, and spend time preparing for her new job. But destiny, again played out its little game as it does with human lives, twisting her future in a completely different direction. A month after her parents departed Patricia received a telegram with the news about their fatal car accident. Both girls were devastated. Francesca was unconceivable, but Patricia knew that both of her parents would rather go this way, together than to live a day without t each other.

The biggest surprise was her father's will – he left everything to her. House, money, family valuables, and art would stay in her possession. If she ever decides to sell, half of money would go to Francesca. Patricia lived her whole life in deep belief that her father never loved her very much, but now she knew he cared, and she was touched. He probably thought that she was not attractive enough to catch a rich husband like Francesca, who by marrying a wealthy man had nicely secured her future. By his standards, he had to take care of the one who was less fortunate. Dear dad did what he believed was right, and Patricia was trapped in the security of money, solitude of a farm, and the image people had of her.

She offered to Francesca to split in half everything, but surprisingly turned out that her sister knew all about the will. Father discussed it before hand with Francesca and both thought it is the best solution for everybody. *To them I am pathetic looser with nothing in my future.* Patricia was not flattered, but her own opinion about herself was not any better.

Of course, she had to decline the teaching position. First, Patricia was now quite rich and there was no need to work, and second, she believed that it was her obligation to keep Lucie's garden as her mother would have kept it herself. To keep Freddy, on whom Lucie depended so much was first thing she have done. People in town missed Lucie and felt sorry for the girls, but the consolation was that girls put their lives quite nicely together.

While Francesca was preoccupied being wife, mother and social busy bee, it turned out that Patricia's engagement on the social plane was even bigger. People somehow believed that she lives in wealth and idleness. Therefore, it was not only perfectly okay, but an act of graciousness to involve her in organizing, participating, and working on every public event including a number of private ones. Every charity auction, Fourth of July parade, Christmas meal for the homeless, could not be coordinated without her. She was a member of the school board, Big Brother and Sister's, boys' choir. In addition, naturally, after Francesca gave birth to the twins, Patricia spent endless hours caring for them which she did not mind loving them dearly. Every evening she would have dinner with her sister's family after putting kids to their beds. In the beginning, they invited her over every day so she would not be alone in her parent's big house, brooding over their death. but soon The Baths' got used to having her around, pleasant, helpful, down- to-earth kind of girl with no demands for herself.

Life in the Baths' big extravagant house was not exactly Patricia's idea of a comfortable existence. Two maids, a gardener, and Flora as a cook and housekeeper were busy all day keeping everything tip-top in the house. Flora was a very capable housekeeper and the older Mrs. Baths and now Francesca never had any need to intervene in the everyday administration of the household. When the Baths would entertain, which happened often, Flora would use one of the several catering businesses in town. Suddenly Patricia found herself in the middle of that bustle after Flora had an accident. There was nobody to instruct her as to what to do and how to run this big house. In addition, everyone expected, she would resume taking care of the children just as she had done before. It was overwhelming for a while, with Francesca buzzing around in attempt to be helpful, while in fact she was lost more than Patricia. In time, she settled in with ease and life once again fell into a routine.

Patricia's public work suffered a little, but everybody understood her present situation. Actually, most of her friends were of the opinion that her sister and family treated Patricia as a servant. They kept their suspicions to themself knowing her too well – she would never accept the idea that the people she loved pushed her into something against her will. Once she took a grip of her new duties, Patricia was very content. With the help from two maids, all her domestic duties were finished during the morning when her niece and nephew were in school. She would dedicate the afternoons to them, helping with homework and playing with them.

Patricia loved to spend time with Timmy and Puppet. When they were very small she used to read them stories, acting out characters using the whole bedroom as a stage, which amused the children tremendously. As they grew, they became bored with the same old stories so she began making up fairy tales about herself as a little girl. They were adventurous tales, full of danger, pirates, robbers, bad witches, good fairies, and her dog Marcus-Aurelius. Patricia always wanted a dog but her father was allergic to dog hair, so she fulfilled her childhood desires through this tales. On the children's fourth birthday, she was persuaded to enact her stories in front of all the children invited to the party. The stories and the way she presented them were such success that no birthday party could fare without her attendance. At one of these parties she met the aunt of the birthday child, who was a publisher from New York. Her name was Paula Kirkpatrick, who ended up completely enchanted by Patricia and her stories. Without ever thinking of becoming a writer Patricia found herself putting down on paper everything she ever made up about little "Patty". Timmy and Puppet were a big help because they remembered, better than she did, all the adventures and strange names of the characters she masterminded. The kids' excitement in anticipating their aunt's first book, made Patricia even more nervous about herself. She did not know what to expect. Long preparation for publishing included several revisions and close work with Michael Brooks, the illustrator. At first, the illustrator being a male, took Patricia little aback, not being sure that a man would be able to capture Patty's sweet toughness. However, she was wrong. Michael was gentle, nice and a very perceptive man. He drew Patty as a tomboyish, pretty, freckled little girl whose features strikingly resembled her as a child. That proved Michael as an artist and his observing ability. The book was a success, and she signed a five-year contract with Paula's company for two books about Patty a year.

Patricia's series of books about Patty established her as a writer, made her life meaningful, and brought two new good friends in her life. Paula was an outsider and adviser while observing Patricia when it came to her life and her family's tendency to use her. Michael found, in Patricia, the woman he had always wanted.

When she would spend time in New York working on illustrations and final touches before publishing, she and Michael always had a great time. He proposed to her many times, and always her answer was not what he wanted. He hoped that in time she would change her mind telling himself that he just had to be patient. Patricia liked him more then she wanted to admit even to herself. He was funny, cultural and very easy to be with as long as he has things his way. Their endless walks down the Broadway, Central Park, dinners in Italian dinners, theater shows and musicals were the spice of her staying in New York, but she wanted all or nothing. Deep down in her heart was buried a little romantic Patricia who ached for the prince on a white horse. The prince never appeared to sweep her off her feet and make her heart to flutter, especially not Michael. She loved him dearly, and on many occasions, she would imagine their marriage. Long walks, long talks, even long love making. They had so much in common; life with him would probably be very pleasant, secure, interesting and above all very productive. He had all these plans about them as a team, writer and illustrator. They would create magnificent children's books together, become famous and rich, living happily ever after. That was an exciting picture and not far from her own wishes, but something was missing. Foremost, she wanted children of her own, not just to write for them, and Michael was a big child himself without any desire of becoming a father. On the contrary, he was almost allergic to children, avoiding children as much as he could. As an illustrator of children's books, he was obligated to go, from time to time, on book promotions and give speeches in schools. Michael was never good in these situations, turning into a drama queen, so Paula usually used Patricia for these kinds of functions.

Patricia had Michael on the fringe of her mind the whole day. While preparing dinner she made all sorts of plans as to how she was going to coordinate taking care of the house, kids and Michael, who had arrived yesterday from New York to work on her latest book. It was the first time that he had come to Church Hill, and only because she roughly cut him off after weeks of explanations as to why she could not come to New York this time. He is very spoiled, she thought while mincing tomatoes. Only at his apartment did he feel safe and content. Maybe that was part of his charm but that make her feel more like his mother then a prospective bride.

The slam of the door announced Francesca's return from one of her projects. Patricia felt relief. It was not very often that her sister came home on time. Now that dinner was ready, she could leave to work with Michael as long as he wanted. Tomorrow she would not have a minute of time with all the cooking and kids at home whole day, and to her dislike, she will have to participate in entertaining the guests – no doubt, all rich, dull, and deeply aware of their importance. Michael, of course, could not understand what could be more important than working on the book. When she was commuting to New York, they worked without any disturbance, and now he had to play second fiddle to whatever her obligations were to her impossible family or whoever chose to use her at their convenience. He could not understand why she is so stubborn and simply would not marry him?

While Francesca's chatter was going on and on about the events of her afternoon, Patricia was preoccupied with a conversation she had with Michal last night, and if it continues like that this evening she will explode. *Why could not he understand that her life does not revolve around writing? I do like to write and make children happy and influence their lives hopefully for the better and to work with him. But my nephew and nice, my house, garden, memories of my parents, all the obligations toward the people in this town are my life. Furthermore, I like it! I do not know what I would do in New York all the time. To go there a couple of times a year is fun, but more than that would be hard for someone who loves nature and the tranquility of the country.*

"Tomorrow Tim's best friend from college is coming, as you know. Tim talks about him almost with reverence, but I think he is a big bore, George Edmond Hammond!" Francesca was pronouncing the words slowly and with mocking seriousness, which made Patricia smile. Her sister liked to mock everybody. "Even his name is a bore. But, Tim admires him and I am resolved to love him too."

"How could you judge a person by his name? Timothy is a stuffy name too, and you have three of them in your own family. How do you live with such an amount of boredom every day, I can't understand. Oh, I pity you my dear sister from the bottom of my heart!" She mimicked her sister's mocking voice, but her generous disposition kicked in and she started to enjoy this conversation with Francesca.

"Oh, go ahead and make fun of me, but as you very well know I am seldom wrong about people. You may call it a sixth sense - the same as I am right about your blowfish Michael! I'm afraid if I come close to him, I'll be pierced with his pricks. And, on a top of that, he despises everybody and everything!"

"That is not true, Francesca! He is not used to kids or big families. He is an artist and has lived alone too long having things his own way. You can't blame him for that." *I'm defending him for the same things I don't like about him. Strange how criticism from other people sounds harsh but makes things clearer. Francesca is right, I could not be happy with Michael just as he could not be happy with me.*

"Well, if you don't need me any more I must go and work with "Blowfish" himself in hopes of not being poked and burst as a balloon. Also, as for tomorrow evening, I'm taking it upon myself to entertain the distinguished Mr. George Edmond Hammond! You can relax and spill your charm over the rest of your guests. I'll do the hard part as always!" Francesca threw a dishcloth after the laughing Patricia only to hit the slammed door.

As Patricia expected Michael was edgy and hostile, pacing his hotel room back and forth with frown on his face. "Don't be a baby, Michael! This is my life, and I'm tired of repeating myself. I want you to calm down. Tomorrow you will come to my sister's house. We'll have fun, good food, you'll meet my friends, and that's it! We can have one day away from work, and the world will still revolve." She tried to be patient, and tried not to sound like she was patronizing or making fun of him. He would not take it lightly, and another provocation would only intimidate him more, which was the last thing she needed now.

"I know you might think me selfish, but I'm a professional and when I'm working, disturbance is not something I can deal with easily!" *Oh, my God he even sounds like a little boy. What a preposterous assumption: I might think he is selfish. I think I never knew a more selfish person in my life. I wonder if spanking would help like when Francesca used to spank Timmy when he would nag too much.*

"And… I'm not sure that I want to meet your friends. They are all most likely like your sister! She frightens me! How can such two different people like you and she be sisters, I don't understand. In addition, those nephew and niece of your, they are like a little buzzing flies. Buzz here, buzz this, buzz there. How can you stand it every day? No! I don't want this nonsense! You have to marry me, get away from here and save your life!" He was really upset. Patricia did not know how to calm him down, and with horror, she realized that her own blood started to boil. She could not remember the last time she was this mad.

"Michael, you're acting like a child! I don't need to run away! I'm free to do what I want and my life here is what I want. Listen to me Michael, do not ask me to marry you again. I can't, and I don't want to!" His eyes were wide open in disbelief. His lower lip started to curl out and up, make him look as if he is ready to burst into tears at any moment. *That's it! Patricia was fed up. I am leaving now, and if he doesn't start to behave as an adult, Paula will have to find me another illustrator.*

Michael helplessly stared at a furious Patricia grabbing her purse from the chair and marching to the door. She did not even give him a second glance as she slammed it behind her. On the way home, she relaxed a little. Waiting for the green light at the intersection, she burst into laughter visualizing Michael's childish face. It was beyond her comprehension how an adult man, and an artist could act like such a brat.

CHAPTER 3

From the early morning, the whole house was turned upside-down. Timothy did not go to his office, which was most unusual. His beloved friend was coming and he wanted everything to be perfect. Francesca was involved in preparing the dinning-room for the evening. The florist arrived early this morning with a variety of flowers, and Francesca was for hours arranging them in exquisite crystal vases. While she was supervising the preparation of the guest room for Mr. Hammond, Tim was constantly underfoot making her nerves, so she exiled him down to the kitchen where he was reduced to kitchen help. Patricia made him slice tons of onions, carrots, tomatoes and, according to him, the rest of the vegetables grown in Chrich Hill just for this occasion.

"I'm a respectable businessman Patricia, not some kitchen boy, and these onions are burning my eyes out of the sockets. I thought my wife was a merciless little dictator, but you Johansson sisters, are the same - a couple of slave drivers!" Patricia smiled knowing that Tim was crazy about his wife, and she believed that he was beginning to like her, too. In fact, that was the truth. From complete indifference toward Patricia in the beginning, he grew to first respect her, and then like her so match that he could not imagine his life without her. Time after time watching these two women together, he thought if he could combine them into one person he would end up with the perfect woman. Francesca was beautiful while Patricia was warm. Francesca was natural with people, charming them all, while Patricia's graciousness with ability to listen made everyone love her. Francesca was a perfect wife for a rich businessman, while Patricia an enchanting mother type and housewife. He could go on forever studying and comparing them. They were not aware of it, but Francesca did catch her husband more than once watching her sister with admiration. It was beyond Francesca's comprehension, who worshiped beauty above everything else, that any man would think differently and even worse, prefer Patricia to her.

Mixing different varieties of lettuce, Tim went on and on about his friend." You should see him with this horse! I flatter myself to being a good horseman, but he and the horse are one..."

"Oh! A regular Centaur! Remind me to serve a little bit of hay tonight! Universe knows we are serving everything else!" Tim looked at her with a smile. That was another thing about Patricia he liked. She had witty sense of humor.

"Preferably with Italian dressing!' He joined her in laughter, but it did not stop him, "And, he was a devil with women. Just wait and see. I've never met a single one who could resist him when he put his mind to charm her."

"Better and better! Mythical beast and plain chauvinistic male pig, all in one! Well I'm ready to extol him for all his rare qualities!" She tried not to burst into loud laughter.

Tim stopped what he was doing for a moment looking at her with a gasped mouth. That was too much even from Patricia. "I'm talking here about my best friend with no success whatsoever. I'm trying to make you understand how great a person he is, and you are turning my every word to create a picture of some monster. I know you like to joke, but it's disturbing how purposely you are seeking fault in poor George, from great into awful!" He would never understand the workings of a woman's mind if he lives to be hundred. Patricia unsuccessfully tried to stifle her laugh under Tim's disapproving glare.

"Patricia, stop it! You don't know him. He is very serious and proper. He can't help that girls threw themselves at him. He was engaged to a girl back home even before he started college. Everything was arranged for them by their families while they were still children, or something. He loved her though. Who wouldn't! I saw her picture. She was a knockout!"

"Was? What happed to her? She married him and turned into an ugly duckling? With his mythological ancestry and magical attraction he probably possess some witchcraft powers, too?"

"She died!" Tim stopped her flatly.

"Oh, I am sorry, Timothy! Sometimes I can be such an idiot! You'll have to tell Francesca, or she'll say something stupid, too. Why didn't you tell us this before? God knows you told us everything else about him!"

"Oh, I don't know! George never wanted to talk about it. I didn't see him very much after her death. They had three children and he took it upon himself to be their father and mother, I suppose. This is the first time he has accepted my invitation. You know that I invited him dozens of times, but no, he always had some family crises or other. He declined to come to my wedding. The youngest child had fever or something, and he wanted to stay with him. People in that wretched town of his think he behaves like this because of a bad conscience. Nobody talks about it, but I think they believe that he is somehow responsible for her death."

"Goodness, he is a real mystery man. Now, *I am* interested to meet him. Three kids you say? He must have some help with them?" Patricia's basic nature of nurturer spoke again.

"I'm not sure whom he has now. Before, I believe, a string of nannies and governesses passed through that big house of his. Well, if I were you, I wouldn't ask him anything about it. He is a very private person, and if he knew I was talking about his personal affairs, he would break my nose. Therefore, you and your sister will have to be perfect ladies… for once!."

"Oh, really! Wait until I tell Francesca about not being Lady! You are dead meat, for one, and second, I promise to talk to him only about the weather, gardening and cooking. Those are probably the only thinks that women are capable of discussing in the minds of chauvinistic men." Patricia decided to treat George indifferently. After all, he will be here only a week and there is no reason to get any more involved in his private life than is necessary.

A couple of hours later Patricia, while taking a shower, was thinking about a few more things she will have to do before the guests start coming. An hour ago, when she barely reached her bedroom, the door -bell rang and she knew that *big* George Edmond Hammond had arrived. She was happy having some time for herself before she met Tim's friend. Now, when she was alone, Patricia could not stop thinking about those three little motherless children, and how their lives could not be easy. Their father sounded like a complicated man and then all those nannies and strange people marching through their lives.

She slipped into her black evening dress and added only a string of her mother's pearls. Patricia loved those pearls and not only because they reminded her of Lucie. Remembrance on time when her father took her with him when she was about eight years old, her father took her to buy a birthday present for her mother. Father had in mind diamond earrings, but when she saw the necklace, she begged him for almost fifteen minutes to buy it for Lucie. The sparkle in her mother's eye that night proved, to both of them, that the choice was right. Lucie wore the pearls more than any other piece of jewelry. Now, Patricia was doing the same. They felt so good around her neck and mother will approve entirely.

Patricia glanced at her image in the mirror for the last time and ran out of her bedroom. It took her longer to dress herself than usual. *With age, I'm becoming vain or this might be my sister's bad influence.* She knew Tim would laugh at this thought saying that the sisters are not so different after all.

Running down the stairs, deep in her thought, Patricia stormed straight into something big, hard, and what's not supposed to be there. Two strong hands grabbed her arms to steady her. The grip was hard and painful, lasting longer than she could endure. Patricia tried to twist herself free without success. Finally, she opened her eyes. She stared at broad chest several long moments before she was fully aware of what was happening. She was in the grip of an unknown man, or was he that unknown? Of course, she knew that this could only be *the George Edmond Hammond* himself, but somehow she tried to prolong this embarrassing revelation. Patricia's decision to keep all interactions with Mr. Hammond light and impersonal as possible burst into a million bubbles. Now, she probably looked silly and foolish, and it was impossible to regain her dignity in the manner she would have desired.

When her eyes, at last, reached high enough to look straight into his, she became aware that he was taller that Tim said and much, much more frightening. For a long moment their eyes were interlocked, his cold and mocking, hers wide open and anxious. He released her only for her to make a bigger fool of herself. Patricia literally ran from the hallway without a word. *Oh, how absurd can I be?* She wanted to smack herself. *I acted like a seventeen year old with a big crush on the star football player.* Her hands were shaking as she pulled food out of the refrigerator and off the stove. She was so mad at herself that she could explode. *Why am I so ridiculous about all of this? He has probably already forgotten the stupid episode. But why should I care? He will be out of here in a week, thankfully never to see him again in my life.* This thought calmed her a little. The voices coming from the living room were loud and sounded relaxed. She took a deep breath and slowly entered the room hoping nobody would notice her. Uncommonly, like magic, all eyes instantly fixated on her and the silence paralyzed her at the door.

"Well, Patricia, finally!" Tim's voice and smile were like a warm breeze. Her cheeks were burning when Mr. Hammond's eyes caught hers again. *Darn, he did not forget anything.* Tim put an arm around her shoulders nudging her toward his friend.

"George, may I present to you my most beloved sister-in-law. This is Patricia!" She found herself standing in front of this very tall man for the second time in a short period, feeling even worse than a few moments ago.

"You mean your only sister-in-law, Tim. But, old boy, you are too late as usual!" George with his deep voice was talking to Tim, but looking at Patricia quizzically. "I had an infinite pleasure of meeting your sister-in-law already." He took her hand bending down, all the while looking straight into her eyes like a snake in the eyes of a paralyzed rabbit. His lips on the cool skin of her hand felt more like a bite, and she trembled, cursing him and her own weakness at the same time.

Why can't I pull myself together and be calm and reliable old me as usual?

"No kidding, George?" Francesca was shifting eyes from him to Patricia, lifting her eyebrows in curiosity, "When on the earth did that happen?"

George finally let go of her hand turning toward Francesca. "Oh, just a few minutes ago in the hallway. She floated into my arms wishing me a welcome. She is small but very strong. I had a hard time preventing her from kissing me. Tim, old boy, you did not tell me that your women are so warm and friendly!" Patricia was staring at him with an open mouth. *I floated into his arms to kiss him? How can he even say such a thing with a straight face?* She was gasping for breath, trying to sound out some words of denial and protest, but she did not have a chance.

Tim was laughing his heart out knowing that George was toying with Patricia. Even funnier was the stoned expression on her face. Than he glanced at Francesca, who looked equally shocked as her sister. He threw himself on the sofa holding his stomach laughing. George acted as Tim did not exist, observing each of the sisters in turn.

"Well, ladies, what will it be? Sherry or something stronger? His slow stroll toward the bar gave Patricia time to close her mouth and helplessly look in the direction of her brother-in-law, hoping for some help from him. Francesca did the same. Tim spread all over the sofa still with a big grin on his face looked so self-satisfied that both sisters were getting angry with him. Of course, they knew he was enjoying all this more so, because they made fun of his affection for George. This was his five minutes of glory and revenge. Tim was gloating. They should take his friend seriously and not make fun of his warnings about George's way with women.

Patiently waiting, George was standing beside the bar, for the sisters to make up their minds, while Tim tried to stand up still in disarray from all the wild laughter.

"Francesca will have a martini, and my precious Patricia, the big seductress, a glass of white wine, George. You always tried to convince me that the shy and quiet ones are the most dangerous, and finally I can see what you meant." He took the glass of wine from George and handing it to Patricia said, "My dear, you should wait at least until tomorrow to make moves on George. I can't believe that after all I've been telling you, tsk, tsk, Patricia. I agree that he is handsome, charming and a very good catch, but a little bit of decorum would be required from my sister-in-law. I can't think what would please me more than the union between my best friend and my dearest girl."

Patricia knew he will go on and on like that, which she could not allow him to do. This embarrassing situation had lasted way too long. Pulling together all of the strength she had left, she made calm disinterested face, controlling her voice the best she could while turning to Tim.

"My dear Tim, you can't blame a girl for trying from time to time to practice her moves on some unsuspected poor man. As you mentioned yourself, you talked way too much about Mr. Hammond, so I thought if I can seduce His Iceberg Highness himself, I can have any man on the earth!" She spoke slowly and with every word, her old self was returning to this confused Patricia.

Poor Francesca, unfortunately, was receiving shock after shock. She never heard her sister speak like this, not sure if Patricia was just jockeying with two men or being downright serious. George placed the martini in her hand with a puzzled expression, having his eye fixed on Patricia. It was his turn to be confused. Is there more to this not-so-attractive girl than on first glance? Her features were plain, nothing of her sisters exciting beauty; but her eyes were large and exceptional, her voice calm and soft, her small tiny body in a simple black dress moved gracefully, and the way she was lifting the wine to her lips made him tremble. He did not feel like this since his teens, and he didn't like it.

Tim was having too much fun to dismiss this great subject so fast, especially after Patricia's reaction to his teasing and with such elegance.

"I always felt sorry that I didn't have a sister to marry her off to this gorgeous brut and make him a family, but now I have a sister-in-law! My dear Patricia, the two of us will have to find a way to make him fall feverishly in love with you, and then he is ours for good!" He looked at his friend with a big smirk, and then his expression changed. This all was a joke. Would it be so far-fetched for George to fall in love with Patricia? What is not to fall for? She is the best creature he ever met. She was funny, clever, and great with children, a talented writer and a divine cook. He suddenly did not feel so light hearted. If she do go away for whatever reason, he'll be miserable. Tim suddenly realized that his attachment to Patricia is more than love for his sister-in-law. Like a lightning bolt struck him that if he had met the sisters later in his life and had time to know them better he probably would have chosen Patricia over Francesca. That was confusing and he did not know from where this was all coming, but he could not lose her. She was too valuable to him.

"Well on the other hand" - he tried to sound equally jocular, as before, "I don't think that you, George, deserve my Patricia. She needs someone nice and adorable as I, and until we find another me, she'll stay here under my protection" Just then, the doorbell announced the arrival of their first guests. Patricia silently thanked her lucky star for that little favor, and carefully avoiding furniture and George she moved toward the door.

The dinner was a success. Patricia engaged herself in caring for everybody's needs, which did not gave her a single second of time to be idle, while all the time she was on guard to avoid George and not to be too obvious about it. She caught him staring at her a couple of times during the dinner as well as afterwards in the great room, while the guests talked having fun mingling. He is no doubt a hideous man, annoying her a great deal, most likely on purpose He is trying to make me sweat for that stupid accident on the stairs. Consolation was that she had her emotions under control promising herself, over and over, never to lose it again, not over Mr. Hammond for sure.

To have her frustrations enhance even more, Michael persistently tried to be close as possible to her, expressing his disappointment over her rejection and announcing his determination to do everything possible to change her mind. Most of the guests noticed their closeness commenting how they look perfect together and that Patricia deserves such a nice and successful man.

George at last found Tim alone. The whole evening was a pure torture, answering endlessly who he was and how he knew Tim. "Tell me, dear boy, is this Michael your choice for Patricia? I mean is he this charming and adorable man who is deserving of her?" His voice was casual, even a little contemptuous.

"Stupid idiot – that's who he is. Don't worry, she'll never marry him!" Tim sounded like he will like to be more sure himself of that statement.

"How do you know?"

"I know, because she is too clever not to see through his ridiculous act" Both men were watching Patricia and Michael. He looked agitated and Patricia was trying her best not to look annoyed. other guests wondered what two friends talked about far from the crowd. In that moment George noticed Francesca on the other side of the room observing them, too. He was curious if she was aware that her husband was in love with her sister and herself at the same time. *Is Tim aware of his love for Patricia, and if he is, what will he do about it?* He recalled the episode earlier this evening when Tim first jokingly proposed Patricia marry him, and the next minute jealously decided to keep her close to himself. This visit will turn out to be more interesting than he anticipated.

Tim was still scrutinizing Patricia and her friend as Francesca worked her way toward them with a smile on her lips but not in her eyes. *Oh, Oh! Storm on horizon!* George felt compelled to do something fast. Slapping Tim on his back, "You never told me that your wife is so beautiful!" He said it little louder, so that approaching Francesca would hear. Tim snapped out of his lament, only to find himself being studied by his wife cold eyes. The guilt he felt puzzled him. Something is wrong with him, he knew that, but what? George's voice refocused him on Francesca.

"Tell me Francesca, what kind of favors and manipulations did this worthless football player used to lure you down from Mount Olympus?" She smiled. Francesca was used to compliments, but she could always handle more, especially tonight when somehow it looked like everybody were preoccupied with Patricia, and she would be dammed if she knew why. There was nothing special or different about her sister tonight than any other time. The same dress - the same necklace - the same hair – the same old plain Patricia. George did not give her time to ponder over it any longer. He took her arm under his, bending down to look into her beautiful eyes. His expression telling how beautiful she was made her forget all about Patricia and her own husband.

Patricia also noticed that something was different about this evening. This whole day had turned out strange. First, Tim stayed home to help with dinner, quite unusual, than this wretched man accused her of - she was not sure of what - and then Michael with all those temper tantrums! A decision was made. First, she will have a serious talk with him, following one with their publisher. It was clear that their long lasting collaboration was coming to an end. She was relaxing stretched in her bed knowing she would never forget this day as long as she lives. As she was slowly drifting in sleep, her last conscious thoughts were of George.

CHAPTER 4

N ext morning, half-awoken Patricia's first though was of George. That thought made her disgusted with her fixation on that hideous man. *Six more days.* She rolled her eyes. *It will pass sooner than it seems right now.* Patricia comforted herself. Besides, she will be too busy with endless chores during the day, which will gave her no time to deal with him, except every wretched evening during dinnertime. Furthermore, if she is lucky, some evenings Tim will take him out. *Good thinking girl, I just have to make Tim think it was his idea in the first place.*

To her great satisfaction, when she came down, Francesca informed her that Tim and their guest had left for Baths' corporate building half and our ago. *Yes!* She almost yelled out loud. *I am acting like a silly high school freshmen, while in reality, I am thirty-two years old, educated and a very clever woman who has many duties and obligations which I, unquestionably, manage to everybody's approval. Therefore, I will definitely survive this week in spite whatever Mr. Hammond choses to throw my way.*

Francesca was unusually quiet, and Patricia assumed she had one of her imaginary headaches.

"Yesterday's dinner went well, don't you agree?" She tried to find out what was bothering her sister. Francesca would never tell her straight out. Being used to, and frankly liked these little games of trivial questions in order to discover what was the latest problem inflicting misery in Francesca's life.

"You do?" Francesca raised her left eyebrow, which meant that she disagreed.

"Sure! Everybody was pleased with the food and the after-dinner activities were great. Tim thinks that George enjoyed himself, and we didn't break a single dish!" A little bit of humor would not hurt, but

Francesca refuse to buy into it.

"Yeah? Tell me, who cooked the dinner? You! Who entertained guests with all those men-head-swirling-around-little-Patricia routine? Finally, as far as George goes, his enjoyment came primarily from looking at you the entire evening. Don't play innocent with me! You did it on purpose, which is silly, because this man will never fall for you no matter how many times you fling yourself into his arms!" Her voice was a voice of little Francesca, when things did not go as she desired.

Patricia was astounded. Even Francesca, with all those imagination of hers, never before made up such a wild assumption.

"Fling? Me? In his arms? On purpose? Men's head swirling? If you are referring to Michael's tasteless exhibitions, I would not call it swirling but nuisance! Oh, for Pet's sake, Francesca, what are you talking about?" Patricia suddenly lost all energy for Francesca's riddles.

"Oh, nothing!" Francesca realized she sounded like a jealous spinster. To be jealous on her plain sister would never happen. She, on the other hand, has it all – beauty, manners, gorgeous hair, beauty – she said that already – rich husband!

The children rushed into the kitchen fighting over having misplaced something or other from the day before. Patricia turned to prepare the breakfast for screaming kids, asking them what they would like to do the rest of the day. Usually, every Saturday, they would go to the park or zoo, but today they will stay at home because of their guest.

"You will have to help me with the apple pie, then we'll go to the grocery store to buy some more meat and veggies. The first one done with breakfast will get to choose which kind of ice cream we'll have after lunch! Okay?

The kids mumbled something through full mouths, while their mother made a dignified retreat to her bedroom.

Tim called from the office begging Patricia to make stuffed peppers for dinner, his favorite meal of all. This was demoralizing news for Patricia - all of them coming home for dinner, and Tim probably bragging about her stuffed papers. *Darn, darn, darn!* She will have to outdo herself – she would not let *that man* think Tim exaggerates about her culinary talents.

During the course of the dinner, she wished from the bottom of her heart, that she had cooked the worst meal of her life. What Tim was swaggering about her cooking, she did not even want to know, but she will scream from the top of her lungs if she hear one more word about her best stuffed papers ever. George was devouring his plate full heartedly agreeing with Tim. Patricia's suspicious glances in his direction did not confirm or dispute his sincerity. *He is mocking both of us, me as well as silly man Tim. One thing is clear – big Mr. Hammond thinks I did it to impress him.*

Dorn, *I will not survive five more days!* Fried chicken with German potato salad was insisted upon for dinner tomorrow evening by Tim, so persistently, that she started to protest. There was no way out of it, unfortunately. Patricia rolled her eyes on the thought that if the meal turns out good, that impossible man will think, again, she did it to impress him. On the other hand, if she makes it mediocre, he will guess it was for the purpose to deny that he was affecting her on some strange way. Patricia was confused with these conflicting emotions overflowing her every though and action since George showed up, and that stupid encounter on the stairway. *What is all that about? I do not even like him a little! Overbearing, contemptuous, self-important and he thinks Tim is a big child. Whatever I do, I can't win!* Patricia shrugged her shoulders in resignation.

"Tell us George little more about your house and property? Tim described it as an old English manor, but he is not to be trusted when you are in question!"

Francesca was radiant tonight. Her sister was looking at her carefully. Always spending a long time in front of the mirror was Francesca's forte, but today it looked as if she spent a whole day pampering herself at the beauty salon. Francesca was really acting like a jealous woman,

41

but way? *What does she have to be jealous of? My cooking? Francesca detests everything in connection with the kitchen and was always happy that someone else messes with it. Tim has been praising my food since the first time he tasted it, which never bothered his wife before now.* On the contrary, she would wholeheartedly confirm that her little sister has a talent to wear an apron. What was happening with Francesca was the thing Patricia would like to know? *Can it be George? Is it possible she has a crush on him? If she does, she would never let anything interfere with her life so nicely put together. Francesca would never jeopardies her position, power and money which comes with being Tim's wife.* Patricia was intrigued all over again. George's laugh pierce through her conscience, so she looked toward him.

"We don't use it at all. Then there are the horse stables. When my great-grandfather bought that piece of wilderness, he first built a house for his wife. She was born into a rich old English land proprietor family, disgracing them by marrying my great-grandfather, who was… I really don't know what the origin of his wealth was, but he had money… Anyway, the story goes he made the replica of her family's house!" He smiled glancing toward Patricia again, "Womenfolk find that very romantic! Then, he was concentrating on the second most important thing in his life horses the stables, and boy, built them to last forever!' He was still smiling at Patricia, now raising his eyebrows. She snapped out of her lethargy, realizing that he was aware she did not hear a word he said.

"Horses! Yes, I do remember those blasted horses!" Tim was staring at his wine glass remembering his first visit to the Hammond estate immediately after they finished college, "Wild beasts! Everything is wild in that dammed place. Natives call it a ranch. Believe me, it was anything but an ordinary ranch. The house is big, Tudor-style house surrounded by the original English gardens, believe it or not and looks a little out of place in such a rugged northwest part of the country. I liked it, though, except those crazy horses!

"I don't blame you for hating them after your harsh experience!"

"Harsh experience, that's what you call it? My dear girls, this man tried to kill me in the cruelest way! He put me on that wild stallion of his. Wind Dancer, that's how you call him? Well, it was not a dance, but he can run like the wind, I grant you that. That beast couldn't be controlled and I'm a good rider as you girls know. For two hours I suffered the worst ride of my life" George laughed hard.

"It was not more than ten minutes."

Tim threw him disgusted look, turning to his astound audience, "And, this big brut pretended he couldn't catch up and save me! To recover from all the bruises and cuts, it took three months, but my crushed pride is still in bandages." Tim tried to look as if he had just gone through the experience all over again, while George laughed out loud shaking his head.

"Ha, ha, ha… Don't believe him, ladies! Wind Dancer is a pussycat. Miss Patricia could ride him with no problem, small as she is. I'll tell you the truth. He bragged for four years when we were back in college, what a great horseman he is, genuine riding talent. Consequently, silly me, I believed him. But anyway, for starters I gave him a calm horse" He started to laugh even harder at Tim's painful expression and open mouth in disbelief what he was hearing. George tried to control his laugh, "Don't think for a moment that I had fun chasing after you through mile after mile! Cuts and bruises were just the excuse to make us pity you. But don't worry, you built yourself a reputation which will last long after we, dear boy, perish!"

"Reputation? What are you talking about?" Tim looked at his friend through squinted eyes, trying to guess on which other way his friend will try to humiliate him now.

"The boys, in your honor, call every beginner rider "Tim's Dancer"!" Tim's open mouth and incredulity in his eyes made the women burst into loud laughter

"If I knew you'll try to discredit me in the hearts of my girls, I would never have invited you in the first place!" The laughter became louder.

"George, tell us more!" Francesca tried to wipe off a tear without ruining her perfect make up.

"I don't think he told you about Maffin. No? Well, Maffin is the girl from a neighboring ranch. Very beautiful, if a man likes tough women. From the first moment Tim saw her, he was smitten. She is a real western girl. She could throw poor Tim over her shoulder and have her way with him with no problem. I think that was the attraction, genuine love at first sight. Remember Tim, dear boy?"

"What Maffin? As I remember *all* the tough girls and not-so tough ones were crazy about you. Oh, you cruel man, you are putting your sins on my back, making my girls suspicious! Oh Patricia, my dear girl, will you have some mercy on poor me and stop this awful man!" He got down on his knees beside Patricia's chair. A little bit of wine, the cozy atmosphere, all the memories of the best years of his life, made Tim dizzy and very relaxed. He took Patricia's hand and putting it over his heart whined like a little boy, "made these bad people go away". Two of us know what cold-hearted woman your sister is, but now my dearest and oldest friend has joined evil forces with her in order to ruin me in your eyes. He hugged Patricia together with the chair she was sitting in, pressing his head to her chest.

The laughter stopped. Patricia felt her sister's icy stare and the puzzled expression on George's face. In attempt to restore the easygoing atmosphere from a minute ago she playfully pushed him away, "Well Tim you know that nobody can make you more ridiculous than you can, and for your riding mastery, I always thought that good riding is little more than staying on the horse for more than five minutes!" Tim jerked his head up. He knew something was wrong. This was not Patricia's kind of joke. It was a warning. He glanced toward Francesca – her face was a mask he could not read. George tried to look relaxed as before, but his questioning scowls made Tim feel uneasy. For a long moment, they just looked at each other, then to Patricia's relief, George ended the awkward situation.

"Well Francesca, you promised me an evening view from the east terrace and if we can persuade Patricia to pour us a couple of martinis, this evening will turn out to be one of the funniest and most enjoyable of my life!" While talking in a low seductive tone, he pulled out Francesca's chair helping her up. Patricia rose too, rushing to pour the drinks, thinking how this man could be very dangerous, but in this moment, she was grateful that this potentially uneasy situation is under control. Handing a drink, first to Francesca then one to George, she looked into his mocking eyes. He knows how to manipulate women, using his charisma and calculating mind. A sudden thought froze her in a moment – he doesn't like women very much, but why? He put Francesca's arm under his and then circled the other one around Patricia's elbow, leading them toward big French door to terrace, "In the meantime Tim, dear boy, you'll have time to wash the dishes!" Francesca burst into laughter again, and Patricia looked at George with a newly developed respect. She never before saw anybody change her sister's mood so fast and successfully as this man was able to, not even her father. Tim laughed too, happy that Francesca was not agitated any more, but resolved to be careful what he was doing from now on. He was thinking back to the evening, trying to figure out what went wrong. What did he do out of the ordinary?

Later, in her room, Patricia was also pondering over the evening's events. She most likely would not think anything of Tim's behavior toward her if Francesca did not act so weird this morning, not to mention this awkward moment after dinner. It must be Tim's exuberance about his beloved friend's presence and all the memories he brought. One thing was clear, something definitely changed between all of them, and she was afraid it would never be the same as before. She wished, for who know what time that this wretched man never showed up. Only the knowledge that Flora would be back soon, and she will be free to return to her own house calmed her down a little, so she fell asleep painfully aware that her last conscious thoughts are full of George's deep voice and his seductive manner.

The next four days passed, more or less, without any incidents, and Patricia reluctantly credited George for that. He was charming with Francesca and did not mercilessly tease Tim anymore. What bothered her was the strange glances in her direction when he thought nobody was watching. *It felt as if I was guilty of something, but what?* It was confusing and uncomfortable, and she was not used to men giving her that much attention. Fortunately, the fact that he did not talk to her very much made it easier to go through the day.

She spent as much time as she could with Michael working on their book. He was edgy and refused to accept Patricia's rejection of marriage. He convinced himself that Patricia developed a childish infatuation with George, while it was obvious to him that George was "in love" with her. Patricia was tired of all that drama and of trying, repeatedly, to convince him that neither George nor herself felt anything for each other except contempt. Therefore, she invited him to dinner in hopes he would see for himself and calm down so they could finish the book.

Well, that turned out to be another mistake, and she has been making too many of those lately. Michael tried to provoke George throughout the evening to do something to prove to Patricia he was right about George's feelings for her. That annoyed Francesca to the point that she became rude toward Michael, which, in turn made Tim angry taking it as insult to Patricia. George, to make her feel worse, was watching her with more scrutiny than ever, which was proof for Michael that George is in love with "his fiancé".

Life became too complicated, and Patricia could not wait for George and Michael to leave so she could go home, and then slip back into her normal and comfortable routine.

The day before his departure George invited them all out for dinner. "Patricia has been cooking every day and she needs a rest, and I want to be seen in the public with one of the most beautiful women I've ever seen!" He looked charmingly into Francesca's eyes keeping her happy.

"Well George, we will be delighted to show you off in this pitiful town. The ladies around here don't have many chances to see such a handsome and charming man too often." Francesca happily accepted the invitation, but things did not go as planned.

First, Patricia had to work with Michael to finish the book before the due date. Because of all the nonsense according to Michel, which was going around here, the two of them were for the first time in danger to be late with delivering the manuscript. Second, it turned out that one of the most important social obligations Francesca had been going on the evening in question. She was not happy, but Tim reminded her of her status in town and obligations, which goes with that position. So, George and Tim had to dine alone.

The two men, sitting in a dimmed elegant dining room of the best hotel in town, talked about old times, the girls they dated in college, their lives since then.

"Can you explain to me, Tim, what are you doing?" At one moment, George changed the tone of his voice, but Tim did not understand what he was asking.

"What do you mean?

"Are you in love with your wife, or is it just her beauty and image the reasons you married her?"

"Of course, I love her! What kind of question is this?" Tim still tried to guess where this inquisition was going.

"It looks like you are more in love with Patricia then with your wife!" He finally spilled out what was on the tip of his tongue and in his heart from the very beginning of his visit.

Tim looked at him with a dumbfounded expression. George kept looking at him with patient determination and fortitude to get to the bottom of his suspicion. Little by little, Tim's countenance changed. At first, he wanted to laugh, but then he realized that George was not joking! What is it that he is trying to say? Did he really love Patricia as a woman and not only as a dear sister-in-law? To be honest with himself, this probability was not so impossible. He was thinking more about her lately than about Francesca, and definitely he liked to spend his time in her company more than in his wife's. He loved Francesca. He was sure of that. Having everything in her was all that a businessman and someone of higher social status needs in a wife. Even his parents, after their first shock, excepted her, and now his mother thinks she is a perfect wife for him. What she lacked was Patricia's warmth and easiness to be with. He looked back at George, who was closely studying his face and changes on it.

"I don't know, George!" He finally breathed out.

"Maybe you don't, but you're acting towards her like a man in love. Even Francesca noticed your strange behavior. For her and your sake I hope she didn't guess the truth. Not yet. She is smart, but her vanity, fortunately for you, is too strong that she could not imagine you, or any man, would prefer Patricia over her."

"Yes, you are right! I just can't imagine my life without Patricia. You probably can't understand this, but it's something about her that makes me want to protect her, listen to her voice, be with her. She is great with kids, with people, with animals. You don't have to guess what mood she is in or acting accordingly like with Francesca. With my sweet little sister-in-law, you always know where you stand. It is so easy. I do love her!" He finally admitted it to George and to himself, "I'm in love with my wife's sister! What do you think I should do?"

"Tim, you have a family, a wife and two small children. What do you think you should do? Do you want to make everybody miserable? Do you think that Patricia is the kind of woman who would live happily ever after by breaking up her own sister's marriage and happiness? Do you think she'll consider for a moment to take away the father of those two children she adores?" The persuasive voice of his friend made Tim see the picture so realistically… It was not pretty. This was more than just a complicated situation.

"Why have I not seen this before? I'm jealous of men talking to her and I was never jealous of anybody over Francesca! I hate this Michael character! I hated him before I ever met him! She used to talk about him with admiration and I boiled inside! I should guess why. I was even mad with you when you were talking to her. Can you believe this? Why would you ever want somebody as plain as Patricia? Francesca is more your type! I was furious at you because she cooked the best meals ever, for you. I know she didn't cook it particularly for you. Frankly, I don't think she likes you very much! It is stronger than me-" George cut his rambling:

"Is she so poor that she has to live with you?" George realized that he knew nothing about the woman.

"Patricia? Poor? Lord, no! Actually, she is very well off. She has nice property and hefty trust fund and, those books of hers bring her a nice sum through royalties. The people in town think she is a gift sent to them!" It was George's turn to be surprised.

"But she is almost a servant in your house! I don't understand!"

"That is Patricia! She is where help is needed. When our housekeeper broke her hip, it was natural that Patricia would pitch in. But Flora will be back soon, and Patricia will return to her own house!" Tim was speaking slowly, feeling sadness in his heart.

"Your wife mentioned that Patricia is over thirty. Why is she not married?"

"I don't know! In the beginning, I thought of her as cold and not pretty! Now, I know better. She will be a perfect wife for some lucky guy, who most likely will treat her awful and make her miserable, like this Michael creature. He wants to entrap her in a marriage just to boost his career." Tim did not try to hide his anger.

"You think she'll marry him eventually?" George was persistent.

"Probably! If she has to get married, I wish it would be somebody who will respect her and care for her. Somebody who would deserve her! But men are idiots! Look at me! I had to marry the most beautiful girl in town. Do you know that it did not once cross my mind as to what kind of person Francesca was. I was doing it to hurt my parents, to make others envious, to forget Lisa." He hadn't mentioned that name since the moment his college girlfriend had betrayed him.

"You never told me exactly what Lisa did to hurt you so much. I never saw anybody so deeply in love as the two of you!" George decided that it was time for old skeletons to be pulled out of the closet and buried, hopefully, forever.

"You mean, you've never seen a man so much in love. Yes, I loved Lisa with all the passion of a young heart, but she was with me only for money. There is nothing more pathetic than a man in love! Makes you blind."

"For money? It's hard to believe her to be so calculating. She was such a sweet girl!" George was surprised.

"Well, who can understand the darkness of a woman's heart!" Tim meekly smiled at his bitter joke. "If you have to know, I'll tell you! When my dear father found out that I was planning a marriage to someone so *beneath me*, he decided to buy her off. In my presence, he informed her that I'd be disinherited if I married her, but if she left me, he would pay her fifty thousand. She looked at him for one minute, and a tiny minute was enough for my beloved Lisa to choose the money over me. I wanted to kill her that moment. He was writing the check with such delight that I wanted to kill him, too! You should have seen how she grabbed the check from his hand. She didn't even look in my direction. Just picked up her purse. That was the last time I saw her.

Francesca was revenge. Surprisingly, somehow, she made my parents love her. She made me love her. Although, I do not flatter myself she married me for me either. My money and position were her major motivation. I have to say she turned out to be a good wife, and I learned to love her. Until I got to know Patricia, I believed that all women are little mercenaries. Well, there are not many women like Patricia. I am sure she can love a man for what he is, not what he has!" George finally understood his friend; he knew all too well that the wrong woman could make a man's life miserable.

The next morning Tim took George to the airport. He said his goodbyes to Francesca, Patricia and the kids. Patricia was relieved,

Tim confused and devastated, and Francesca would definitely miss his charm and flattery.

*****

The next morning Tim took George to the airport. He said his goodbyes to Francheska, Patricia and the kids. Patricia was relieved, Tim was confused and devastated, and Franciska would definitely miss his charm and flattery.

On the surface it looked as everything was normal, but all of them knew that their lives had changed, on some subliminal unobtrusive way. The two women did not know what exactly had happened, but everything just felt different,

Francesca was sorry that George had left, and she thought that was the reason for her sadness. On the other hand, Patricia was relieved to see the last of him. He profoundly disturbed her perfectly adjusted life. Besides, George was a type of man she never liked. He was one of the worst she ever encountered, so sure of himself, cynical in displaying his contempt for most of the people around him. Tim did not know what to feel. He had wanted for so long for his friend to come, but now he was not sure this visit turned out to be a good or a bad thing. George definitely made him look into his life, and what he saw was nothing short of disturbing. He has to be careful for a while and decide what is most important in his life and the lives of the people he cared for.

The same day the book was finished, Michael tried for the last time to change Patricia's mind about marrying him. To his complete dismay, Patricia informed him that she had already spoken with Paula and asked for another illustrator. Deeply hurt and insulted to the point of almost hitting her, Michael blamed it all on George. All the way to the airport, he did not open his mouth, nor through boarding the plane. Patricia knew he would never speak to her, nor she will ever see him again. This chapter was closed. Patricia was embarrassed that this thought brought her relief, being fed up with that childish man.

Thanks to Universe, Tim's parents were coming back the next week, and even better Flora too. Patrecia was more than ready for her quiet life, back on the farm. Returning to all her regular endowers was appealing and comforting – working in Lucie's garden, painting kitchen cabinets and putting down on paper some new ideas for her next book. Paula made it clear that she could not continue to write about Patty anymore with a new illustrator. Patricia knew it was time to outgrew little Patty and create a new character, maybe something for older children.

CHAPTER 5

Midsummer brought scorching heat. Patricia was back at home diligently working on her new book. Paula approved the idea of writing about three sisters whose father was an anthropologist working in exotic countries around the world. The possibilities were endless. If the first book sells, she can turn it into a series, relocating the girls in every book in a different country. It will appeal to kids between the ages of eight to twelve years old. Through the adventures of the three sisters, children can learn about countries, customs, people, geography and so on. Patricia was very excited and spent many hours researching about Uganda, where the first story will evolve.

She still went, almost every day, into town to spend some time with her niece and nephew. Francesca was busy with her activities. Patricia did not see very much of Tim, mainly because she would leave before he come home from the office. The Baths did not invite her to dinner as much as they used to, but she did not mind. What she did mind was that Tim avoided her. In the beginning Patricia did not think much of it, but as time went by, it became obvious that he was trying to be in her company less as possible. When they had to spend time together, he did not joke with her anymore, nor speak to her much in general. What she missed the most was that nice cozy relationship they had before - yes, the one they had *before* George came into their lives and changed it all.

Patricia did not think about George very often. Annoyance was all she felt when she did. Knowing very well that it was not his fault for the strange situations in which she now lived, but it was easier to blame him than Francesca or Tim or herself. The only comforting thought was that she would never have to deal with him again.

Before the summer reached intolerable temperatures, old Mr. Bathes and his wife left for their annual cruise, this time north to

Alaska. Francesca got into her head that Tim and she deserved a similar treat. For a couple of weeks, she tried to convince Tim to go to Hawaii. Finally, when Patricia supported her sister and promised to move back into the house to take care of the kids, Tim agreed. Francesca booked a week in Maui and spent three days in Chicago shopping. Patricia took the children to her farm during this time, guessing that Tim would be happier if she did not stay in the Bathes mansion.

Francesca returned from Chicago shopping spree refreshed, exuberant and with a truckload of new clothes. Everybody in the household happily concluded that they had not seen her like this in a long time. The trip was what Tim and Francesca needed desperately; Patricia concluded with satisfaction. That evening, Tim was thinking the same while watching his wife trying on new dresses, chatting endlessly about Chicago, Maui, bathing suits. For months, he was battling his feelings for Patricia. He tried to stop it but up till now, he had to admit to himself that he was not having much success. He tried to stay away from her as much as he could. When she was around, he wanted nothing more than to talk to her, laugh with her, touch her. Oh Lord, he wanted to be with her, and he hated himself for that. Knowing very well that Patricia did not have the slightest idea about his feelings, and how hard he had to fight not to show them. Now, watching his wife, he hoped that this week on Maui would restore his feelings for his wife and lessen his love for Patricia, at the same time.

Being back in this big house with Timmy, Puppet and Flora, Patricia planned a lot of activities for the kids. It was quiet and peaceful. The maids and Flora got their vacation too, now when all adults were away. Patricia would spend mornings playing with kids, swimming in the backyard pool, or reading to them parts of a story she had written the day before. Afternoon, while they were napping, she would sit in the back yard and write in the shade of the big oak tree, feeling content again after such a long time.

Then, the unthinkable happened.

Two days after Tim and Francesca's departure, she was peacefully writing a chapter on Sara's – the youngest of three sisters – dangerous encounter with an old lion in the middle of the hot savanna. She lifted her head to think about a better word for big fear, and there he was. Petrified, she stared into his cold calculating eyes. She slightly cringed with the thought flying through her mind. *It looks like he despises me even more than before.*

"Flora told me that I'd find the mistress in the garden. Somehow, I expected to find Francesca!" Even his voice was colder than usual.

"Well, I imagine that it would be a bit of a disappointment for anybody to find *me* instead Francesca!" Her voice was cool and ironic. It was obvious that he understood her hint and tried to control himself.

"May I join you?" He sounded almost civil. She blushed. Darn, he did it again. *Why around him, do I always make a fool of myself?* She pointed to the chair, "Of course, Mr. Hammond, please sit down. What brings you here this time… I mean… Nobody told me you would be coming." *I am stuttering, darn, darn…Darn!*

"Nobody knew I was coming!" He said slowly, placing himself on the patio chair, "I didn't know that you were still here!"

What did this darn man mean by that? "Yes, I'm here. Where else would I be while everybody is out of town!" She snapped. *He can think whatever he wants; I have no patience with him anymore.*

George raised his eyebrows, "Out of town? Will you explain that?"

"The older Mr. and Mrs. Baths are on Alaska cruise and the young ones on Maui" she collected herself determined not to lose her temper again. If he had not surprised her, she would not have lost it in the first place. "Well, will you tell me now, if it isn't too much to ask, what fortune brought you here?" She managed to smile proud of her self-control.

"Some unfinished business o, better, the business I need to attend to!" He studied her face carefully, "But, now I'll have to wait for Tim to return home." She looked at him surprised that he was not upset.

He is not a man who easily changes his plans. Something is fishy about his behavior.

"By the way, when are you expecting them back?"

"In five days. You probably would not have time to wait that long." She was hopeful.

"Oh, that's perfectly all right. My kids are in a summer camp. I'm not needed whatsoever!"

You are not needed here either. Patricia succeeded in not wording it out aloud. She was annoyed realizing she was losing her temper again. started to lose her temper again. *Calm down,* this thought flashed like a mantra again and again. *You can't afford to lose your temper, or you'll make things worse.*

"I can use some time for myself, don't you think so!" His behavior becomes stranger every second. An uncomfortable knot in her stomach turning into a warning bell. *He is up to something. Be careful and watch him closely.*

"Well, there are many nice places around. Some with historical value while several just famous for its beauty It will shorten your waiting!" *If he spends his time anywhere but here, these next five days won't seem like eternity.* She hoped.

"That's great! That's an extremely nice offer, Patricia, to take me around and make my time pass faster. Tim was right in describing you as the nicest person he knows!" His voice was sweet, too sweet. Disbelief in her eyes did not affect him at all. When on earth did she offer anything, especially to entertain *him.*

"But... but... I have obligations to the children. This is why I'm here in the first place!" *He enjoys making me squirm.* Patricia's mind was spinning.

"Of course. we'll take them with us. I know how much you love those monkeys. and I am missing mine, so I look forward to spending some time with those two!" He interlocked fingers over his belly, and with stretched legs in front of him, George was sitting there, as he has nothing else on the world he would rather do. *He must do this just to annoy me*, crossed her mind. *Or he is a total lunatic.*

"It's after five, Patricia, don't you think it's time to get the kids out of bed and feed them? Besides I can use a little bit of nourishment myself." While helping her out of her chair, she felt inadequate again. *Now he is telling me how to take care of Timmy and Puppet, and he makes me rude, I forgot to offer some hospitality.* She was mad with herself, glancing into his calm face shifted anger back to him, asking silently: *what's next?*

The kids were happy to see George again so soon. Last time he amused them with stories about his ranch. Now, they wanted to hear more. Besides, the perspective that Georg will spend the next five days with them produced wild screaming, running around Patricia and jumping all over relaxed George. Her thoughts were rushing in circles trying to find some sense in him coming back, scrutinizing his every move. *He is growing more content, while I am becoming more irate.* At that moment, she decided to play his game.

"Okay everybody! First, we will eat and then we'll go to the movies to see "Lion King" – again! Uncle George just expressed his explicit wish to see it. We would not want to disappoint him, would we now?" Another burst of screams and jumping, this time all over Patricia, sealed their destiny for that evening. To her disappointment, George did not look upset with the prospect of spending time watching an animated kids' movie.

While they were eating, Patricia would send George sweet smiles every time he looked in her direction. Suspicion that George was aware how desperately she was trying to provoke him was overwhelming, just as it was clear to her that he was doing everything to annoy her.

To her surprise, George was a perfect gentleman, attentive and helpful with the children, and it looked like he enjoyed their everyday activities. In the afternoons, while the children napped, she would write in the garden, and he would sit opposite her reading newspapers or a book. In spite of that seeming tranquility, Patricia was on guard. She did not trust him, being sure he was up to something sinister. But, what? She patiently waited for him to reveal his true purpose. Has to be something important to justify his unexpected coming, out of character. The most puzzling was his constant observing her every move and word.

The lazy summer afternoon soothed her nerves. She looked up from her laptop. It was almost time to wake up the children. George was reading, leisurely stretched out on the grass.

"Francesca called while we were out. They are coming tomorrow evening." She spoke.

"Oh! Are you happy to see them?" George carefully studied her face.

"Of course, I'm happy to see them! Aren't you? Flora didn't tell them that you are here. She forgot!" *I wish I could.* The hopeful thought died before fully emerged. "Don't worry. I'm sure that Francesca will be more than happy to see you. Your kind of flattery is oxygen to her. Thank heavens Tim is not the jealous type!" She hated him at this moment. It looked to her as if he was protective of Tim in the most subtle way, for some mysterious reason.

He slowly raised himself in a sitting position, looking at her with slightly raised eyebrows. George got up, still looking at her, this time with an upturned corner of his mouth, in some sort of cynical grin.

"Don't be so sure of that…Don't be so sure…" For a moment, he was deep into thought, then he turned toward house brushing some imaginary dirt off his pants. "Let's go and spoil those two angels a little more before we dump them on their parents!" He managed to plaster a pleasant smile on his face as if nothing was amiss at all.

Patricia was confused. What does he mean by that? Why would

Tim be jealous? *We have been dancing around each other for five long days now.* Anxiety and strange fear flushed through her. What will transpire at the meeting of these two old friends?

Francesca and Tim were more than surprised to see George in their home. Tim was bedazzled by George's decision to drop in so unexpected. After years of being unsuccessful in trying to persuade George to visit, he came twice in such a short period of time. Francesca's mixed feelings perplexed her for several minutes, but then she was giddy to have someone who would appreciate her biggest asset, beauty. Over the last week in Hawaii, Tim was attentive, courteous and very generous, but something was missing. He worried all through his vacation, how Patricia dealing with things at home, and are the tweens were okay. He never used to be concerned with everyday household matters.

After the first excitement passed, all of them, comfortably seated in the great room talked casually. Over the course of the evening, Patricia was running around with snacks, coffee, and dish towel to wipe spilled liquids, All the way through it, Tim's eyes followed her around in the most peculiar way, while that wretched man seemed to study both of them intensely. Finaly she was tired and just wanted to go home.

"Francesca, I have to go. While George was here, I didn't have much time to take care of mom's garden. It's summer, you know, plants need more water than usual, and I neglected them a little. George and the kids helped a couple of times, but Freddy was away, nobody else is there to do it. I wish you all good night" She slowly backed toward the door.

"Wait, Patricia! Tim jumped up, "We want to… well we'll tell you all about the trip when the pictures are developed. Do you have your car here? No? It is still in the shop? I'll drive you home. Give me a sec to get my keys."

George impatiently cut him off, "Tim, you must be tired, and I have done nothing but lay in the grass the whole day long. I'll drive Patricia home!" The way he said it, nobody opposed him. He grabbed Patricia's arm above her elbow, pushing her toward the door. George led her out of the room leaving everybody feeling uneasy – her numbing feeling that she was at a loss about what just happened, and Tim with the realization that he is losing the battle.

Patricia was shoved into the car with no fuss. *What did I do wrong this time?* she wondered but determined not to ask. With a squeal of the tires, George sped out of the driveway. Silence lingered for a couple of minutes.

"Why are you doing this?" He finally broke that precious silence, and it was clear that he was enraged.

"No! Question is why are *you* doing this… this charade? You could have let Tim drive me home and both of us would be spared this torture!" George was driving too fast, but she did not want to protest. She will not give him satisfaction. If he is determined to kill them both, that's okay with her, being too tired to care. The glance in his direction confirmed - he is still furious. *What on the Earth does he have to be mad about?*

"Oh, you would like that!"

"More than your bad behavior!" She snapped. For a while they were silent again.

"I still can't decide if you are completely unaware of what is going on or if you are the most deviant person I know!" His voice was tight.

"What is that supposed to mean?" George did not answer, just clenched his teeth. She could not hold her frustration in check any longer. "I sensed from the beginning that you're holding some grudge against me, and I'll be dammed if I can figure out what? Why don't you, for once, just tell me what's bothering you and spare me any further guessing what is it that I did wrong this time?" She could not remember that anybody had ever provoked her so much to lose all of her good senses.

"Okay Patricia! But remember, you asked for it!" He took a deep breath, and then said slowly. "Are you aware that Tim is in love with you?"

Patricia felt something hard hit her in the stomach, and in the middle of the temple at the same time. *This man is not only crazy... he...he...*

"Tim? In love? With me?" When she said it out aloud, it sounded so funny that she burst into laughter. "Oh, Mr. Hammond, I don't know how to respond to this craziness! Tim loves my sister! She is... she is so beautiful! Who would not love her? Even you have a weak spot in your heart for Francesca, and don't deny it." Patricia's brain was working a hundred miles an hour, desperately searching for any reason why George would think something so absurd. "How did you come up with such an unsubstantiated fabrication?"

"It is the truth, Patricia! If you would think more carefully about Tim and your relationship, you would see it too."

Patricia frowned. Tim's behavior has been strange lately and she wondered more than once what was wrong with him? *Is it possible... No, it is not possible!* Then she exclaimed aloud, "Impossible! I don't believe it!"

"Patricia, he admitted it to me when I was here last time. I saw it from the very beginning of my visit. He was not aware of it himself until I ask him if he loved you?" She turned in her seat looking at him in hopes that something on his face would deny this madness. George stopped the car in front of her house.

"You never invited me into your home. Several times I've been here, but never inside. We have to talk. Therefore, I'm coming in invited or not!" Being in shock, she did not understand completely what he was saying, neither was she aware that he was helping her out of the car.

"Of course... we need to talk!" she finally muttered.

A few minutes afterwards, Patricia was seating at her kitchen table while George was preparing tea. "Where are the mugs? Oh here. how convenient. "

Over and over again, those blasted words were swirling around and around her mind. *Tim's in love with me! Tim's in love with me!"*

"Stop looking like the world is falling to pieces. This is not your fault. At least according to Tim, it isn't!" Patricia was upset and surprised by this devastating revelation to think clearly. George studied her face for a while, and he was sure now that she never suspected what was happening and definitely didn't provoke it as he suspected from the beginning. He gave her time to ponder over it all.

"This has no logic. Why would Tim, *anybody* for that matter, fall in love with me? He is married to my beautiful sister and…and she loves him. I never thought that she would love anyone beside herself, but she does love him."

"Yes, she does, but this is not the point. They have two small children. And so far as I can see, Tim was entertaining, for a while, the idea of declaring his love for you, that is, until I told him that you are not a woman to break up anyone's marriage, especially your sister's!" He placed the cup of tea in front of her then sat down himself.

"You are damn right, I'm not!" She wanted to cry, but not in front of this man who had disrupted her life beyond restore. "Oh, what am I going to do?" She was not asking him, she just pondered over what she needed to do next. One thing she knew – she had to make serious changes and decisions in her life and do it fast.

Nevertheless, George answered, "You'll marry and go away!" He said it in a low predatory voice, as if waiting for the right moment to inflict the next stab.

She jerked her head to look at him in astonishment. *Marry? Like this is some everyday occurrence.*

"Think carefully, you have to admit there is no other choice for you but to go away. Right?"

"Right. I'll go to New York or… Chicago, I liked living there while I was in college! I don't have to get married!"

"Be reasonable! Tim will leave you in peace only if you belong to somebody else! You have no other choice. Think!" His persuasive voice was making her hair stand up. She hated to admit it, but he *was* right! To be in this situation without any influence of the outcome was not easy on her.

" You are right, of course!" She got up. While pacing the kitchen up and down she was making quick decisions. " I'll call Michael Tomorrow! I'll tell him I changed my mind. He'll probably give me a hard time just to put me in my place, but he'll marry me!" George looked at her with disgust.

"You will not do such a thing. What life will you have with that monkey! He is a mediocre human being without any passion for life. He hates children, probably animals too. What would the two of you do between books?" The impatience in his voice made her listen.

For an intelligent man he can be so stupid. Maybe Francesca can get five proposals a year if she needs to, but I had one in my entire life, and he managed to make it disgusting in thirty seconds.

"Yeah? Marriage proposals do not grow on the trees. Michael was the only man who ever proposed. Now when you know this, you can despise me more, who do you suggest I marry? You?" *If he does not go away soon*, she decided impatiently, *I will kick him out of my house on his nose.*

"Yes!" his voice sounded like he was confirming he would like another cup of tea. She was not in the mood for more sparring with him.

"Oh, really? Let's recap, shall we? First, even *if* you are serious, which is preposterous, what would make you a better choice than Michael?

He at least, respects me, and second, I believe that he honestly thinks that he loves me. This is much more than what you can offer! I grant you, he is dispassionate and dull, but life with him would be easy. With someone like you just a battle!"

Patricia was standing in front of him asking herself why she even bothered to explain. He was steadily looking at her with no expression on his face.

"Besides why would you marry me? Tim pierced our ears about all those poor women who were throwing themselves on the ground in front of you and I believe him, too! You are the male chauvinistic type who would enjoys that kind of pitiful display. I could never be one of them. Besides, not being pretty enough so that the rest of your male friends would drool all over me and envy you wouldn't make me the right choice at all!" She was steaming and George let her emit her frustration.

"Well, I knew that you didn't think highly of me, but I wasn't aware how much you dislike me! Anyhow, I'm your only chance to help your sister and Tim put their marriage back on track. Tim is my friend, and I'll do everything in my power to help him. In addition, I can assure you as my wife, you can be at peace that he would keep himself under control. He respects me, so he'll never hurt me by hitting on my wife."

"He respects me too, you know! I'll confront him and I'm sure he'll get over this lunacy!" She couldn't give up.

"Are you sure? How much do you know about men? He was already hitting on you, remember, that first evening I came. I couldn't believe it! Even Francesca had her suspicions. Men in love are not to be trusted. Remember that, little Patricia!" *How can he be so calm?* She did remember Francesca's strange behavior during and after George's visit. *Darn man! Why can't she I find some reasonable solution without his help?*

"But marriage? George, can't we come up with some less drastic solution?" She finally gave up fighting him.

He smiled. "I never thought that marrying me would be so dreadful? A low husky laugh escaped his throat for a moment. "I am sorry, but I don't see any other solution. I am aware of this situation for much longer than you, and believe me I gave it a lot of serious thinking. First of all, Francesca will find it natural that you would want to marry me."

"But she won't find it believable that you want to marry me!" She looked at him from under her eyelashes.

"She will. she will when we convince her with a display of all the love and passion we have for each other!" His lifted eyebrows and reassuring smile infuriated her again. He is always so sure of himself. She wished she felt the same.

"What? You propose that we fool them? I have to tell her."

"To tell her that you are marrying me to stop her husband from destroying her life. And stop cutting me off every five words! Just listen! We'll tell them that we fell in love these last five days while we were waiting for their return. Nobody ever questions love, Patricia. Love, my dear girl, struck you and you can't help it. Francesca is romantic no matter how rational she wants to be. She'll buy it. I'm more worried about Tim. He knows that I know, so he might suspect I'm doing this for him. We have to make him believe that he's mistaken, or he could do something stupid. Do you understand the importance of this?"

"Yes, I do! I'm not sure I'll be able to pretend very well, I am a poor actress as you'll see!"

"I know.! You are very straight forward. I don't know if that's good or bad. I never met a woman who wasn't very successful at pretending whenever she found it beneficial for her. You have to think, all the time, about your niece and nephew and, of course, your sister! It would be much easier if you like me just a little bit. Then you won't need to pretend so much. Maybe you can make yourself believe that you do like me, at least try. Okay?" George took her hand in his. Her small fist completely enveloped in his big strong hand, seemed even smaller.

"Oh, I need some time to think about it!" she whispered.

"Time is the only thing we don't have! If I don't tell them something very soon, it will be very hard to explain why we didn't tell them everything immediately. I am planning to tell them tomorrow as a big surprise, after which everybody will be in a celebratory mood! We will drink some champagne and act lovestruck. You'll see everything will turn out okay."

She was staring at him absorbed. *He is very smooth and sickeningly logical.* That thought made her even more uneasy. She did not know what to say. *I am so tired.* Sudden realization drained all of her diminishing energy and motivation to fight him. *I want to go to bed.*

"I think I should go to bed, George!" Patricia whispered.

"Listen! I'll come back here tomorrow morning, early. We'll talk and get back to the Bathes' home before breakfast. Okay?" She nodded.

Patricia was sitting in the same place long after George left. The last couple of hours were the strangest of her life. Her existence was something she was sure would never change. Patricia accepted and embraced what she had – her house, writing, family, and her peaceful life in this little town. She did not desire anything else. Or did she? A long time ago she did.

Remembering herself as a young girl she fantasized about a husband and children, like all of her girlfriends. Several relationships she had in college convinced her very fast, that she most likely will never marry, unless… unless somebody would love her with all of his heart… which, she concluded then, would never happen. Men are shallow worshipers of beauty, like that infatuated army of adolescents who chased Francesca solemnly because she was beautiful. None of them cared about her as a person. They wanted to be seen with her sister to be the envy from the less fortunate, crated achievement of being chosen by gorgeous woman. So many times, as a young girl Patricia felt cheated by not inheriting any of her mother's looks. Through the years of observing her sister and her life, made her realized that Francesca could never be sure if there was a single person who would love her if she was not beautiful. Even her own husband married her for that reason, and now when he got to know her, it seemed he would rather have plain Patricia. Yet again, he wanted a mother for his children, good housewife, companion with a sense of humor, trades Patricia possessed. Even Michael's pursuit was for her writing abilities, not her. Evidently, she has to settle for… What? A man with a strange sense of loyalty toward his friend and their past a man determined to live with a woman he despises. She will not do it. With this decision, she went to bed.

CHAPTER 6

The early morning sun entering the dimness of her bedroom and the birds' vocal response to it were the usual way for Patricia to wake up. However, today was accompanied by a numbing sensation around her heart. Laying in bed, still half asleep, yesterday's events floated up to her awakening conscious.

Patricia jumped out of bed. George will be here sooner then she would like. She will be ready to confront him with her decision. After all she is thirty-two years old, an educated woman with an established life and respect of her community, smart and capable to face and handle every problem. This was a problem she will deal with it on her own, not needing help from some overbearing macho man.

She put on her gardening jeans and an oversized faded t-shirt. *This is me at home, comfortable old plain Patricia, not marriage material for some spoiled rich and handsome man.* George drove to her front door just in time for a fresh pot of coffee and Patricia ready for the duel of her life.

"Good morning, George! I hope you had pleasant dreams! Sit and have a cup of coffee! Had any breakfast yet? No? Neither did I! How about -" Patricia was peering into her open refrigerator under the scrutiny from George. It was obvious to him, from her first word, that she is up to something. "I have cheese, some deli meat, butter, jam and grapefruit!" Pulling everything on the countertop, she sounded and acted as if they had been spending their mornings this way for ages.

"Patricia, what are you up to?" His voice was slow with a warning undertone.

"George, let's have a nice breakfast and then we'll continue our discussion from yesterday!" She looked at him with a sweet smile.

"Patricia!" It sounded like a treat. He crossed his arms over his chest frowning.

"I have a perfect solution for our little problem. Nothing as drastic as a marriage of horror," she pointed finger at him, "and a human sacrifice!" Pointed at herself.

"Human sacrifice? What are you talking about, for God's sake!" He exploded.

"I found it very charming that you are ready to sacrifice yourself on the altar of a friendship and altruism by tying yourself to an unwanted bride!" While talking she loaded food on the plates, placed them on the table and pulled the utensils out of the drawer.

"Okay, I am all ears!"

"I will go away, somewhere far where Tim, and anybody else will not be able to find me" She looked at him under her eyes, "and in time Tim will forget all about me and that... that silly infatuation!" She again looked at him with a broad smile.

"So, let me recap just to be sure I understand you correctly! You'll pick up some of your belongings and disappeared into thin air?" His raised eyebrows annoyed her, although she did expect this would awaken his stubbornness.

"Well, you couldn't say it more brilliantly, but never-the-less that is exactly what I am going to do, and you will help by not interfering and going back to your ranch and businesses, your life!"

"Now, explain to me what everybody you'll leave behind will think and feel about it? People do not disappear without a word or trace. Are you aware that the police will be alerted! That your family will look for you think the worst, that you are kidnaped, raped, killed, sold into slavery!"

"Sold into slavery? Please George don't be so dramatic!" She tried to save her "brilliant" idea, but he was destroying it with such ease.

"Dramatic? *I am* dramatic? I never heard such exaggerated bull… in my life. What is going to happen when you are not found? Think about your sister and her children, whom you love? How are they going to feel day after day, week after week, year after year not knowing if you are alive or dead? In addition, if you left on your own accord, why did you do it without a word?" Patricia was looking at him in horror. Oh damnation, if she only could think of a better way to get away from Tim, but with less dramatic consequences of her action.

"Furthermore, if you decide to go ahead with this silly plan of yours and leave everybody in dismay, how are you going to live your life?" He was merciless in his attack, "Imagine never seeing your family again! Never to know how they live, what they do, how Timmy and Puppet are growing up, what they look like! What they would think about their selfish aunt, when they grow up, who abandoned them without a word so long ago?" He picked up his coffee mug, watching as Patricia's face changed from determination to an expression of defeat.

In deep thought, she was standing beside the kitchen sink for a long time. Finally turning to him she said, "Alright, Mr. Hammond, I'll marry you, but I want to have some answers. I know you like Tim very much, but to marry a woman you don't even like to save his marriage is a little too much, even for a most beloved friend. Why would you sacrifice your future for his sake?" Patricia asked as she scrutinized him carefully.

"I wanted to discuss with you the rest of my motives for marrying you some other time when all this is behind us, but I might as well do it now. You know that my wife died soon after having my youngest child six years ago. Since then we have gone through a number of nannies and governesses, but it hasn't worked out. I contemplated for a while to remarry, only I didn't see any of the women I knew as good mother material, until I saw you with Timmy and Puppet. You are natural with kids and mine have been in need of some motherly attention for a long time. You see, Patricia, we can help each other solve our problems. You can stay in touch with your family, see them and visit them. Every summer they can visit our ranch. Maybe at Christmas we'll come here. This is the best solution for everyone!" His persuasive voice and logic of his arguments made her feel foolish, but her brain was still working overtime trying to find some way out of this craziness.

"What would happen if someday you fall in love with some gorgeous woman?" He felt relief. She had made up her mind. She will marry him. The balm of relief rushed through him. Keeping his face blank, answering her with the same unchanged tone.

"I can assure you – it will never happen!" He smiled with just the corners of his mouth.

Patricia frowned seeing clearly through him. *He is having fun on my account again.* She looked up at him with the challenge in her eyes. "And what happens if *I* fall in love with somebody?"

"Well, I'm hoping it will be me!" he smiled broader.

"Don't be silly. I am not a masochist!" Suddenly all she wanted was to put all the unfortunate confrontations and situations with her family behind her. "We better go. Francesca will be up soon, and she'll worry about what's happened to you." Patricia now knew what she had to do, and her brain was already planning their next move.

"Yes, let's go!" He got up trying to foresee what Patricia could stumble over and jeopardize their plan.

Knowing Francesca's perceptiveness, Patricia's heart twitched in fear. Both of them hurried toward the door at the same time, running into each other. George grabbed her to steady her, and the next second she was in his arms. His lips covered hers hard and demanding. She froze in this moment in time aware of what was happening but unable to move or protest. Then he raised his head looking into her eyes, just as they had the first time they met on the stairway. Patricia regained control over her mind and body, feeling how all of her blood rushed to her face. Jerking herself away from George. She was furious.

"How dare you?" … you… you beast!" She was losing her breath, painfully aware of her crimson face, fast heartbeat. She opened her mouth to put him in his place, but George interrupted her before she had time to think any further.

"Thank heavens I did it here. I was afraid you'd react like this. What will Tim and Francesca think about our undying love if you react in front of them as you did just now? Pull yourself together, Patricia! People in love can hardly keep their hands off each other. How do you think we'll convince your family that we are in love?"

Patricia was blinking her eyes in confusion. Why should she be so upset over one insignificant kiss? She'd been kissed before, but not like this. The scary thought started to creep in her mind. *Is she* angry because of the kiss, or how it affected her. A dilemma she will have to think about some other time.

"You… just surprised me!" Patricia snapped, "Why didn't you warn me? Just tell me that we need some practice… I'm not a little teenager without any experience… I have been kissed before; you know, but you grabbed me like… like…?"

"A beast?" He laughed, "I'm sorry! You are right, but we were in a hurry and I… Oh, It's not important. Let's go and face the firing squad!" He took her hand leading her to the car.

"Patricia, do you understand that we have to get married fast?" George asked slowly.

"How fast?" She was afraid of the answer.

"Very fast! As soon as possible! I can stay four or five days more, then my children will be back home. I hope we'll be able to organize everything on the shortest time possible." She could not believe what he was saying.

"Do you propose to get married in four days? It is not doable! I have so many duties and obligations in town, with the kids, then the farm! I have to find someone to take care for the garden besides Freddy, house, the whole property! No, no! Four days is not enough, George, you have to see that!" Patricia started to understand the wider effect of their decision. A person never knows how complicated life is and how immensely connected to so many people until some handsome rich man comes and sweeps you away. It was funny and ridiculous, but she did not have the energy to laugh.

"We'll see. I'm sure that everything can be handled to your satisfaction. Let's do one thing at a time. Agreed?"

"Agreed!"

*****

They were approaching Bath's mansion. Patricia was not ready to face her sister and Tim, but George was already helping her out of the car. The entrance door opened, and Tim's smiling face appeared.

"Francesca! Here he is. He went to fetch Patricia, just as I told you. The two of you are very mysterious. If I didn't know better, I would swear that you are in love!" He was joking. The love between George and his sister-in-law was the last thing on Tim's mind.

Francesca was in the kitchen feeding the children. She looked at them and instantly knew something was different.

"What's wrong?" She looked directly into Patricia's eye.

"Oh Francesca, nothing is wrong. On the contrary, things can't be more perfect. Listen here Tim, dear boy, and you Francesca. Patricia and I have something to tell you both!" George sounded a little too joyful, putting his arm around Patricia's shoulders at the same time. Raised eyebrows were the only response. nd.

"We have decided to get married!" He said it slowly with a big smile on his lips. Tim and his wife just stood there looking at them in amazement.

"I… I don't believe it!" Francesca finally muttered.

"How did this happen?" Tim went pale, squeezing the back of the chair so hard that his knuckles turned white.

"You are surprised, dear boy? I know, I am surprised that this dear girl fell in love with me too. I worked on that around the clock. She stole my heart the last time I was here, so I decided to come back and make her love me. Unbelievable as it sounds, I succeeded. She loves me!" He sounded like a man whose biggest wish came true. *Oh, he is good,* Patricia was impressed. *Who would dare not believe him? He made me believe him too for a moment.*

Tim and Francesca stood motionless in place watching them in disbelief. George bent down and kissed Patricia passionately and playfully on her lips. This time she accepted his kiss more gracefully by looking down at the floor.

"Well, won't you congratulate us! You look like I'm not good enough to be your brother-in-law!" George moved toward the paralyzed couple, dragging a flustered Patricia with him.

"Of course. Congratulations! My dear Patricia, how great… how unbelievable!" Francesca hugged her sister still carefully watching both of them. She half expected they would burst into laughter and tell them it was all a joke. Tim looked at Patricia with troubled eyes, and then he hugged her too.

"Congratulations, my dear! I hope you'll be happy as much as you deserve!" Tim kissed her on the cheek, keeping her close a little longer than necessary. George pulled her away laughing.

"Tim, do you remember how many times you wished to have a sister I could marry so we could be a family. Now your wish has come true. We'll be a family, dear boy. Life manages to put all things in order!" George could not stop amazing Patricia. He genuinely looked like the happiest man in the world.

Patricia had a harder time keeping up with George, looking exuberant and accepting George's hugs, holding hands, and some short kisses from time to time, with equal eagerness as he bestowed them on her. She must be doing something right because Francesca embraced this new situation, already deep in plans for the wedding. With a pad in her hands, she was making a list in which order the event would unfold, because of the short time they had to organize everything. She even called Tim's parents on their cruise, excited about the wedding, they promised to be back in time for the ceremony.

Tim, on the other hand, did not look excited at all. Patricia caught him, over and over again, staring at her and studying her. It was more than obvious how troubled he was. Tim did not know what to think. Is this just George's scam to take Patricia away from him, or has he fallen in love with her? Knowing George, that was not very believable. Francesca was more his type. He was always falling for beautiful and glamorous women. Nevertheless, Patricia became so special and dear to him that he did not doubt for a moment that any other man could love her, too. Is George that sensitive and perceptive to see deep into Patricia and found all that beauty and treasure there? Conflicting emotions were sweeping through his heart. In one moment, his soul twisted in pain with the thought of George possessing his precious Patricia! Then, the next moment, he felt grateful that she would be going and making it easier for him to forget her. Ultimately, the questions of George's motives for marrying her would put him into another state of torment. If he is doing it for his, Tim's sake, it would be a terrible thing to do to Patricia. She was so naïve and easily hurt, but watching George's tender care for Patricia made him angry. It felt like George was stealing his most precious possession. Damn, how is he going to endure all that and stay sane? With loathing, he looked at George who was whispering something into Patricia's ear. She smiled and nodded her head.

The next few days were a test of everyone's endurance. Francesca, with her sense of style, wanted perfection to the last detail, which of course, was not possible with the lack of time. Patricia was using every second to put her public work in order. Fortunately, everyone was happy that their favorite person finally getting married, and to such a handsome and darling man, so there were enough volunteers to take over all of Patricia's duties. The hardest task was to find someone to take care of her house and Lucie's Garden. George carefully suggested that the property be sold, but Patricia fiercely refused. That surprised him a little. Patricia did not expect him to understand. In her mind and heart, selling was not an option. This property was all she owned and, if marrying George meant leaving Church Hill, it was okay with her, but she needed something to wait for her if things went wrong. The house and garden were part of her entire existence. She always felt secure here, the only place in the world which belonged to her, and she will never give it up. George did not mention the subject again, realizing that things were moving too fast, and Patricia would need more time to make such a decision.

The day before the wedding took place, the older Mr. and Mrs. Bathes came home. Both were very excited, which did not stop Mrs. Bathes from trying to change Patricia's mind.

"My dear, marriage is a very serious matter. How well do you know this man? I have to admit, he is very handsome, and Tim insured me that he is very rich. I hope you understand, my dear, that you have to be sure what you are doing. He has three children! Do you know that? And, what about his first wife? She is dead! How awful! Did you see "Rebecca"? Terrifying movie! You have to be very careful. I want you to promise me if over there you find anything, *anything* suspicious, you'll come straight back. Nobody would blame you. Promise me, my dear" Mrs. Bathes was at her best again, Patricia smiled.

"Of course, Mrs. Bathes! One stuffy servant and I'm back before my suitcase has a chance of being unpacked. Don't you worry for one second, I'm sure that everything will be perfect!"

I wish I felt this confident. Patricia knew she was afraid, not that she would be tormented as poor Rebecca, but there were so many uncertain details, unknown things, and no time to find them all out. Mr. Bathes was genuinely delighted. In his opinion the only duty and calling for a woman was to get married, have children, and take care of house and her husband. With fluttering anticipation, he approached Patricia the second they arrived home.

"My sweet girl, now that you no longer have a father and I'm the only male relative of proper age, I hope you'll allow me to give you away to this lucky man?" Patricia loved Mr. Bathes who always tried to make her feel like a member of his family, so she accepted his offer with a throb in her throat. The whole day she thought of her mother and father, wishing them here with her on this uncertain day. She was grateful to Mr. Bathes after her parents passed, who did everything so Francisca and she would not miss their parents too much.

Not sure she would be able to sleep tonight, Patricia was surprised she slept soundly as if she has no problems in the world. The same happened in the morning, puzzled how calm and composed she is on the very day she is sealing her destiny forever, not knowing what awaits her so far away across the country. While taking a shower she realized all the strings that held her here were severed with one strike. Her life will not be simple and under her control anymore. To live as a married woman with a man she did not like very much will be trying. They will have to come to a certain understanding about their personal relationship. These passing days were filled to the brim with hundreds of little and big tasks and decisions, thus reducing seeing George to only in passing for few minutes at a time. Arrangements of mutual satisfaction will be snap; after all, he did not like her very much as well. One thing that make her feel easier - he was not such a selfish man as she thought before. This extravagant gesture of marrying the woman he despises just to save his friend's marriage shows that he possesses a dissent amount of compassion. Furthermore, his desire to provide his children with the best possible mother told her more about his character than anything else she knew about him. A fear of her future life was eased by the anticipation and prospect of being a mother for real. Resolved for some time now she would never have an opportunity of having her own children, she dedicated herself to Francesca's kids. One thing was clear – those children needed a mother, and this was her chance to be one for real. She will try to do all she can for those children, Patricia promised herself. As to what kind of wife she will be to a rich and influential man posed a big question mark in her heart? Definitely, she will try to be a presentable wife and keep her part of the bargain.

Francesca nervously knocked on her door.

"Patricia, are you awake?" Barely having time to open her mouth to respond, her sister was already in, fussing over her.

"Look at yourself Patricia, you are still in your pajama. You should be finished with breakfast by now. The man will be down soon and as you know, and as you know it's bad luck if the groom sees the bride before the church. hurry, hurry! I spoke with the pastor. He assures me that the church looks absolutely beautiful, even better than at my wedding, which is hard to believe. but if it is, I'm happy for you." She was dragging Patricia still half-asleep down the stairs chatting tirelessly.

While forcing on Patricia loads of food, Francesca was calling caterers, florists, bridesmaids and others, checking, instructing, and rushing everybody. After stuffing more food down her throat, just to pacify the flustering Francesca, Patricia was slowly climbing the stairs thinking how much time will pass before she sees this house and its inhabitants again. Tim's voice snapped her out of her lament.

"Patricia, may I have a word with you?" She turned and her heart went out to him. He looked troubled and drained.

"Of course, Tim! Come up with me. If Francesca catches me wasting time, she'll spank me. She's my older sister and she thinks she's entitled to it." Discovery that she still can joke with him as she did before was like sweet music. They entered the bedroom and a splash of yards of white satin was lying all over her bed, this stopped them for a moment. The maid must have put it there while she had her breakfast.

"Beautiful dress!" Tim mattered.

"Well, nothing that I would have chosen, but Francesca insisted on buying it, so I agreed to the

one she wanted. But yes, it is very beautiful!"

"Tell me honestly, are you, sure that you're doing the right thing?" He finally asked.

She knew he would ask that sooner or later, so she was ready. "Of course, I'm sure! Tim, do you remember when you and Francesca were getting married? Everybody doubted your decision and all of us were wrong. Look at the two of you now? I don't know a couple happier and more suitable for each other. George and I can only hope to come close to what you and Francesca have."

He looked confused, not expecting this kind of an answer, turning even more miserable. Patricia continued calmly, although she was far from being at it. His peace of mind depended on what she would say these next few minutes.

"On the other hand, you are responsible for this! First of all, you told us all those fantastic stories about George, then you brought him here. What could a poor girl like me do but fall in love? Then George told me how you filled his ears with numberless, no doubt imaginary, good things about me until he fell in love with me. You must see, it's all your doing. Therefore, George and I are grateful to you forever, my dear brother!"

"Well, I'm happy for both of you, and wish you the best of everything!" He almost ran out of her room, making the approaching hairdresser jump backwards to prevent from being knocked over.

This was the first time she was completely sure that Tim was in love with her, and that realization made her finally except what she was doing is right on so many levels and for so many people. Patricia was almost happy.

The hairdresser was a miracle worker! She transformed her hair into an elegant swirl, which made her look sophisticated and even pretty. Francesca ran in again. and from that moment, events were flying faster than Patricia could follow. From being stuffed into her gown, dragged downstairs and shoved into a big white limousine was the least of it. The church was packed, so many had to stay outside. The crowd cheered to her as she got out of the flashy big car. Her heart was overwhelmed with contrasting emotions. The love for these people, the beloved town she was leaving, the uncertain future and questionable happiness of her family were rushing through her heart. Mostly she was afraid, but things were unstoppably advancing. Mr. Bathes led her proudly toward the altar, where George stood, handsome and so calm, waiting for her with a smile on his face. Glancing toward Tim, who was standing beside the groom as the best man, her heart twitched in compassion. He was not so calm, but she saw determination on his face. It was obvious he would manage to go through this without any outbursts, and his secret will stay safe.

The ceremony stayed vague in her memory; the pastor's words were like background noise. The waterfall in her ears hushed every other sound. She did not remember saying "I do", but she must have done it; the ring was on her finger, George's kiss followed with loud clapping and cheering, and his reinsuring hand on her elbow helped her walk her toward the bright door opening. More cheering outside of the church awakened her senses, so she waved to her fellow citizens and friends.

The reception was in the biggest hotel in town, in a huge ballroom extended by white tent into beautiful grounds on the back of the elegant building. Patricia was grateful for a big breakfast forced on her by Francesca, for she did not have time to do anything but receive good wishes and tearful goodbyes from hundreds of people.

Several hours later, she took her seat beside George in the airplane flying to her new home and new life. She did what she had to do, and there was no way back.

George was sitting beside her reading some documents. *I don't even know what he does jobwise. Is it ranching? I don't think so. He has a big house, but who lives there beside his children? What are their names? He mentioned it once, when he visited the first time, but I didn't even want to remember, thinking I'll never see them in my lifetime. I was sure I'll never see him again. How strange life can be?*

On impulse she turned to him.

"George, will you please tell me a little about your house, your children, your ranch, what you do there, and the people who are closest to you. Somehow, they will expect me to know these things." He looked at her with annoyance. *Damnation is this the way he's going to treat me from now on., Well, I don't care, but when I want to know something, I'll ask, and he better answer it promptly.*

"George let's put things in proper perspective! We both know why we are going through this charade. And I can accept the need to pretend, how you called it, oh yes, to be *passionately in love*. When we are alone, I will be more than happy not to talk to you and be invisible, but when I ask a question, which is closely connected with all the things I just mentioned, I expect some courtesy from you by answering my question!" As she was going on with this tirade, she became calmer and more thrilled she did not cave in and let him intimidate her.

He looked at her with surprise and maybe a little remorse. "I'm sorry, Patricia! I should volunteer all the information which you need to know as my wife. Well, let's see, first my children. Andrew is eleven, Lindsay is nine and Mark just six. Millie is my housekeeper and cook. Peter, her husband, is the gardener and groundkeeper. They are more family than employees. They live in a small house down from my main house… our house. We have two girls who help with housework. They are the wives of my cowboys. My job, as you put it, is, well, I own several companies, which I manage. I have many interests in a wide array of business around the world. The rest you'll see by yourself and meet everyone in time." He returned to his papers forgetting all about his surroundings. For the rest of the trip Patricia occupied herself with anticipating the kind of welcome she would get when she arrives in her new home.

CHAPTER 7

After the fiasco in the airplane, Patricia refrained from more questions, or any other observation. She did not care for him and looked like she never would. Therefore, it is good that he does not want any close relationship. For her it was never hard to find friends, among normal human beings, that is. She will also find them here. Mainly, she will spend most of her time with the children, and naturally, she will dedicate herself to writing.

They changed airplanes twice. The last was a small plane, because Sheridan, the closest airport to George's ranch, had a small-capacity runway. Peter waited for them with the big Cadillac to accommodate all of their luggage. He was a man in his early sixties, short but strong in build. Overexposure to sun wrinkled his skin, while a broad smile seemed to be a permanent fixture of his face including the twinkling sparkle in his small friendly eyes.

"Welcome home George!" He slapped his boss's back not to gently in Patricia's opinion, turning toward her, "Well Mrs. Hammond!" *Oh, dear me, this is the first time I have been called by my new name.* It felt strange and little bit frightening, but she did not have time to lament over it, "Welcome to your new home! Oh, my, my, this big fellow did not tell us how pretty you are. A real lady, this time, my boy!" While talking to George, he was eyeing Patricia up and down from her toes to the top of her head. The elegant suit she used to wear during her New York visits, made her feel a little out of place in this small provincial airport. Although Peter's openly scrutinizing glare was somewhat intimidating, but his disarmingly charming demeanor put her instantly at ease, so she was sure she will like him. Patricia extended her hand smiling warmly.

"Thank you, Peter, for your kind words. I'm glad we have finally arrived. I didn't realize that this... this place is so... well, small and that we didn't have direct connection. But we are here and I'm looking forward of seeing it all!" *Oh, I'm mumbling like a schoolgirl*, she thought in dismay, while feeling more than seeing a cynical smile on George's face. That shut her up, but she kept her friendly smile directed at Peter.

"Okay, folks. Let's go! This will be the last leg of your journey, Mrs. Hammond. This big car is pretty comfortable. George insisted on this one. I planned to come in the truck. Somehow, I thought you'd have much more luggage, but he knows best." studying his boss through squirming eyes, "It must be nice to be so much in love! Don't think for a moment, young lady, that I forgot how is to be in love. One day I'll tell you a story how I kidnaped my Millie and, made her love me. Hah ha." Astonishment on Patricia's face amused him, so he laughed even louder.

"How come I never heard that story? If it's the truth?" George's voice was flat.

"Because you don't have a single molecule of romance in you, my boy! You wouldn't be able to understand the fine distinctions in romancing a woman. You'll drive?" Peter looked at his boss teasingly. Patricia marveled at the ease of Peter's dealing with her new husband.

"I'll drive, you old fool!" George snatched the keys from Peter's big hand.

"But I am a romantic! I would love to hear that story and I don't care if it exactly true or not!" George grudgingly responds to totally unaffected Peter. Patricia started to relax a little, thinking she had to do her best to make these new people in her life friendly. *As few enemies as possible*, rolled like a mantra on the back of her mind.

All the way to the ranch, Peter was pointing out interesting and beautiful points while telling her wild stories from the past. The landscape was green and lush, spackled with slow moving cattle.

"What are those? They look like a… lamas?" She could not believe her eyes.

"Of course, they are lamas! We use them for packing, you know at hunting time. They can go everywhere and carry heavy loads at the same time." *I am going to like this country and maybe I will even make George my friend.* Her natural optimism won over and she sat deeper into her seat ready for whatever was ahead.

They entered the most superior-looking woods she'd ever seen, then she realized that it was not a woodland but a huge park. Tim's description of George's estate was a mansion in the middle of a beautiful English garden, and finally it made sense to her. Then, the sight of the house suddenly appeared in front of her, taking her breath away.

"This is the most beautiful house I've ever seen!" She heard herself exclaiming, while looking ahead with an open mouth.

"What you thought that we lived in a mountain cabin?" George's voice was like ice, making Peter look sharply at him, which remained George that Patricia and he are supposedly madly in love.

"Well Peter, if you don't stop trying to seduce my bride I won't only fire you, I'll fill your hind full of buckshot!" He looked at Peter with a comical murderous expression, which made the older man laugh aloud again.

"The boy is jealous! That is normal! Young people in love are the most unreasonable creatures in the world. Jealous of me? Wait until I tell Millie!" Peter's insistent laugh made Patricia laugh too. In that moment, they stopped in front of the house. Patricia spotted a short plump woman standing at the big entrance door. She waived at them descending the large stone steps.

"Oh, you are finally home! Dinner was ready half an hour ago, and it's not my fault if it is spoiled now! George, you could stop Peter from blabbering and wasting your time. You know him better than that! When he sees a young face, he loses all his marbles!" She finally reached the other side of the car where Patricia was standing not knowing what to do.

"Okay George, this is your new bride? Well, you were right, she is pretty and small!" The short intense scrutinizing was over almost before it started, "My dear, you look like somebody starved you on purpose. We will change that in a jiffy! Good food and fresh air will fill you up, as a woman should be. Welcome, my dear. I just know you'll be happy here! And, if those men give you a second of trouble, you just come to me. I won't feed them for a week, and they'll be mellow as puppies. A bit of advice, my dear, don't believe Peter's stories, he is losing it. I bet he told you how he kidnaped me and made me marry him. Ha, Ha." She took Patricia under her arm, leading her toward the door.

"How come I never heard that story in my life" George was annoyed again trailing after the rest of them carrying language. These people he has known all his life, in the presence of this woman were turning into strangers.

Peter did not listen at all, he happily dragged Patricia's suitcases up the steps constantly repeating, "She does remember how I took her away… she does remember…"

George was hopelessly looking at Peter's back, "Everybody went crazy in a single week while I was absent! I'm afraid to see the kids. They probably turned into aliens, or something!"

"Dad, you are talking to yourself again! What did you bring me?" A tiny voice turned him around.

"What did I bring you? You little greedy monster! And I don't talk to myself. I nag out loud and with good reason. Come here and give me a kiss!" He lifted up into the air a small boy who was kicking his legs and screaming with laughter. Then he saw his other two children running toward him.

"Dad, Dad! You are here at last! Did you bring-!"

"Stop right now! All you want from me are gifts! This time, I brought you a new mother as I told you I will!" They stood there looking at him. "Don't look at me like I'm sending you to boot camp.

You need a mother to put you in order."

"We don't need any mother! We haven't had one for a long time, and we are okay with it!" Andrew said sharply, "You can bring seven wives, but none of them will ever be our mother!"

"Andrew, I'm warning you! You may think whatever you want, but don't fill the ears of the youngsters with it, and behave towards Patricia with respect, or else." Andrew just looked at him with pressed lips.

"Where is she, Dad? We'll see her today?" Lindsay was curious about the new mother. She agreed with her older brother about not needing one, but she was very interested in seeing her anyway.

"Listen to me guys, as I told you the other night on the phone, you don't have to call her mother if you don't want to. Actually, I didn't discuss this with... my wife. Maybe she won't like you calling her mother just yet. These things will need some time to work out. But, please, give it a try before you pass on your judgment, okay? Andrew?"

"Okay, Dad!" Andrew responds, looking at the ground.

"Actually, she is very nice and, did I tell you, she writes children's books!" He smiled at three   surprised faces. *I shouldn't use executive boardroom tricks on my kids, but I always felt more at home dealing with sharp businessmen then with my own children. One thing I'm sure about – my children needed a mother, and I know that Patricia is the best choice.* "March, you wild cowboys, I'll introduce you to Patricia now and you'll see how great she is. Andrew, you count to ten before you find it necessary to open your mouth!" George started up the stone steps in front, and three children obediently followed him.

In the meantime, Millie led Patricia through the big lavish hall and up the stairs to the first floor, chatting tirelessly, "After he built this house the way his wife wanted, he let her furnish it any way she liked. Money was not in question, so she ordered the best furniture from England. It took months to deliver it here. At that time, these parts were just territory. First, the boats needed a month to bring it to

Boston and then from there several more months in wagons through wild and rough country. Indians and bandits swiped several shipments. Old Mrs. Hammond was one persistent lady, you have to give her that. The mistresses after her added some new pieces, but the majority of the furnishings are from that time. Oh, here we are! Your bedroom!" Millie opened the door of a beautiful big room painted in a light blue color, white furniture was gilded in gold, a huge French window led to the balcony with a spectacular view of the mountains. Her eye caught a big king size bed. *Oh! Lord, we never talked about sleeping arrangements.*

"Millie, this is one beautiful room!" She started carefully, "Somehow, I can't imagine Mr. Ham - George in this room."

"Oh, no! George slept, since his wife died in the west wing. After he was back from Church Hill that first time, he said he was getting married and ordered this room to be remodeled for the two of you. He said blue is your color and I must say he was right!"

A pang in her stomach straightened Patricia's back. She frowned. *He planned to marry me during his first visit. This is not possible!* Her mind was racing at light speed back in time trying to remember a single hint of anything else but impatience and disdain toward her. *But he remodeled the room. How did he know I would agree to marry. Bustard! He played me like a violin*, "Millie, will you show me the rest of the house? I want to see everything, kids' rooms, yours and Peter's, in case that I need something in the middle of the night, kitchen!" She needed to be distracted, not to show how disturbed she was by these new revelations.

"You are an eager young bride; I agree hundred percent with you. The best thing is to take the whole enchilada into your hands from the very beginning. Those four need some order in their lives. Come, I'll show you the kids' bedrooms. Over there, down the corridor. This one is Andrew's. I think it is too messy and all these crazy posters, but he is getting into that rebellious age, and George lets him get away with everything. This one is Lindsay's. I like it, a real girl's room. Too many books, maybe. She turned to the books after her mother, you know, and the little one sleeps here. George buys him too many toys, perhaps because the boy never had a mother, and George is away from home too often. Every time he comes back, he brings him some of those big plush animals. He spoils him!"

Millie started down the stairs beckoning to Patricia. "Kitchen, great room, playroom, library, and conservatory are downstairs. Swimming pools are in the back. The indoor one is used almost every day by the kids. You will have to sit there during swimming time. George doesn't let them swim without supervision. It was my job, like it would help Hahaha, I can't swim, you see."

They entered the most beautiful conservatory she had ever seen. "You see that little piece of roof down among those trees? Yes? That is mine and Peter' house. Please come to see it soon as you can. During the day, I'm mostly here, but I like to spend my evenings at home. The older I get, the more I like to spend time in my own space. I hope you don't mind. I was so happy to hear George was getting married! I'll have more time for myself and Peter. And I'm sure you would like to spend time alone with your new family. Getting to know the kids and George, too. I can tell you, he is a different person at home. Don't worry, you have your whole life to get to know them!"

Approaching, they heard the voices coming from the great room.

"Patricia, Millie, where are you?" George yelled.

"Over here, George, we are coming!" Millie yelled back, "Come, my dear, I can hear the voices of my darlings."

Patricia heard them too. She was afraid, nervous, agitated, but determined to go through it as soon as possible. She did not know what to expect, trouble or acceptance, or?

"Patricia, you toured the house. That's good! Good! I would like you to meet my children!" George sounded too cheerful. She suspected that he clashed with the children over her already. *Good for them! Bringing a new mother home like broccoli or cabbage and dump me on them. What a nerve!* She looked at them. Three pairs of eyes watched her with curiosity, fear, and maybe a little hatred, especially visible in Andrew's eyes.

"Kids! This is Patricia, my wife! That's means she'll live here with us, and you will obey her as you obey me. Patricia, my dear, this is Andrew, Lindsay, and my baby Mark!" Patricia slowly approached.

"Hey! I don't know how you handle Millie, but she already made trouble for me. She dumped onto me her duty to supervise your swimming activities. I didn't dare to say no, although, I can't swim. I never had the guts to try. My only hope is that you will teach me and have patience with my fear and clumsiness!"

The kids, as well as George, looked at her with surprise. This kind of beginning nobody expected.

"Naturally, we'll help you, won't we?" Lindsay glanced at her brother.

"Don't you worry, Andrew is a great swimmer. He won't let anything bad happen to you. He taught me how to swim with great patience!" Mark looked at her with big dark eyes like his father's. Her heart leaped in her chest. This little boy is acting like an adult. She wanted to run to him and take him in her arms, but it was too soon. They expected some kind of response from her.

"Oh, that's great! I'm such a chicken when swimming is in question! I just hope, Andrew, that there is some shallower part in the pool, or I will have no courage to get in!" She slowly got closer, casually putting her hand on Lindsay's shoulder. Mark squeezed her other hand in comfort, and she gently enveloped his tiny fingers. She looked around not being sure where to go.

"I don't know about you, but airplane food is terrible and I'm starving now. Will you show me the way to the kitchen. Millie said something about dinner, which had been waiting for a while. If it's not eatable, you can help me prepare some brownies."

"Brownies for dinner? Don't let Millie hear you. She'll flip on her back!" Andrew was laughing.

"I don't believe this kind of food is right for dinner every night, but from time to time when our real dinner is spoiled, some brownies and milk can't hurt. Although we have another reason for an unusual dinner. Today is a special day, for me at least! Coming into an unknown place, meeting a number of people who are strangers to me is very unnerving. So, some sweet treats like brownies - which are, by the way, one of my favorites – are comfort food, as food like that is called. I think you guys are in the same situation! I came here to become a permanent member of your family. You don't know me, I am a stranger to you, so I think you are entitled to comfort food, too!"

She was speaking slowly with a smile, more like she was telling a story. The kids looked at her almost mesmerized, nodding their heads in agreement. George was standing in the same place during this interaction between his children and his wife, thinking how Patricia is a very clever person who knows a lot about children. He was ready to endure a big scene, including insulting Patricia, tantrums, maybe even crying; but somehow, she turned things around without any effort. He slowly followed them toward the kitchen. Millie would not be happy with the invasion of her kitchen, but he could not stop them now.

He stayed for a moment behind still expecting trouble, but when he finally reached the kitchen door, he saw Millie and the kids helping Patricia find all the ingredients for brownies. Millie was going on and on about her mother's lost recipe for the best brownies in the world. Lindsay tried to make Patricia promise to put in double the amount of chocolate. Andrew and Mark were fighting over which pan to use. Mark was pulling out of the cabinet the turkey pan ignoring his brother's protests that the turkey pan is too big. To top this commotion, Peter burst in wondering what all the noise was about. With the word brownies, he instantaneously turned into a big child, approximately Mark's age. *How is she doing this?* George wondered, amazed by how the potential disastrous situation was transformed without any struggle by this strange woman into a pleasant family evening. Feeling a little bit out of place, and definitely ignored by everybody, he decided to go upstairs and take a shower. He knew that problems would arise sooner or later, and he would have to deal with them, but tonight he was off the hook.

An hour later, after a long shower; George put clean clothes on, thinking about the talk he will need to have with Patricia about... The loud summoning forced him to run out of the bedroom in a panic.

"What happened?" From the gallery he saw Mark impatiently beckoning him down.

"Dad, Come! Come fast! The brownies are done, and we'll open the champ... champ... Just come, and hurry!" Mark yelled and rushed into the kitchen.

"Champagne, you dork!" Andrew affectionately rubbed Mark's hair with his knuckles. Patricia was cutting the cake, placing the slices on the plates, while Millie and Peter were arranging the glasses on the table quarreling about if the children should have champagne or not.

"Millie don't be such a nag! This is a special occasion! Their father just got married, and they got a mother. What can be a bigger thing that this?" Peter was placing glasses on the table, repeatedly, after Millie would put them back in the cabinet. Mark was picking tiny pieces from the side of the cake while looking at Patricia from under his long lashes, suspecting she pretended not to see what he was doing.

"Patricia, can we have just a drop of champagne?" Lindsay asked casually, placing plates with brownies on the table.

"Let's wait for your father to make that decision, okay!" Patricia decided that diplomacy was the best call.

"If *You* ask him, he won't say no!" Another diplomat in the family, she smiled looking at the smug expression on Andrew's face.

Standing behind the door for a while, George listened to all that excitement inside, not wanting to spoil it. His kids were not so relaxed forever. When he finally entered, he pretended to have no idea what was going on.

"It is obvious that you guys are celebrating my wedding without me!" A big smile on his face mimicked the ongoing bustle inside, "And, you turned my bride into a cook! Ha? I won't be surprised if she picks up her things tomorrow and runs back east!" He approached the apron clothed Patricia, putting his arm around her shoulders and lovingly pressing her close to him. The impulse to kick his shin was strong, but under the five pairs of curious eyes, she made herself smile sweetly and circled her arm around his waist.

"Oh, George! I wondered where are you? We are having a little soirée! I love brownies, and this was an excuse to have some and not feel guilty! And, as for leaving here, forget about it! I'll be too tired in the morning to move, and I'll postpone another flying experience like the one I had today for at least a week!" Laughing, she playfully pushed herself away from him urging the kids toward the table.

"Let's seat, the brownies are the best when they are warm!" Everybody rushed to their places stumbling over each other. Andrew and Peter were the fastest, which made Millie roll her eyes and Patricia like him more. The frightening prospect from this very morning turned out to be one of the most pleasant in a long time. She looked at George, "Come dear, you must try my brownies!" She was pure honey.

"Well, George, here is a bottle of champagne I bought when you called that your dear Patricia agreed to make you the happiest man in these woods!" Peter was holding the bottle up in the air, "Now is the time for you to open it! Before that, you have to solve a little problem we are having here. The kids should toast their new mother, that's what I think!" He looked at his wife making a significant pause, "Millie thinks they are too young to be corrupted in such a decadent way! Patricia is playing it safe and wants you to decide. Well, the ball is in your corner!" The eager faces in front of him filled his chest with hope after a long time he had none. Some strange reassurance entered his heart, that everything will turn good, and that he made the right decision bringing this woman into his home and family.

"This is a special occasion, and it is bedtime anyway, so, I think they should have a little bit of champagne. But until they reach eighteen there will be no more important occasions to repeat this!" Loud cheering followed his speech. He took the bottle from Peter's hand. A loud pop and a stream of bubbly liquid rushed out. Everybody was laughing, pushing tall flutes under the golden stream.

The cake was eaten, champagne disappeared, but chatting was going on and on. Mark was first to give up, sleeping curled up in Mille's lap. *Okay! That's it!* George stood up, "Millie, hand me the boy! I'll take him up to his bed. You two, straight to your rooms. Millie, Peter, don't rush in the morning. This outfit will not need breakfast before nine." He marched toward the door carrying his youngest son.

"Good night, Millie, Peter. George is right. Nobody will get up early tomorrow morning, so you can cuddle a little longer. Thanks for everything!"

"It was our pleasure! Good night, Patricia!" The old couple left through the back door. The whole day's exhaustion surfaced like a tide, made her feel weak and all she wanted was a long and peaceful sleep. *I am so tired, and I still have to talk with George.*

Patricia was standing in the middle of the big bedroom not sure what to do. There was not a trace of George. *To hell with him! I'll just take a shower, maybe that will refresh me enough to be able to sort things out with my new "husband" and survive this evening.*

When she entered the bedroom again, George was standing beside the open balcony door looking at the mountains. The beautiful night wrap she wore, chosen by Francesca of course, felt somewhat out of place. *I will be damned if I let this intimidate me more than George already has.*

"Millie brought me here pointing out this will be the room where I will sleep. Maybe I didn't understand correctly, but she left me with the impression that we'll share it. I know that you have no desire to sleep with me in the same bed any more than I do. Now, the question is how are we going to make everybody else believe in our *undying* love and stay out of each other's hair at the same time?" She said it with more composure than she had.

Now it was his turn to make the situation easy as possible for both of them. *Darn man, is he going to stand there the whole night just staring at me?* She could not show any sign of weakness, so she stared back at him for a long time. What Patricia wanted the most was to turn around and hide in the bathroom, but she had to stay and endure this, or she will lose this little bit of self-esteem she still had left. Then he moved.

"I figured it all out before I went back for you. I chose this room because it is connected to a big dressing room. That was my great grandmother's original bedroom. She wanted a large dressing room, so her husband built it for her. The following ladies of the house preferred the bedroom on the west side of the house. You'll sleep here and I will be in the "dressing room". When I ordered the redecoration, I turned the dressing room into sleeping quarters for myself. Unfortunately, we'll have to share the bathroom. But I will try to use it when you are not around." He headed toward the door on the same wall as the bathroom, then he turned around one more time. "This door doesn't have a lock, but don't be alarmed I won't use it during the night or when you are in the bedroom."

"I'm not alarmed, I know you won't." He looked at her for a long moment then disappeared behind the dressing room door.

Patricia took a deep breath. That went smoother than she had hoped. She silently thanked her good fortune, slid under the sheets and instantly fell asleep.

CHAPTER 8

The next morning Patricia woke up looking at the light blue celling thinking, *where on Earth am I?* In an instant she remembered everything. She sat up in her bed and scanned the room. Again, her eyes were drawn toward the bright window. It was a nice sunny day full of promise. Patricia jumped out of bed.

The bathroom was damp. *Oh, George had showered already! But how did he get in here?* Turning around she noticed the narrow door in the corner of the bathroom. Slowly she opened it, half expecting to see George, but the room was empty. It was much smaller than her bedroom, but she liked it. If she didn't know that was George's bedroom, she'd think it was an office. The colors were warm shades of browns, okras and greens. There was a desk with a computer on one side of elongated space and a day bed on the other, then shelves with books were neatly lined at opposite wall, projecting the feeling of a cozy workplace from some past times transported here and now. *How clever of him! He can comfortably sleep here, but to unsuspecting eyes, this was just a nice office for some late-night work.*

After she finished her morning ritual, it was after nine. From the staircase, she heard loud voices streaming from the general direction of the kitchen. Before she reached the hall, the kitchen door opened wide, and three kids ran fast as they could towards the conservatory. *Oh God, I didn't know how* embarrassing will be to face these people again. She stopped for a moment in front of the kitchen door to collect her thoughts and calm her tattered nerves.

"I know, Millie, that we should have a proper honeymoon, but I took time to visit Tim last month, then over a week this time to marry Patricia. I didn't have that luxury at all, as you know very well. Tomorrow, I have to be, *have to*, you understand, be in Denver, on Thursday in San Francisco. I'll make it up to her. She is very understanding. And, I really think it would be a mistake to take her away right now!"

"Why a mistake?" Millie was curious.

"Did you see how she handled the kids last night? I was so afraid they'd give her a hard time. I don't know her that well to… I saw her with her sister's children. They adore her, but they have known her since they were born. Anyway, I think it is more important if first Patricia and those monsters get to know each other better. The honeymoon will have to wait."

The silence lasted long enough for Patricia to enter the kitchen and not to be suspected of hearing any of their conversation. "Good morning, everybody!" She put her happy-casual face on, grabbed the coffee pot asking, "Where are the children?"

"Back yard!" Both of them answered simultaneously.

"Oh, great! I'll go join them soon as I finish this excellent coffee!" She looked at Millie approvingly, "I think I should spend as much time with them as I can, you know, to get to know them better, and give them time to get used having me around. I'm sure that you, my dear, have a lot to do, having been absent from your job for so long! You must be anxious to dive into your corporate puddle soon as you can. Millie, may I have one of these Danish? Thanks!" She sat at the table eating with enjoyment.

Millie and George looked at each other. Patricia surprised them again.

"Yes, I'm going to Denver, then San Francisco. I have no idea how long it will take!" George looked at a relaxed Patricia, who gave the impression she lived here for a long time, and this was one of her normal beginnings of the day. To him she looked like a creature from some other planet.

"Oh, that's okay, George! Millie, we'll talk later about lunch! I'm going to join the kids!" She started toward the door, then turned back, "Have a nice trip, George darling!" Patricia bent down and quickly pressed her lips on George's forehead. He reached grabbing her hand, pulling her closer to put his arm around her waist, before she could run away.

"I'm leaving in a few minutes, my pet. I want to give you a proper goodbye!" While talking, George got up, scooped her into his arms, just hard enough that she could not move, and planted a passionate kiss on her lips. Patricia was incapable of moving, not only because he held her tight, but some strange numbness froze her into the moment. *Oh providence, make him stop.* George loosened his hold on her. His smiling face was so close when she opened her eyes. "I'll be back soon as I can! Millie take care of my girl!" He backed toward the door and disappeared.

Millie was smiling, "That's my boy! Honey, he'll be back in no time. Imagine, I was afraid he'll never fall in love again!"

And, you were right, Patricia almost babbled it out aloud, but instead she just turned and left the kitchen. *I have to control myself better,* Patricia was angry with herself remembering George's kiss. *One second longer and I would have made a complete fool of myself. This man has some strange power over me.* With every step, her decision was stronger, not to think about it anymore.

With George out of the picture, Patricia plunged herself into getting to know everybody on the ranch, to became familiar with the immediate grounds of the property and to study these children placed in her care so unexpectedly and permanently.

Andrew, by her opinion, was a young man with great potential but somewhat troubled. Only he remembered their mother well. Up until now, he avoided talking about her. Patricia was ready to wait for him to open up long as it took. Lindsay liked to believe that she also remembered their mother, but Patricia doubted that. The girl was then barely three and it is most likely that her wish to remember made her believe in it. Most of the time she pretended not to care about being without a mother, but on the other hand, she was very eager to talk with Patricia about all those things girls usually discuss with their mothers. Immediately she liked a little girl, knowing they would get along very well. The biggest problem was Mark. He never had a mother and really did not understand what mothers are good for, as he proclaimed seriously. What troubled Patricia was that he did not act like a boy his age. Most probable his solemnity is a result of spending most of his time with adults rather than with children. His brother and sister were, most of the year, in school leaving him home alone.

The school was in Sheridan, which was over an hour's drive from the ranch, so they never came home before five o'clock in the afternoon, and then homework had to be finished before dinner. There was never enough time to play with Mark, talk with Mark, or pamper Mark as a small child should be treated. He just could not wait, since he remembered, to go to school himself. At last, that big event will be this fall. Until now, his life consisted of spending time between playing by himself most of the day, and spending time with Mille and Peter. What he liked the most though, was to be around the stables and *work* with the "Boys", how Peter called the stable workers and cowboys.

The kids made a game of showing Patricia around the property, including showing her all the ropes of ranch work and life. The thing they liked the most and had the best time was in the swimming pool. Andrew took it upon himself to teach Patricia how to swim. In return, she tried her best to be clumsy and frightened as possible, hoping that Andrew would never find out about her high school swim team glory days, and being a swimming instructor for handicapped children, which she did during her college years. All three of them were excellent swimmers, on the insistence of their father, who was concerned for their safety. Apparently, nobody on the ranch knew how to swim beside him, and he was not around all the time.

"Who is hungry, guys? I'm starving! Andrew, you are merciless!" Patricia pulled herself out of the pool exaggerating slowness emphasizing exertion and hunger. Children were laughing imitating her, dragging themselves, toward chairs towered with towels, on all four. They were still laughing while approaching the main house. Millie watched them with tears in her eyes, thinking again how George could not have chosen better than this smart girl. She turned to Peter, who had just entered the kitchen with a basket full of vegetables. "Patricia is a good influence on kids, don't you think so?"

"The "Boys" think the same! I swear, all of them are in love with her. You won't believe it but yesterday they fought over who will teach her to ride the horse. She doesn't ride, you know. Thus, Sam got it into his head to teach her himself. Then Chuck stared to laugh, how the worst rider in the outfit could teach anybody to ride. And, of course, you know Chuck fancy himself to be the best rider here, but only by his opinion, ha, ha, ha."

"And the biggest flirt! Did you hear the rumors about him and that girl? What was her name? Rachel? Well, everybody says she's pregnant! And, naturally, Chuck is the number one suspect!"

"Don't believe everything you hear. Hence, I put the Boys in their place. George will teach his bride how to ride. After all, he is equally as good a rider as Chuck, if not better. Hey, you wild Indians! How's swimming lessons going?" Peter turned toward loud children rushing in the kitchen tailed by an equally giddy Patricia.

"We are thirsty!"

"I'm hungry too."

"Patricia is tired and hungry because Andrew is merciless!" Mark calmly placed himself on his chair at the table.

"She would be much better if she let herself go, but…" Andrew stuffed his mouth with a whole cookie, pushing Lindsay away from the pitcher of lemonade.

"Andrew!" Millie cried snatching a cookie jar and placing it on the high shelf out of the reach of the children.

"Patricia will be better if Andrew doesn't push her so hard… Yes, you do!" Mark was looking at Andrew with serious disapproval.

"She'll learn in no time, Peter!" Lindsey exclaimed, then whispered in Peter's ear. "I'm sure she pretends to be worse than she is, just to make Andrew feel important!" She winked at Peter pouring a second glass of lemonade.

Watching those people, so new to her, but already so dear to her heart, having such a good time. Patricia felt a pang in her chest, the school would start soon, and the kids will be away more than she would like. She would have more time to write, which she neglected up to now, more than she could afford, but spending time with those delightful little people held bigger enchantment for her. For now, she was reading them parts of her new book about the three sisters in Uganda. Lindsay loved it immensely, but Andrew and Mark thought that a story about the boys would be more interesting. Patricia defended herself by pointing out that she did not know very much about boys, having no brothers herself and never had the opportunity to be acquainted with boys until now. "But, if the two of you will be good maybe I'll get inspired and one day write a book about you! How would you like that?"

"And a book about me!" Lindsay shouted.

George, being away, did not forget to call every night to talk to the children and Patricia. The kids would chitchat at the same time describing all the happenings of the day, while Patricia would mostly listen under five pair of watchful eyes, answering simply: "Yes dear… of course, my darling…naturally… I will, dear…" and so on.

After the kids would go to bed, Millie and Peter went back to their home; Patricia would retreat, with her laptop, to George's "bedroom". It had a full west exposure with a breathtaking view of mountains and spectacular sunsets, dressing the room in reds, oranges and dark warm shadows, imposing on Patricia some unfamiliar restless mood. She was very content with her new life. Every night before going to bed she would thank her good fortune for her new situation, but with an underlined feeling that her new experiences had some unknown sensations creating turmoil in her heart and mind. She felt as though something was missing, and that something was just beyond her reach, but what? Patricia remembered having similar fervors as a young girl fantasizing about a glorious and adventurous future of great love, success and exploration. The reason might be those majestic mountains, unspoiled nature, and this beautiful estate filled with all these unusual people.

A smile brightened her face at the memory of the "Boys" fighting over as to who will be her riding instructor. At first, she thought they were joking just to entertain her, but after Peter's interference, she realized that they were deadly serious. The conversation with George was necessary, soon as possible, about the best way to avoid similar situations in the future. As time was passing, it became more apparent that George missed explaining about the people, their customs and the way of life, which had now become part of hers. Two weeks after his departure, George, instead of calling home that evening, showed up unexpectedly during dinner. Everybody was happy to see him, expect Patricia. She was surprised and alarmed although he, her husband, was a stranger to her. Watching him now, it seemed even more so. They were at the dinner table, noisy as usual when he rushed in with a big smile and arms full of packages. The kids jumped up shouting like one, making it impossible to be understood.

"Stop, you wild cowboys, nobody gets a thing while this howling lasts!" He lifted his treasure up and out of their reach. Patricia studied his face. He enjoys this as much as the kids do. Threat had an amazing effect. The children went dumb in a second, showing their impatience only by jumping from foot to foot. George, ever so slowly, placed a package in each child's hands. They ran to the sofa in the great room tearing and dropping wrappings on the floor along the way. George did not pay any attention to that behavior, obviously used to this kind of homecoming, already approaching Mille handing her a paper bag with a seductive smile, "The worst thing about business trips is not having your culinary delights every day," He plastered a loud smutch on her plump cheek, "fish stew tomorrow, pretty please, Millie!"

She looked at him over her shoulder as he was some buzzing fly, "Can't do. You could save yourself some money, my boy! My doctor appointment is tomorrow" Fussing with the bag she finally unearths some ugly looking bulbs exclaiming with a sparkle in her eyes, "For one, George, you did something right. Patricia cooks tomorrow, so don't waste your charms on me! Look Peter, these are the ones I was talking about! If they survive the winter, in several years we'll have some number of them in the south meadow."

"Don't listen to that babbling woman, Peter! Here, it's some of that tobacco you were begging for. I had a hard time finding it. To spare myself that ordeal in the future, I made a deal with the owner of that tobacco store to send us a box whenever you call for it!" Peter snatched the box from George's hand faster than Patricia thought he was capable and held it to his nose with blissful expression of a toddler getting a new toy.

"Patricia, my darling!" George approached her with a pathetic expression on his face. "I missed you so much, girl ... come here and give me a kiss!" He reached for her, but she moved back, "Nobody is paying any attention to us, George... There's no need for this... this...!"

"I have a present for you, too! Maybe then you'll be nicer to poor me and try to make me feel a bit welcome!" Bending to her ear, he whispered, "They are always paying attention, watching us even when they are not around!" Playfully kissing the corner of her lips he extended a small package. Patricia hesitantly excepted the box thinking that he was acting as a spoiled brat, but always have appropriate respond to her silly behavior. Patricia was holding the gift not knowing if she should just take it and go with the flow or shove it down his smiling throat.

Millie saved the day by saying straight into her ear, "Go on. Open it! Open it!" Patricia looked around. Everybody was looking at her with expectation. George was right again – her new family did pay attention concerning everything that goes on between her and her husband. She knew they wanted her to be surprised and happy so she opened the package. The long leather box announced the jewelry. *Oh, dear Universe, please don't let it be something expensive.* It was! A beautiful diamond tennis bracelet sparkled, laying in its whole glory on black velvet... and, the diamonds were huge, screaming an equally huge price tag. Her first reaction was to give it back, but the screams and comments from Lindsay, who pulled the bracelet from the box and wrapped it around Patricia's wrist trying to close the clasp, prevented Patricia to do anything.

"Let me do it honey! Jewelry like this has some kind of secure clasp. That old witch, who sold it to me, tried half an hour to teach me how to do this. Now, watch how clever your father is!" He winked at Lindsay taking Patricia's hand and bending over it, he was explaining to his daughter the trick of the closure. The bracelet looked stunning around her delicate wrist. Collective awing of approval would not allow her to protest.

"Oh Dad... this is beautiful! Patricia, don't you think so?" Lindsay studied the bracelet with an open mouth.

"You see, Millie," Lindsey turned her big shiny eyes toward old woman, "this is what I was talking about. Dad is romantic! Men can be, too, but only when two people are in love."

"In general in love, or in love with each other?" Millie was deathly serious pretending not to understand, but Lindsay did not buy it. She continued, as she had not been interrupted. "Girls are romantic probably all the time, but real romance is when two people are in love with each other, as you very well know!" Millie and Lindsay were progressing down the hallway, while George and Patricia listen not believing their ears.

"I could never figure out where she picking up these things. Boys are so easy to understand. How are you getting along with those monsters? Are they behaving?" He took her hand leading her up the stairs.

"Oh yeah! They are very special children. Andrew is a little uptight and rebellious, unfortunately. It's going to get worse," She added slowly.

"How do you know? What do you mean by "worse"?"

"He is approaching the awkward phase of growing up. Teenagers! You've heard about them?" She tried to sound casual, but all the time she was thinking about the best way to return his gift, which was burning the skin on her wrist.

"Of course, I've heard about them. I hoped mine would go straight from kindergarten to college postgraduation. You just broke my bubble, Patricia. As a penance, you will have to suffer with me through those upcoming hellish years!"

They entered the bedroom laughing. Patricia still did not have a clear idea what their lives will look like, but it would not be boring, for sure.

"Let's go in my… in dressing room and have a glass of something?" *Why does he have to look like a little boy every time I need to be strong and stern.*

"Okay! I want to talk to you anyway?"

George went in front of her started to talk about his trip. *We look like an old married couple, not like newlyweds who met for the first time several months ago.*

He handed her a glass of sherry. "You wanted to talk with me?"

"Yes! First, about the children! They are great kids, as I already said, but they spend too much time with adults. Andrew and Lindsay are in better positions because of school, but Mark, I think he will have problems in school this fall. We will have to keep a close eye on him. Then, there is that problem with the "Boys"!"

"Boys"? You don't mean my cowboys?" His expression was so strange that she felt guilty not knowing for what.

"Yes, your cowboys! They have put into their heads to teach me to ride. Sadly, some of them didn't say see eye to eye about who should be teaching me. So, they…" She did not know how to put it delicately.

"Fought? You are here two weeks and already managed to make

my cowboys loco! I was under the impression that you were not into seducing every man on your path!"

He is acting like a jealous jerk, Patricia frowned. "Don't be silly! Peter and I explained that you will teach me to ride, and you'll do it. Don't think even for a moment that I'll be the center of some rivalry between big egos of some... some..."

"Wow! Patricia! I'll teach you. It's good to know how to ride. Riding is big around here and those kids need more practice. Peter is too old to chase those little Indians on horseback. The "Boys" are too busy. I'm not around enough. I warn you, be careful with Chuck! He is a womanizer. If he chooses to seduce you, he'll try like a hell. You are my wife, and I won't allow anybody to make a fool of me!"

Patricia could not quite pinpoint the strange undertone in his voice.

"Nobody tried to seduce me up till now. Maybe I would like it!" She tried to loosen up the growing tension with a joke, but his murderous look in her direction reminded her why she is here in his bedroom. "I'll do my best in spite of my fear of horses. There is one more thing, but I don't want you to take it wrong. About this bracelet, it is the most beautiful piece of jewelry I've ever seen, but I can't take it. It must cost a fortune, and what will I do with such a piece, anyway?" With her every word George was getting more mad. *This time he would not win.* She was adamant.

George took a deep breath trying to be calm as possible, "Listen to me Patricia, you are my wife. What we do, or let's put it this way, what we don't do in our... your bedroom is entirely our affair. But to everybody else, we are a normal married couple, and let me remind you, *a couple in love.* From me, it's expected to buy expensive gifts for my wife. Besides, don't worry about it. You'll have plenty of opportunities to wear your bracelet, as well as all the other pieces I plan to give you! While we are on this subject, I also plan to take you, very soon, on a shopping trip. Your clothes are not what I consider suitable for my wife. No offence!" He spoke slow and convincing, but the worst for Patricia was the logic behind it. She hates it when he was so unquestionably right. All of hers so clear and reasonable objections were shredded in pieces in a matter of minutes. Dignifying retreat was the only reasonable thing to do.

"Well, we'll discuss the rest some other time, George. I'm beat, all that laughing and running with kids the whole day. Good night, George!" Before she shut the door to her bedroom behind herself, she heard a low, "Good night, Patricia!

*****

School started and Patricia found herself with an enormous amount of time to her disposal. George ordered a new computer for Patricia's writing. He installed it in the library, remembering how much she admired the room the first time she saw it. It was a pleasant room enveloped with shelves and shelves filled with the books. From the very beginning, Patricia enjoyed its tranquility, giving her a sense of peace and providing a feeling of belonging in these big unfamiliar surroundings. Now, being alone most of the day, she would retreat there to write and reflect on the happenings in her life, people she just started to know and love, as well to where her life is going.

It was so easy to slide into an imaginary world of her characters. The hours would pass unnoticed until she would be pulled out of it by children's voices in the hallway. George had an office building in Sheridan from where, through fax, telephone and internet, conducted his businesses around the world. He made a point of driving the kids to school in the morning and bringing them back in the evening.

A week ago, George asked her to put on some jeans, comfortable shoes and a hat. Her riding lessons were about to begin. Patricia was excited and uncomfortable about it, not knowing what to expect from George. Married or not she still knew next to nothing about him. The moment she thought, she had a glimpse into his character, he would do something atypical, which would throw her off. *Is he going to be patient or unyielding as he is with the kids and sometimes even with his staff.* She was nervous about it, but more because of her fear of horses.

She mentioned it to George, doubting now that he heard a word she said. For someone like him, who grew up on horseback, he probably felt that this kind of attitude was an alien as spaceships. Therefore, she toughened up, and obediently followed him down to the stables. The big selection of extraordinary horses made her even more uneasy. The "Boys" were everywhere, occupied with imaginary chores, but when two of them showed up, they plainly stood in unabashed curiosity. Chance to see boss' wife first riding lesson was irresistible. How the little lady, they grew to like, will handle the horse she is afraid of, and how will their boss handle his wife.

George tricked them, which came as no surprise to Patricia and greatly amused her the "Boys'" disappointment in seeing them slowly walking away from the stables on foot with horses trailing behind them. George saddled the two horses casually talking to Patricia about Deer Creek Canyon, one of the most beautiful wanders of nature in this region. Then he took her hand leading her and the horses toward the east slopes of the property, sheltered from snooping eyes by small clumps of tall trees. Patricia became more relaxed with every step listening to stories about horses, their sensitivities, and the ancient connection between the horse and the man. She was intrigued by this unusual man, walking beside her, more and more as time was passing. Every word he spoke proved his respect for horses, nature and love for the outdoors. It took her a short time living here to see his love for his children, his obvious huge attachment to this rugged country and the slow pace of life on the ranch. With a smile on her lips, she had to acknowledge that her first impression of him was very much different than now.

Half an hour later he made her climb upon the horse, teaching her what to do so the animal will know what she wants from him. Patricia tried hard to remember how to use her knees, ties, bridles, body shifting, and so on. Then she forgot it all. George laughed at her frustration, teasing her that she has her whole life to learn and he has enough patience to keep teaching her.

When they slowly rode back to the stables, the "Boys" were still there, accompanied by the children who ran up to them the second they appeared among the trees.

"Hey, Patricia! You look great on that horse!"

"How many times did you fall off?"

"Can I go with you next time…"

George was laughing, not offering any comments, just helping Patricia off her saddle. She did not say anything either. Her smiling face felt like a mask. Every muscle and bone in her body was in agony of pain. She walked slowly, the only way she could, conveying the real state she was in. For the next three to four days, she suffered with every movement and was grateful, for the first time, that the children were in school, so she could mend her aches unobserved.

George would look at her searchingly, ever so often, but she would rather die than show how uncomfortable she really was. Nonetheless, the most terrifying thought was she had to do it all over again this upcoming weekend. To give up was not an option, not for the sake of the kids, nor for her own sake. Patricia expected a number of possible problems she might encounter in her new environment, but never did it cross her mind that so many people would constantly be watching her every move, judging her, and waiting for her to make a mistake. It was not a hostile or hateful observation, just a curiosity about the new mistress, the greenhorn from the East, unaccustomed to their ways.

Even worse than back horse riding was a prospect she will have to face this upcoming Saturday. George was throwing a party for her! She did not say a word when he announced it, but the next day she tried to find the best possible reason to stop it by talking with Millie.

"Do you think the party is necessary?'

Millie looked at her like she was out of her mind. "The whole county is burning up to see you. You can't imagine how many telephone calls I got, not to mention George, since you arrived? Hundreds! George is one of the most important and influential men in this part of the country. Everybody knows him, and it is only natural that everyone wishes to meet his new wife. After Tiffany died it was expected of him to -" She glanced at Patricia, "It looks to me as though George didn't tell you much about his first wife? After all, you haven't known each other for very long… Her mother will come, of course. Laure. Tiffany's mother is a bitch, but the rest of the crowd will be nice. I'm more worried they'll eat you alive with kindness. Only if… no, no, she is in New York, and I hope she'll stay there forever. George is taking you tomorrow with him to L.A. to buy some new clothes and things. So, take advantage of it! Don't make the mistake and buy simple. Has to be elegant and expensive!"

Sometimes she could not follow Millie's rumblings at all. *Who is "she" Millie wants to stay in New York forever and why?* What unpleasant behavior could she expect from Tiffany's mother? Fortunately, Millie was busy around the stove and did not notice the distress on Patricia's face. *Oh boy, what a torment this party will be? Granted, nothing compared to the trip to Los Angeles.* That thought created the eruption of regret through her mind. The refusal of Francesca's offer to accompany her in a quick shopping excursion to Boston was a bad decision. She would now have something to wear, and this wretched trip would not be necessary. She never cared for fancy clothes, which was not imperative in her life. Realization that she had to know better, being the sister of a rich man's wife, should make her aware of what would be expected of her.

Tuesday morning Patricia sat in the car together with the children and George along with heavy heart. Knowing that her usual, bargain-hunting way of shopping was out of the question made the whole idea troubling. How she was going to accomplish what was expected of her in the huge, foreign town of LA was beyond her. Since George proposed - *commended* her to marry him - she realized that her life would completely change, but she did not have time to think about every single detail. *I will have to sacrifice more than just my freedom!* Thet thought was disturbing.

"Patricia, the dress has to be blue!" Lindsay's voice snapped her out of her glum, which she was thankful for. "It's my favorite color, and dad said you are the most beautiful in blue, although, I think that you are beautiful in any color. But…. You know, the people who don't know you as well as we do, will need some help to figure that out in one evening!" Lindsay was smiling up at her. Patricia felt a rush of some strange sensation in her chest. She knew then that she'll love this little girl her whole life no matter what happens between her and her "husband". Andrew looked distant and cold. *I worry that he could be hurt that I'm leaving and turning my back on him or is this just a teenage faze he is entering.* She glanced at Mark, seated between her and Andrew, completely content like always. The ache in her heart sharpened. It was clear that he likes her, but he most likely did not waste a single thought about her absence for a whole five days. To have her around was great, just as being without her. *Does he feel the same about his father's absences?* She wanted to hug him and tell him how much she'll miss him, but it would be useless. It will not mean a thing to him.

Being in deep thoughts again, Patricia did not notice that they were approaching Sheridan. George abruptly stopped in front of the school, and before she had time to say a word, the children jumped out shouting goodbyes. "Blue!" Lindsay cried one more time, turning toward her, before running after her brother. George started the car equally as fast, so she just sighed and tried to concentrate on the ordeal ahead of her. Until her return home, she would need to resolve any developing damages in her relationship with the kids, which could develop during her absence. Presently, she have an equally big problem on her hands.

The trip lasted almost a whole day. Three connecting flights reminded her on her first trip with George. It was twilight when they arrived at their hotel. The big and expensive looking building made her feel uneasy, but ridiculously lavish insides were plainly intimidating, which reminded her of her sister's in-laws, who would not put foot in place without five stars. George entered the lobby unaffected by this exhibition of wealth and lack of taste. In a matter of seconds they were surrounded by the men in crimson coats, talking the language, waiting to lead the way to their room, asking George how the their trip was, and wishing them a nice stay in L.,A. It was obvious how well known he was in this establishment. Patricia, at last, snapped out of her stupor, realizing how funny the situation really was. Francesca would have enjoyed this tremendously. That thought made her smile while they were carefully stashed into the elevator.

George looked down into her face. "Are you okay?"

Her eyes were shiny with a spark of humor in them. *I have to write about this hotel to my sister and poor Tim will have to bring her here promptly.* "Of course, I'm okay!" She looked up at him and something in his eyes confused her.

They stood there in the elevator with locked eyes for a long moment. Then the bell announced their floor, and the ever so servile crimson coats led them down the corridor. Moments passed, and confused Patricia, was puzzled by the expression in George's eyes. She brushed the feeling aside and was ready to tell George how much Francesca would enjoy all this while entering their suite. She stopped at the door not believing her eyes. It was the most elegant room she ever had seen in her life. *Like an old Hollywood movie,* she thought and smiled again. Everything was in royal blue, white and gold. George promptly deposited tips in the men's hands and they disappeared without a sound.

"Do you always stay in this -"

"Yes, this is a hotel my father always used. I have no desire to go around in search for something less pompous." He put his attaché case on the desk with a frown on his face.

"No, I mean in this suite. It's so not you at all!" Her attempt to clarify her notion did not work well, so she changed the subject, "You should get two rooms, nobody is here to watch us, and we don't have to pretend. I think this is the best part of our trip, not to have to act all the time." George looked at her with a bigger frown.

"I usually take a less elaborate room!" He snapped. "And we can't occupy two rooms as you would so desire. I'm still juggling between are you afraid I'll lose my control and rape you, or my presence irritates you more than I thought. If you really have to know, my secretary reserved this ridiculous suit because it's her job. When I realized what she did, I asked her to change it to two rooms because I knew you'd complain, but she looked at me like I'm crazy, so I lied that I don't want to disturb you with my frantic schedule. Well, she said that she booked this suite with two rooms so you can have a retreat while I'm overloaded with work. Patricia, we are always observed, don't forget it!"

"After I agreed that the suit was a perfect solution, my secretary ran out to tell everybody, in tears if I may add, that I must be the most considerate husband in the world. It is puzzling how the rest of the world thinks of me as considerate"! George turned to study his papers. During his speech, Patricia felt guilty. She never feared that he'd rape her, *how can he even suggest something as preposterous as that*? But somehow, she always feels uncomfortable in his presence when they were alone. She could never understand why, but the truth was she didn't like to be with him very much. He was fun, the kids loved him and the rest, as he just pointed out, thought the world of him. She desperately tried to find something witty to say to pull herself out of this uneasy situation.

"How can you even say such a silly thing, George. Rape me. I *do* think you are considerate. I just didn't want us to bother each other. We have too many things to do in the next few days and I... Oh boy, I just hope you'll get out of this absurd mood before we go back home!"

While looking at his papers he replied, more or less, in a normal voice. "It's okay Patricia! I was just thinking the same. We do have many things on our agenda. It's sort of no-fun-just-work trip, so let's have a nice dinner tonight and collect some strength before we dive into our duties tomorrow." George raised his head with a question in his eyes and maybe a little provocation.

"Yes, I think that's good idea, as long as I don't need to wear something too dressy. I have my black evening dress and my -"

"Your mother's pearls!" He finished her sentence smiling. "That will be perfect. We'll just dine here in the hotel. The chef is excellent, but don't mention that to Millie!" Patricia was still standing in the same place looking uncertain as to what to do. When he raised his head again, she started slowly.

"Well, which room should I take?" Her glance was shifting from one side of the living room to the another, where were the doors to the bedrooms.

"Whichever you wish, Patricia, I really don't mind."

An hour later, they were entering the beautiful dining room on the top floor of the hotel. The view was spectacular and Patricia, for the first time since they left home felt relaxed. Tranquil music from the piano muffled the noise of the conversations in the big space. They were following the head waiter towards an expertly set table, when a deep voice stopped George and made him turn around.

"Hey George, I don't believe my eyes! Is that really you?" A tall elegant man pushed the chair away from the table they were passing by, grabbing George's hand, shaking it with pleasure.

"Bill? Old pal! What a surprise! I am the one who shouldn't believe my eyes. To see you in any other place but Manhattan is mind shuddering. I remember a young designer who thought to be in any other place on the globe but New York was beneath human existence!" George was laughing.

"Oh, youth is always obnoxious! I did live like that for a long time, too. But George, join us! Please! Here is someone you won't mind seeing again!" Bill waived back toward his table. George glanced in that direction and met the beautiful eyes of a gorgeous woman.

"Hey, George!" The seductive voice made a forgotten Patricia look closer at these strangers to her, especially the girl.

"Alicia! How nice to see you!" George smiled widely while

approaching the table and extending his hand toward the woman. She slowly placed her elegant narrow hand in his, then in one smooth move flowed straight into his arms. Alicia embraced his neck, looking at him from a distance of only a couple of inches.

"Long time no see! We have to sneak off to some secluded place, then George, you will tell me everything!" She continued to stare into his eyes without blinking. *Like a cobra,* Patricia irritatingly thought.

"Alicia, leave the poor man alone. Your claws scratched him once and I'm sure the scars are still visible" Bill pulled her away from George, and not so gently by Patricia's judgment. Gesturing toward the table he repeated the invitation.

"Come, let me introduce you. These are my friends and managers of my West Coast department. Slim and Moraine O'Sullivan. Guys, pay attention! Here standing a man, without whom you wouldn't have a job, neither me, for that matter. He was the only one who believed in me, some ten years ago, and graciously invested in a starving young designer when everybody else thought I was a loser!"

George nodded his head at the couple seated at the table, remembering at that moment his wife standing behind him. He turned back, reaching for Patricia's hand. "Allow me to introduce to you this lovely woman. This is Patricia, my wife!

Bill raised his eyebrows in amusement, but Patricia was more interested in Alicia's reaction. For a second the girl's eyes shot poisonous darts at her, then she sweetly smiled.

"Again George, I thought that one wife was more than enough for you?"

George turned to Patricia, "Don't pay any attention to Alicia's impetuousness! Dear, this is William Gilbert, an old acquaintance. Warning don't believe a word he says about me. You know how artists are totally irrational and have a tendency to exaggerate!" Bill grabbed Patricia's hand.

"Glad to meet you! Now, you *have to* join us for dinner!"

Without much fuss, he placed her in the chair between him and Moraine. Alicia got up again, poking Slim on the shoulder, who occupied the chair beside George. "You, George, sit beside me. We have a lot to catch up on! Slim, move!"

Slim jumped to obey, looking apologetically at Bill. Patricia had the urge to grab Alicia's expertly twisted hair and... *Oh, what's wrong with me? This has nothing to do with me. We are not married in the right sense of the word. So, why do I feel I could kill this barracuda with pleasure.*

George was staring into Alicia's long eyelashes, which strategically flickered with every move of her perfect lips. *What is she saying to him?* Patricia pondered gravely. He was drowning himself in her eyes, oblivious of everything else. *I should kill him instead of her. Oh damn, I'm acting like a jealous woman.* Suddenly stricken by that realization, felt like a lightning bolt. *But that is not possible. I should be in love with him in order to be... No, it's impossible!* Confused, Patricia turned her head in the other direction and met Maurine's questioning gaze.

"Patricia, are you okay?"

"Oh, yes! Why?" *Is it so vivid on my face how I feel,* she feared.

"I called your name twice, but - Oh, well, you are probably tired. I was admiring your pearls. A present from your husband?" The pleasant voice pulled her back to reality.

"Oh no, they belonged to my mother. My father and I bought them for her birthday when I was a child." She smiled at Moraine, thankful that she can occupy her mind with something else besides George and Alicia. "I always wear them!" She lowered her voice and with a little humor mocked herself. "They are so flashy that nobody notices the dress!"

"Don't be so sure, my dear!" Moraine whispered back with a crocket smile, which softened her frankness, "You should go shopping soon as possible and buy some new dresses. L.A. is a right place for that, if you know where to go"

"That is exactly my problem. I came here to do just that. But, I have no idea where to go and what to buy. I'll make all the wrong choices. My sister Francesca would know what to do. I did contemplate calling her to come and help me, but, She is nothing like me. Francesca is beautiful , elegant and so sure of herself, especially when it comes to buying clothes!"

"Come to our store tomorrow, and I'll help choose the right clothes for you. With your figure and complexion, I'll have no problem finding the perfect wardrobe!" Moraine tapped her hand in assurance.

"Will you, Moraine? If you will, you'll save my life!" Patricia felt such a relief that she forgot about George and Alicia. The two women chatted pleasantly during the dinner, interrupted just here and there by the men. Alicia made sure they were completely dedicated to her.

A few hours later Patricia and George were in the elevator on the way up to their suit. She happily jabbered about Moraine's offer to help her with her shopping. He studied her face, puzzled with her disinterest in Alicia's odious behavior. He saw dozens of times how Alicia managed to turn the girls ballistic with similar exhibitions, but somehow, Patricia seemed unaffected. She was surprising him routinely now.

The following morning Patricia insisted on taking a taxi and laughed at a frowning George, telling him that she was used to living and moving around the big city long before she met him. So, each of them went about their business.

Promptly at nine o'clock Patricia entered a luxurious shop on Rodeo Drive. Barbie doll look alike girls were slowly fixing already perfectly arranged clothes. She hesitated at the door not sure if this was the right place.

"Patricia, my dear, right on time!" Moraine was ambling down the stairs, fresh and graceful in fashionable attire. She looked more like a model than the shopkeeper. Moraine turned on her way down, o the Barbie Dolls.

"Girls, take over the store, I have a special assignment today!" Barbie Dolls nodded and continued their pointless jobs.

"Maurine, I hope this will not disrupt the routine of your normal working day!"

"Darling, this is my routine. My job is to find beautiful clothes for the rich and *sometimes* beautiful women. Today I have an easy and pleasant duty to accommodate a customer who is rich *and* beautiful. It will be fun, I promise you. Unlike most of my regular customers, I like you, my dear, very much. We going to shop, shop and shop!" Giddy Maurine slid her hand under Patricia's arm leading her upstairs.

"Oh Moraine, I need just several things and everything here looks so expensive." Patricia hesitated uncomfortably. Her companion laughed again, waiving her hand in dismissal.

"Don't look at me like that. George called me a few minutes ago and gave us a green light to buy whatever we please, regardless of price. You have one hell of a husband!"

The time flew by. Moraine was a real expert, and at the same time, an excellent teacher. She showed Patricia how easy it is to put coordinating articles of clothing together, and how to choose the best color to enhance her natural features. For the first time Patricia enjoyed shopping. Actually, she felt like a new person. With Moraine, everything was like a game, and Patricia's inherent sense of humor accepted it as such. Her biggest nightmare turned out to be one of the most enjoyable events in her life.

"Now, my dear, let's be sensible! First, I won't tell you how much lighter your husband's bank account is from this morning's shopping, which won't hurt him at all, and second, we deserve a big lunch after all that work. This great new restaurant with food to die for is our next stop!" Moraine was looking at a big pile of clothes with a satisfied smirk on her face. Patricia realized how hungry she was and that she had not felt this perfectly happy in a long time. Feeling guilty for this enormous spending was muffled by beautiful, soft, elegant, and the colorful wardrobe she just acquired.

The restaurant was so chic and charming that the girls, already accelerated by a fun morning, felt at ease and a little frivolous. They were giggling while Moraine was flirting with the waiter, innocently, but with pleasure.

"Moraine, what would Slim say if he saw you? Patricia laughed

"Oh, Slim!" Moraine made a face, "He is just a man. All of them are the same. Women and control, that's all they want. Don't take me wrong, Slim is not bad, better than most I know, if I may say so for my own husband, but he's just a man. Just a man!"

"Are you trying to say that Slim chases women? That all men chase women?" Patricia suddenly remembered Alicia.

"No, not all of them! Some drink, some gamble and some spend all the time with their pals watching sports. Take a pick, which is your preference?" Moraine started to giggle again.

Patricia would usually find this disturbing, but she too, burst into laughter. "Well, am I to presume that Slim is a womanizer? She teased.

"Slightly, very slightly!"

"What's that mean? I need a little input here, being a fresh bride with no suspicions until now!" Patricia made a face to resemble Alicia's pouting lips and flickering eyelashes.

"Oh yea, Alicia! That woman makes me furious. In the beginning I had the urge to strangle her, but I'm over that one!" Patricia looked at her with questioning eyes.

"Now, I think she deserves nothing less but medieval inquisition torture!" They giggled again.

"Although, she thinks she's irresistible and wants everybody to think the same, which she manages most of the time, I see now how shallow she is. She never succeeded to keep a man, although she pretends not to be interested in serious relationships. It's so obvious how desperate she is!" Moraine was stirring her coffee remembering with a smile some of Alicia's stunts.

"I'm not sure! She seemed to me so secure, and may I add successful. Our brave knights last night were smitten by her!"

"That's the talent she possesses. Her ability to lure men under her spell is strong, but, as I pointed out earlier, I doubt she's equally able to keep any of them. Interesting thing is that men start to interest her when they are not free!"

"You mean a married man.?"

"Or engaged! Let me tell you a little story. When Bill decided to expand on the West Coast, he wanted Slim for all of his organizational and promotional skills. But, Slim has no fashion awareness. He's a big shabby mouse. You should have seen him before I took him into my hands. Even his best friends didn't recognize him afterwards. Well, the story began when Bill came from New York to find a location for his L.A. store and to coach Slim how to run a fashion establishment. Slim is a genius in the world of business, but fashion? Spare me. Well, Bill was coming and Slim realized that he didn't have a suit that would appeal to someone like his new boss. And, as sometimes things fell at the right time in the right place, it happened that he drifted like a lost sheep into the department store where I worked.

One of my male associates tried to help him choose a suit. It was disaster after disaster. He hit the slow time of day, so I amused myself for a time watching those two masters in action. Then of course, I took pity on them and offered my services. Well, what can I say, I have a soft spot for overgrown idiots. The result was a metamorphosis. An ugly caterpillar turned into a moth, but a handsome and elegant moth.

He was overwhelmed by the results. I have to admit I didn't want him to go and never to see him again, so I suggested a good haircut and designer shoes would be the next logical step. He looked at me as if I was sending him to fish piranhas with bare hands in the Amazon jungle. Again, I *had to* offer my help.

The next day I took him to my friend Alexander, a genius with scissors, then in search of shoes. As a reward, he took me to lunch, where he, as every man, was endlessly talking about his new job, his new boss and a whole truckload of problems because of his ignorance of fashion. Patricia, I knew instantly that was a job made for me. I was sick of being just a sales person in a department store, possessing a diploma from art school, and being very good in styling the wardrobe. Therefore, I started to comfort him with advice for his need of an assistant with taste, fashion sense, and experience in selling clothes. Imagine this! He moaned for a full fifteen minutes that to find someone like that would be next to impossible. Then he glanced at his transformed image in the mirror behind our table and opened his mouth in a revelation. I let him try to induce me to accept the job for the next half an hour. Then I said yes with upmost modesty.

When Bill arrived a week later, we were ready with a complete business strategy, which was Slim's masterpiece, and my presentation of displays and sales pitch. Bill was more than pleased, and since then things had been going very well. In the same moment the *spider women* Alicia herself came on the stage. Slim knew her long before he met Bill, but she never showed any interest in him, not until she saw me, that is. I fell in love with that big log in a matter of days, but men are slow in their heads. I wanted him to love me back without using my womanly strategies. I knew it would happen in time, when it became clear to him that he couldn't do without me. So, I was patient! The thing was he called me "my girl", more as a compliment and comradely between two colleagues, not out of an awareness that I was a woman.

When Bill came, Alicia was tagging along, and the simpleton she is, she thought that "my girl" meant how it sounded. Oh, Patricia, she made a real spectacle of herself. Poor Slim found himself woven into her spider web until he couldn't breathe. Don't think for a second that he resisted. Falling like a log has a profound meaning. For a whole week, she was all over him and poor Slim was like a teenager drooling over every Alicia's word. In addition, don't think I took it as easy as I talk about it now. One second I wanted to kill her, next him, but the rest of the time I contemplated suicide. It was the worst week of my life, and then it hit me. She is not interested in Slim; she is not interested in any man. She liked a hunt and conquest. *Certain* types of conquests. She was under the impression that Slim and I are in a relationship. For the normal person that would be a signal to stop. That precise fact evoked her need to prove, again, how irresistible she is. She thrives in breaking up couples! As I said before, Alicia never noticed Slim before, but with me in the picture, he was hers to fry. Then, I knew what to do!" Maurine sipped her vino.

"You were able to do something?" Patricia was picturing George in a spider web and Alicia circling around him ready to pluck his heart out.

"You bet!" Moraine nodded extending her neck to see what was on the dessert cart pushed by the waiter to the next table. "That evening all four of us went to dinner, against Alicia's wishes of course, to discuss the last detail before they left for New York. Alicia was full of plans to come over as much as she could to help Slim with the store opening, and with everything else. Slim was dribbling over her every word. And then I strike like a cobra. I was leisurely eating my Tiramisu chatting friendly with Bill and turned the conversation up to a more personal level asking him if he'd rather be married or have a serious relationship. He went on about his one and only mistress, the art, and finally asked the question I was leading up to the whole evening.

"And what about you, Moraine? Is there some lucky guy in your life?" Alicia was feeding Slim carrot cake with her fingers, and it looked like she didn't know we existed, but I knew better."

"Steven! Tall, blond, gorgeous, my high school sweetheart. I have neglected him since you arrived, but he is so understanding. My big bear! I don't know what I would do without him. Oh, Patricia you should have seen her. She sprang away from poor Slim as if he just developed scarlet fever. I pretended that I wasn't aware of those two, and I was going on and on about my beloved Steven. Slim, the idiot, was stunned by Alicia's sudden transformation into an iceberg. He, for real, didn't hear a word of what Bill and I exchanged. He just looked at Alicia's murderous expression while she barked at me why I'd never mentioned my boyfriend before. I turned my big baby blue innocent eyes in her direction and sweetly replied that she never asked. She abruptly got up hissing through her teeth something about packing and going to bed so she would be fresh for tomorrow's early departure for New York. Slim was forgotten like a squashed fly, and by the way, he in that moment looked like one. He never knew what hit him. Bill laughed, hugged me, and whispered " Smart girl!" Moraine finished with enjoyment.

"You believe he knew that Steven was a fabrication?" Patricia equally enjoyed that account of the victory over Alicia.

"Certainly he did! He still sometimes asks how Steven is, and I always make some little anecdote about him, especially if Alicia is around.

"I bet you do!" Patricia watched her new friend with admiration, "And, how Slim survived that ordeal?" She couldn't resist.

"Oh, I hate to look back on that time. He moped for a whole month, walked like a zombie, talked as if he had a toothache, lost fifteen pounds. The whole business was on my back. The first week I wanted to strangle him, Then I planned to buy a crocodile and lock them together in the basement. Even that long and painful torture seemed too light of a punishment. In fact, I worked and hoped he'll snap out of it. One day he came and ask me, out of the blue, what he did wrong to insult poor Alicia so much that she didn't want to talk to him. In that moment I went ballistic. How could this smart man be so stupid? I couldn't believe my ears! You should have seen it: I jumped and trashed in his face the whole ugly truth about his *perfect* beloved. He looked at me with an open mouth, and then accused me of being jealous of her like every other woman who knew her. That turned me into an evil witch. I asked him who told him that every woman is jealous of Alicia – Alicia. Why she never showed a shred of interest in him before - because he was single. Why she dumped him so abruptly – because of Steven. And , if he didn't believed me, he was free to call Bill and ask.

"He moped for another week, but this time evaluating everything I said. Then, he called Bill. I guess whatever Bill said was not very flattering for his ideal woman. The result was another a couple of months of an even harder life. He went through the world hating women with a passion. The problem was that his job was to interact with them daily, to flatter them, dress them, and admire them. From time to time, I felt sorry for him but, truth be known, he deserved it. To be so stupid and fall into Alicia's web was a male thing to do, but to languish over it for months was pure imbecility." Her eyes were shooting balls of lightning.

Patricia's affection for this woman grew more by the minute.

"How did he ultimately get over it?" She could not resist.

"Well, with the overdose of the same medicine. The business started great, but no thanks to Slim. Bill decided to come and see what we were doing to have such a success and what could be done from his side to make it even more successful. In this business you always have to be one step in front of your competitors. So, Alicia was coming too, which threw Slim into another fireball of torment. His biggest fear was she'll mess with his head again, and he will not be able to resist. Every spare moment we had, he was making different plans as how to withstand Alicia's charms. On the end he asked me for advice. First I asked him whether he just wanted to resist her, or maybe inflict a little bit of revenge. He agreed that some pay back would restore his self-esteem. I suggested a little performance for Alicia. The idea was that he'll find a girl who will act as his girlfriend, which will mess with Alicia's sick mind and try to win him back. Revenge would be his complete preoccupation with his *girlfriend* so much so that he wouldn't "notice" Alicia and her advances."

"I hoped he would ask me to be the *girlfriend,* which I would do with pleasure. Fat chance! That dope was walking around for two days evaluating every female he knew since kindergarten. In the end, a day before Bill and Spider Woman were coming, he burst into my office and almost commanded me to be his girlfriend. Well, what can I say? As much as I hated the last visit from our boss, I must say this one was one of the most enjoyable of my life. Slim was nervous, but when they appeared at the airplane exit, and he saw Alicia's predatory glance toward us, something happened inside his sorry brain. He transformed into Cary Grant! Wherever possible his arm was around my shoulders, he opened doors for me, ordered food "knowing" what I liked to eat, called me every possible lovesick name."

Maurine joined Patricia in a full-hearted laugh. "Bill was delighted with our performance, while Alicia was confused. After a couple of hours Bill casually asked what was happening, and how Slim managed to win me over from Steven? Slim was great! In that moment, I decided I'd marry that big log. He calmly answered that after he tried everything to make me love him, he finally succeeded by making me jealous pretending to be in love with Alicia. I almost died of delight, realizing that he finally read *Spider Woman* through and through. She almost died too, realizing that she was used by a man to captivate another woman. Bill almost died of amusement that somebody had at last put Alicia in her place. Of course, she tried every possible trick she knew to restore her impeccable reputation, but Slim didn't cave in. Since then I'm her biggest enemy, and I'm sure she vowed to get even one of these days. So, Her Majesty, The-Big-Seductress is not completely invincible!" Moraine concluded with a satisfied smirk.

"Bravo, Moraine! Next time you'll have to tell me how you made him fall in love with you for real, because, I can tell he is head over heels in love with you!" They exited the restaurant looking for a taxi.

"No my dear, next time you'll tell me how you managed to captivate George. Everybody can see how much he is in love with you. Last evening after you left, Bill went on and on about how nobody believed that George would marry ever again. He was even more surprised to see him so much in love, concluding that you must be a truly exceptional person to melt the heart of that refrigerator."

Patricia stared at her totally bewildered. She opened her mouth to protest, but that would give away the secret of her marriage. In that moment the taxi stopped in front of them, and Moraine stuffed her into the car, promising to call tomorrow after she made an appointment with her hairdresser.

Patricia was deep in her thoughts replaying in her mind all she heard from Moraine, especially about her last remark, which was brain-tearing.

How had they got the idea that George is in love with her. According to Moraine, it was so obvious. Bill too, and he's known George for a long time, and supposedly he knew him very well. Must be that old saying, people see what they expect to see. George is everything but in love with her, and that was a fact. During yesterday's dinner, he barely paid any attention to her, so how could everybody be so convinced of his love for her? Oh dear, and on top of all this confusing situation she has to worry about Alicia. That woman is willing to do any craziness to succeed in the only important thing in her life. The next thought froze her heart. Alicia couldn't afford another defeat in front of Moraine. Nothing would stop her from proving superiority over other women. *But maybe she has some other reasons? I'll have to ask Moraine about the history of George and Alicia.* Somebody was betrayed - that much she gathered - but who? George or Alicia or third person?

Their hotel suit was dark and empty. Patricia did not know where he was, nor did she have a way to find out, but there was no doubt with whom he was. She shook her head with a feeling of hopelessness. *I'm too tired of all this! He can do whatever he wants! I'm going to bed.*

The next morning there was a note from George lying on the coffee table in the suite's beautiful living room.

Dear Patricia!

I hope you had a fruitful day. We are invited to dinner this evening.

Be in the hotel suite before seven. If not join us in the restaurant.

Love, George

He did not bother to say who invited them to dinner, probably presuming she would know. Who else but Bill and Alicia, and I bet it was her *sweet* idea. Some strange uncomfortable twitch in her chest reminded her of Moraine's account of her distress. She marched decidedly into the bedroom. *I'll put one of those elegant dresses, enjoyed the meal, and to hell with Alicia. Maybe I'm jealous, maybe just possessive, but I'll be dammed if I'll give her a second of the pleasure of watching me suffer. I have to pull myself together and play ignorance.*

While waiting for Moraine's call, Patricia was going through her newly acquired clothes for this evening. *I'll have to choose something sophisticated and crisp to keep me on guard,* she reminded herself several times. She smiled happily. *Today, I'll have myself another wonderful day with Moraine.*

That was exactly what she had. First, they spent a big portion of the morning at Moraine's favorite beauty salon. They were giggling and making jokes about a *fame fatale* who is busy keeping in suspense three men, while they enjoyed themselves having mud baths and massages. Skillful masseur's fingers were tireless, relaxing Patricia's muscles and nerves to the point that she was able to think calmly again.

"I spoke yesterday evening with Slim about George and Alicia." Moraine was purring like a lazy cat. "Well, he doesn't know all the details. It looks like Alicia was very interested in George, or as Slim thinks, in his money. George's wife, I mean his first wife was still alive, but such minor details never bothered Alicia. At that time, she was involved with some big-shot lawyer. He left his girl or fiancé for her. Slim thinks that the guy was serious about Alicia. He bought a big flashy ring, and everybody thought that Alicia finally found herself a man. But George was wealthier, more handsome, which made him too big of temptation for Alicia to resist. So, she put her moves on George, neglecting her fiancé.

"George responded with equal amount of flirting, treating the matter as a game. But, Alicia was serious. One evening her fiancé waited for them in front of her apartment building. He pleaded with her to reconsider and come back to him. That was a moment she made a fatal mistake, She laughed in his face that she found a better man and she'd enjoy more being the next Mrs. Hammond then the wife of some New York layer. The poor man was left in pieces, but George made her regret it in a matter of minutes. He calmly told her that he had a wife, and if he ever chose another Mrs. Hammond, she, Alicia, will be the last on his list. Slim assured me that this story is still circulating around, burning Alicia's ugly heart".

"Truth or not, you can imagine how mad she was. After that fiasco, Alicia tried to patch it up with her lawyer, but evidently, he managed to resist. Lucky devil. All of us knew that George's wife died, but his marriage to you was a total surprise for everybody who known him. I was thinking about all what Slim said and I wouldn't take it lightly. Believe me, she'll do every imaginable dirty thing to revenge herself. You and I, my dear, will make sure that she doesn't succeed. Is that clear?"

Moraine turned into a determined little schemer. "Don't take me wrong, my dear, George loves you too much to fall into Alicia's web, but I think that she's begging for another lesson.'

"Yeah, and do you have any idea how we'll do it? Patricia wanted to know.

"You are more beautiful them she. You are honest and fresh, she is shrewd and has been playing her games for too long. We must let her destroy herself on her own!"

"But, how?"

"First, we'll go to Alexander's and let him work his magic, then professional make up, and when you put on one of the dresses we choose yesterday, Alicia will turn green."

Listening to Moraine everything seemed so easy, but she knew she couldn't compete with Alicia. In this moment, she did not care. Moraine's spirit overwhelmed her and she will try her best not to disappoint her new friend.

Pushing the tight itinerary, they were running late. It was after 6:30 p.m., and they were still in a taxi slowly advancing through L.A.'s streets. Five minutes before seven the girls rushed into an empty suite. George had been there, the bathroom clearly showed that, but he was probably in the restaurant by now.

Sifting fast through Patricia's evening dresses was not a chore for Moraine's trained eye, completely ignoring Patricia's choice from this morning. She had chosen an elegant, but not too sexy dress by Patricia's opinion. It was red and shimmery, tightly outlining Patricia's slim body.

Patricia had never worn anything like this in her life, and quite frankly, she could not believe she was going too now. However, she liked it. It made her feel like a different person, someone who could stand up against Alicia and feel confident. While she examined her image in the big mirror, Moraine was putting on a beautiful silver dress chatting how fortunate it was she didn't have time to go home and change into one of her own. To borrow from a friend was always more fun. Her endless energy wouldn't let her stop for a second.

In half an hour both of them were ready and eager to face the barracuda herself. Exactly at 7:30 p.m. they glided into the dining room. Everything was the same as two days before, but seemed different. The music was playing, the waiters were discretely strolling around the tables, the guests were chatting amongst themselves.

Then something happened that Patricia had never experienced before. As they entered, the guests and working staff stopped whatever they were doing and stared at them. For a minute Patricia froze in fear that something was wrong with her gown or professional make up from this afternoon, but unmistakable expression of admiration on their faces put her at ease. They approved! Never before has she evoked such unanimous appreciation for her looks, and finally she was able to understand Francisca's addiction for public praise. Moraine was sweetly purring in the headwaiter's ear, asking for assistants with the party they searched for. Every head was following them through the room, and then, she spotted George and his friends. If she ever desired a moment of victory this was the one. Slim and Bill stared at them with surprised smiles and wide expressive eyes. Alicia was turning from green to deep red, while poison arrows were shooting toward both approaching girls. But, the biggest thrill was George's open mouth and bewildered look on his handsome face. He looked at her without blinking. then the waiter announced.

"The rest of your party is here, Sir!" George and the other two men jumped up with big smiles, holding chairs for the two women. Moraine lovingly looked into her husband's eyes, and kissed him lightly on the mouth. "Hey honey, how was your day without me?"

"Lonely, and you know that, but the sight of you now makes me forgive your desertion these last two days!"

Patricia sweetly smiled into George's face, feeling some newborn security which allowed her to do and say whatever she wanted. So, she pressed her lips to his cheek. This was not the first time she did that, but this time she lingered there much longer, slowly releasing the kiss. Then she withdrew her face from his asking in a low seductive tone.

"And how was your day, darling? I missed you!" At the same time she lifted her small hand and with her fingers tried to wipe off the trace of lipstick from his cheek. When she wanted to pull her hand away, he grabbed it and pressed it to his lips.

"I missed you too, but now that you are here my heart is complete again!" He helped her into her chair, refusing to release her hand. The conversation continued, and this time three men were listening with great amusement to their accounts about shopping, massages, traffic, lunch and everything else that had happened to them. Alicia was a frozen iceberg. She did not even try to involve herself in the conversation, which would be difficult anyway, The girls were jumping into each other's sentences, and the men were asking questions before they were done with answers to the previous one. They were having a great time, and Patricia was in some feverish state of mind and body. George was still holding her hand, and his thumb was slowly stroking her palm. Every caress was shooting some strange shocks up her spine. Their dinner came and with a slow unwillingness George let go of her hand, creating an odd emptiness around her heart. To keep her hand were it was would be worth skipping the dinner, although she was starving.

While they were eating, the piano player left and a small band of musicians started to play dance music. Moraine clapped her hands in delight. "I completely forgot that Saturday is dance night. Oh Slim, let's dance! I haven't had a chance to shake your bones for longer then I like to remember!" Slim stood up helping Moraine onto the dance floor.

"Shall we join them, dear? We haven't had a chance to dance since our wedding, and we need some practice for our big party next week!" George took Patricia's hand again, helping her out of her chair. She just smiled and nodded. The prospect of being in his arms was thrilling, and she did not want to think why she felt that way. Several couples were already on the dance floor slowly moving in waves of dreamy music.

George took her into his arms, playfully swirling her in a circle a couple of times. The music was slow, so he slowed down looking straight into her eyes. Patricia looked back, puzzled how her opinion of him had changed drastically. She never thought of him as remotely handsome, but now she was sure that he is the most gorgeous man she ever seen. This discovery surprised and fascinated her so much that her eyes sparkled making them even more beautiful. George kept staring into them, and she would give anything to know what he thinks at this moment. However, tonight she did not want to analyze her thoughts or feelings, maybe for the first time ever she allowed herself to go with the flow. Slow romantic music, and the wine she had with the dinner made her conspicuousness blurry. Any rational thought which tried to take control of this woozy Patricia was blankly pushed down with the cozy *numbness she was floating in. Without knowing it, she put her head on his shoulder letting herself for* once enjoy the moment. George sighed and pulled her closer into his embrace.

Time was standing still. *To be like this in his arms is dangerous, but I cannot think about anything more pleasurable. It would be nice to belong to him like this for real. To be the wife he loves and Oh goodness, even the wine and music should not make a raving lunatic out of me.* Her rational inner self meekly protested. *Why would I want all that nonsense? I am not an empty-headed cheerleader in love with a school jock. In love? It feels like love. All the signs are here: jealousy, a desire to be attractive. I would never make such a spectacle of myself if - Oh Patricia, girl, don't even think about it. If you fall in love with him, your life will turn into misery.*

"Patricia!" She opened her eyes to look at George's face hovering over hers. "The music stopped. Shall we go back to the table?" Patricia just nodded, and tried to pull herself out of his embrace, but he did not let go. His arm reached around her waist pulling her close to his body. *Well,* Patricia thought, *I am not the only one taken over by the wine.* A couple hours later, more wine and dancing made it clear to be too much for Patricia. George almost carried her to the elevator, listening to her protests how she is more than capable to walk on her own, but she clung to him anyway, feeling a little bit unsteady on her own.

"I thought you could drink a couple of glasses, but I was wrong. "George teased.

"Of course, I can. It was more than a couple, and you know that. I'm so dizzy George." She laughs.

Her husband picked her up in his arms, and that was the last thing she remembered until the next morning.

To open her eyes next morning took some effort. Daylight was creeping through the thick curtains. She lay there for some time wondering where she was and why her head would not function as usual. In a flash everything came to her. *Oh boy, I embarrassed myself last night. Who cares about my head? George must be mad as a hell. The first time he takes me somewhere, I make fool of myself and him.*

She listened for a while. Complete silence ensured her that she was alone. Patricia lifted the comforter to discover, with horror, that she was wearing her night gown. *George? He did it. Oh, how will I ever look into his eyes again. He must despise me even more.*

The note was on the same place as the one yesterday. This time she was not so egger to discover what's in it.

Dear Patricia,

I am wrapping up my business this morning. Hopefully I will be back around 1:00 p.m.

Moraine called, but I did not want to wake you up. So, give her a call. I think you

got yourself another friend. How are you doing it so fast? If you go out with her leave

a message with the concierge, and I will take the two of you to lunch.

Love, George

Love, my foot! After last night, if he does not lock me up in the basement every time somebody visits, I will consider myself lucky. But we are married, and I'll have to face him sooner or later. Better get over with it soon as possible, she concluded and picked up the telephone receiver to call Moraine. *I need a good, long and hopefully comforting conversation with somebody who will not judge me too severely.* She will get that from George in abundance, no doubt. Therefore, Patricia dressed and bravely marched out into the wild traffic of the busy city.

"Moraine, please tell me how big of a fool I made of myself last evening?" was the first nervous question she asked entering Moraine's office. The other woman raised her eyebrows in astonishment.

"What are you talking about? The evening was perfect! Alicia got what she deserved and the two of us earned undivided attention from our husbands. I do not remember the last time I had such an exciting evening! Don't you think so?" Moraine happily moved around.

"I was drunk!" Patricia miserably cried. "You have to tell me how many embarrassing things I have done. Was George mad, or furious, or - I give up! I'll just wait for him to strangle me!" She hopelessly threw herself on the sofa.

"Honey, I still don't understand what you're talking about, but if you are worried about being a little tipsy, it was nothing. All of us had a little too much, but you should have seen Alicia. After you and George left, we remembered *Her Majesty*. She was stoned! Poor Slim and Bill had a hard time dragging her out of the restaurant in a way that people would not notice what a stopper she was in. I was a little happy myself, and had even harder time not to giggle. Believe me, she must have one monster of a headache this morning. She as well had to digest all that poison she produced last evening."

Patricia gave up, realizing that Moraine was a little drunk herself too, and was not a good judge of the situation.

"George wants to take us to lunch. He expects to finish his business dealings around noon. Therefore, we have to call the hotel and leave a message for him where to pick us up. I know you must have some plans!"

"Lunch sounds great! Slim would like us to spend some time together without *Spider Woman*. Today I got a completely new line in for Autumn. You have to see it. I already pulled aside several pieces for you. Let us go and try them on. I'll show you the rest, too, and if you like anything else, it's yours.

Morning went by with lightning speed. Two women had a blast with clothes and accessories. However, as time was passing Patricia grew more nervous. George would come soon, but she was not ready to face him. She made up a hundred different decisions what she will say and how she will act, but nothing made her feel any easier. When George and Slim finally showed up it was worse than her most awful prediction. He was in a great mood, or so it seemed. When he saw her he widely smiled approaching, reached for her hands, then placed on each palm one feather light kiss.

"How are you feeling today?" He encircled his arm around her shoulders, "Moraine told me she selected more clothes for you to try. Did you? I hope you found more exquisite dresses like the one you wore last night!" George turned toward the other couple, "Are you ready guys?" They nodded, so he pulled Patricia closer to him and headed for the door explaining to Slim something. She heard the words but not the meaning. *Does he really not care what happened last night, or is he so good of an actor and waiting for the final blow when they will be alone? Damn, when will this torment end?*

Lunch was passing pleasantly - too pleasantly - when Patricia was concerned, enjoying little too much the fact that George made a habit of holding her hand whenever possible.

She observed Moraine and Slim. It was so obvious how much they cared for each other. Her heart jumped! What she would give if George would love her like that. Then she could be free and open like Moraine with her husband. *To touch and kiss him whenever she felt like it. Oh, Patricia stop it! You just torment yourself with unrealistic dreams. He loved his first wife, and everybody is shocked that he married again. They are shocked to see him in "love". That's telling enough for itself.* If her new friends would know the real reason behind their marriage, what they would think of her, she wondered.

"When is your airplane leaving tomorrow?" Slim asked.

"seven fifteen, which doesn't give us much time. Patricia and I would like to thank you for everything, and we would like if you could visit us soon. For Thanksgiving if you have no other plans?" George looked at the young couple questioningly.

"That will be great!" Moraine screamed, "I'm dying to see your property, horses, kids and, of course, Patricia's cowboys!" Moraine winked at Patricia, George frowned.

"Now I know what you talked about these last three days!" He let go of Patricia's hand, and abruptly got up, "We have to go. I'll call you, Slim, and we can arrange all the details" He squeezed Slim's hand and planted a kiss on Moraine's cheek. Patricia gave Slim both her hands and smiled, "Slim, this was one of the best times I ever had, mainly thanks to you and your lovely wife. I'm expecting you to honor the promise and visit us!" Then the two girls hugged.

"Wild horses won't stop me from getting there and charm all of your cowboys, and then George will not have any reason to be jealous again. But I warn you, nothing will persuade me to get on one of George's beasts!"

"Oh Moraine, you'll fall in love with those horses just as I did. Thanks for everything! Without you, I would have bought all the wrong clothes, not to speak of haircut. Goodbye and I hope to see you soon." Girls hugged again, then they left the restaurant.

Patricia was unceremoniously showed into a taxi. *We are alone, so now we can stop pretending.*

"This was a successful trip; don't you think so? I hope you enjoyed yourself as much as Moraine tried to convince me. But one thing she *has* done - she made sure you bought enough of everything." George interrupted her thoughts, "One of my partners invited us to spend a weekend at his Lake Tahoe vacation house, I didn't have any excuse to refuse the invitation, so, put it on your schedule for the next month." *Damn, a weekend vacation is not a business trip. We will probably have to spend every minute together. How will I survive that?*

"Can we take the kids with us?" The sudden thought gave her hope, "They would love some boating, maybe fishing?"

"I don't think that Martin would be happy with three noisy kids under his feet for two days. Besides, the other partners will not bring their kids, so It will have to be just the two of us. What makes you think the kids would like it? I took them several times on similar vacations, but after that, kids refused to go again. "George was smiling with one side of his mouth, remembering, "Lindsay was seven, I think, when we went to Palm Springs to spend some time with my cousin. After three days, she refused to come down for dinner. I wondered why, so she explained that if another person squeezed her cheeks and called her an *adorable child* shell have to bit their fingers off. Then she informed me that she is a well-behaved girl and biting someone's fingers of will not do, so she decided to stay in her room until we went home. Since then whenever I mention a vacation all three of them suddenly remember something important they have to do, which would unfortunately prevent them from going with me." He laughed completely relaxed again.

The big conversation she expected obviously will not take place, at least not for now. Maybe Moraine was right. Maybe she did not do anything outrageous. All of them drank a little too much. *If George doesn't want to talk about it, that is perfectly fine with me*, she resignedly concluded.

CHAPTER 9

The preparations for the big party were passing her by. Although, she offered her help, it looked like organizing parties in this house was like a performance of a perfectly tuned orchestra. Millie, like an experienced conductor, supervised decorating the house, ordering flowers, choosing a caterer and food, writing and sending the invitations and hundreds of other small and large chores. The children were out of the way, obviously used to similar situations. So, Patricia had no other choice but to follow their example. She kept herself out of everybody's hair and stayed in the library most of the time writing her book. George would come with the kids every evening, listen to Millie's long report, approve or disapprove, then he would go into his room with an excuse of being very busy.

He did not communicate very much with Patricia, and she did not know what to think. Is this behavior the result of her fiasco in L.A? Or, is this how he is going to treat her in years to come? I could not care less, she would try to convince herself over and over again, not wanting to acknowledge that little throbbing in her heart had something to do with it.

Late afternoons were the best. Together with the children, she would go for a swim, or take a walk down to the stables. They would climb on the hay piled in the barn, and she would read them what she had written during the morning. They would made comments, or laugh rolling through the hay until tears run down their faces. Andrew still thought that at least one of the sisters should be a boy, and Patricia promised, again, she will think about it

"Now, that I know how boys can be obnoxious, I just might put

137

in some eleven year old boy who creates more problems than all three sisters together. What do you think?"

"I'm not obnoxious, and I don't make more problems than Lindsay and Mark!" Andrew protested.

"I didn't know that we were talking about you, Andrew! I was just creating a possible character for my book!" Patricia played innocent, "You know, if the character is too boring nobody would want to read the book. Only unusual and special characters could interest a reader enough to wish to know what happens next. So, if I have to invent a new character, he should be all of that and more, don't you agree Lindsay, and you Mark?" Andrew looked confused, and Lindsay giggled in delight watching her brother squirming, finally having someone who knew how to tame him.

"Oh yeah!" Lindsay frowned like she was deep in thought, imitating Patricia, "Boys are not very interesting, as it is, and if you don't make him slightly unusual, nobody would remember that he is in the story." Lindsay acted as she was not aware of Andrew getting upset.

"Why everyone always thinks that for every naughty thing it's the boy that should be blamed?" He just could not give up.

"Because it is usually correct!" Mark calmly replied.

"Oh, what do you know?" His brother looked cross at him

"Well, do you remember when all the horses ran out of the corral? Although, you tried to blame it on the" Boys", I saw you open the gate!"

"Yes. But they needed exercise, and everybody was busy with the hay because of the rain!"

"And, that time when Millie baked a lemon pie! You ate it behind the barn. I know because you were sick all night, and believe me Millie was not fooled for a second that the mountain lion did it, as you suggested!"

"You have no proof for that!"

"I don't need one!" Mark frowned for a couple of seconds in concentration, "How about that frog in Morgan's salad?"

"You could have done it, just as well as I!"

"True, I could, but I didn't. You are the only other one who could!"

"Lindsay could, too! She hates Morgan as much as we do!"

"Right, But she hates frogs almost as much as she hates Morgan!"

"You smarty pants!" Andrew sent a malicious looks toward his brother, "Don't think for a second that I don't know about yours little pranks!"

"Name it!" Mark challenged.

"That false fire alarm last spring! You were screaming your head off that the barn was on fire, but it was a lie!"

"No, that was business. Chuck paid me six bucks to do it. He needed a diversion to sneak out on a date with Sally… no Ruth… Mary. I'm sure… maybe Lisa… Doesn't matter who! He wanted to skip laying barb wire. *But, you* wanted to set a forest fire on the south slopes, just to see how many animals will run out and how many would be cooked. That was cruel, and I had to tell Peter!" Andrew jumped and grabbed Mark's arms looking down at the little boy.

"You were the one! I knew it all along! You little spy…" Patricia and Lindsay jumped at the same time to separate two boys. Mark was calm, as usual, and Patricia, in amazement realized that the boy had an IQ above average. He knew how to provoke his brother, but he also knew that Patricia and his sister would come to his rescue. This boy is too similar to his father. Is that good or not she could not decide just yet. She will have to observe him more, but in the meantime, she will have to handle him carefully. Being so secure in himself at six and a half was not something she would wish for any child.

"Patricia!" Lindsay was calling her for the third time.

"Yes, my dear?" She turned to the little girl with and apologetic smile.

"My dress for the party is, I'm afraid, too small. I know it's my fault, Millie warned me, but I was too lazy to try it on time, so..." Lindsay whispered.

"After dinner we'll go into your room and see what is hidden in the depths of your closet. Trust me, I'm an expert in adjusting old dresses. For me it was always more comfortable to fix old dress instead of going shopping for a new one." Patricia winked at the worried girl, "Come on boys, Millie will be upset if we are late for dinner, again!" She put stress on the word again. The boys, always hungry, did not wait for her to say it twice. They ran as fast as possible toward the main house, while Patricia with Lindsay beside her, proceeded in a much slower pace talking about the dress and party.

The next day, after George and the children left, Patricia was thinking about their rampage through Lindsay's closet last night. That girl is even worse than I was at her age. All of her clothes are tomboyish or bought by somebody who has no idea what is currently in fashion. They did not find a single piece which could be used as a suitable evening dress for an almost ten year old girl. So, Patricia decided to go into town and try to find something appropriate. Since she moved into George's house, it was a rare occasion for her to go anywhere. What kind of stores she will find in Sheridan was a total mystery for Patricia.

Millie suggested taking the old Pontiac which belonged to Tiffany, George's first wife. Millie used it, herself from time to time, to keep it in operating condition. The road was a dirt road, but repaired often enough, so the ride was pleasant. The sunny day made her feel good. She was thinking about her new life, her marriage and kids with pleasure. Surprisingly, she was not afraid any more. Some tranquility overwhelmed her with a thought that everything will work out. George will never love her, though, and be a real husband. Never to have a children of her own, was something she let go of a long time ago. When she would think about it before, it would hurt. Not any longer! Happily she smiled realized that now she has three of them.

God knows they need her more than anybody else ever did. *I will be the best mother to those kids as I possibly can.* That thought made her feel great. Kids are kids, all of them need someone to love them and take care of them.

Fortunately, Sheridan had a big department store. The selection of evening dresses for small girls was not great, anyway Patricia found a pretty dark blue velvet dress. I will take off this lace and shorten the sleeves. It will look just like some of the dresses Moraine forced me to try on. She remembered with nostalgia how they laughed forever as she looked like a teenager in them. Afterward, Moraine confessed that the line was made for very young girls. I learned from her much more about fashion that I thought possible. Now I can teach Lindsay, and have those mother - daughter conversations. She realized that she was smiling from ear to ear making the sales girl look at her with raised eyebrows, but she could not care less. Maybe next time, when we go to L.A. Lindsay could go with us. She smiled even wider with delight at that possibility.

Saturday morning Patricia was awakened very early by the noise of cars, footsteps and voices of strangers. For a moment she just wanted to curl up under the covers and stay there until tomorrow. She refused to think about the party. She was afraid. According to Millie's preparations the number of guests is enormous. The thought of so many people she had never met frightened her. What kind of people were they? Are they coming to meet her or criticize her? But, mostly she was afraid of comparison. Everybody knew Tiffany, everybody thought of her as beautiful, and everybody would, on purpose or not, compare the two of them. Patricia knew she will lose that battle. Be brave, my dear, Patricia was studying her reflection in the mirror, you lived your whole life in the shadow of your sister, and you coped with it amiably. You can do it again. Let them think what they please, she concluded philosophically.

My new family likes me… most of them, that is.

George stayed at home. What for, Patricia could not figure out. She watched him walking around getting in everybody's way, asking questions. In turn he got short answers. He was giving equally numerous suggestions, which nobody needed or heeded.

Patricia decided to retreat to the library with the children. They played the game of pretending to be Patricia's three characters. She would give them an initial situation after which they would have to tell what each of them would do if they were there. It was more fun than Patricia contemplated. She better understood how the kids' brains works, and was surprised how much imagination they possessed. Andrew was the wildest, and she definitely decided to turn one of the sisters into a brother. Andrew was ecstatic! He frantically ran through the library, jumping over sofas, chairs and all the time screaming like a wild cowboy. George abruptly burst into the library with a worried face, but was stopped by the girls' laughter. Andrew, who usually yielded to his father, did not stop for a moment. George had to call his name several times.

"Andrew! Stop this nonsense!" George grew impatient, "What's got into you? For a moment I was sure that somebody was hurt!"

"She'll write about me! She'll write about me…" Andrew started to jump around again shouting the sentence repeatedly. George turned to Patricia with quizzical eyebrows.

"Andrew, stop that right now!" Patricia tried to sound serious. With a smile on her mouth, she addressed George, "He tried for a while to convince me to include one boy character in my book. I know I should wait to announce it when we have less people in the house, but the damage is done, so…" She lifted her shoulders in silent apology. George's face changed, and he looked at her with interest.

"Your book, of course! Is it going to be finished soon? I would like to read it. Your picture books are great, but this one will be for older children, right?"

"Yes" She was surprised that he was aware of her work in such detail... "These three like it until now. It's a good indicator that the most of the readers would too." He was still standing there watching, making her feel a little uncomfortable, and prompted her to speak.

"Are the preparations close to the end, or..."She started.

"Almost! Millie prepared some snacks for the kids and us. She wants to know where we want to eat. I thought... Maybe in my... in the dressing room? His eyes were studying her face.

"I think that is an excellent idea!" She hurriedly answered, and getting up called the children

"I'm sure you are hungry, guys! Let us go into your dad's... into our dressing room. There is quiet and we won't be in anybody's way!" The children rushed out of the library, while George stayed beside the door keeping it open for Patricia.

The light lunch passed in laughter, teasing, and Andrew's endless repeating that he will be famous like Tom Sawyer and Huck Finn. Maybe even more. The atmosphere was cozy and relaxing. This is how it should be, Patricia thought, in an ordinary family. She even forgot about the upcoming evening. Although, she planned to ask George about his guests and what she might expect, but decided not to after all. He could not possibly understand her feelings and fears. She will manage on her own with whatever comes her way this evening.

George firmly insisted that the children go into their rooms and rest, "If you want to stay awake longer tonight, you need to rest now!" They went obediently, but Patricia could not help overhearing Andrew's nagging under his breath that he was too big for an afternoon naps. George turned to her.

"Are you okay? You look a little pale, and Millie is worried that you are sick!"

"Oh, no! I'm in perfect health!" Patricia smiled thinking, if you only knew how the thought of this party is horrid to me, you would despise me even more.

"I'm going to see how Millie is coming with everything!" She just wanted to get away from him, or she will start to cry revealing all of her fears, and make a fool of herself again. She cannot afford any more mistakes. So, she turned on her heels and run down the stairs.

"Millie, is everything as you planned, or do we have any problems?"

"My dear, don't you worry a bit! You have to relax and look gorgeous tonight, and stop agonizing over trivial things!" Millie looked at her, "You appear nervous! Don't tell me that the party makes you uncomfortable? You have no reason for it! These are great people. All friends, and they can't wait to get to know you better. It will take them one look, and they will fall in love with you, just as the rest of us did." Millie smiled broadly.

"Did you? Yes I think that the people on the ranch do like me… Oh, I don't know Millie, it looks like the whole State is coming just… to judge me!" Patricia had to talk with somebody, "George's first wife was from this area, and those people knew and loved her. Tim told me how beautiful she was, and… me being so plain, and… I'm afraid they'll compare me with her… I'll lose big time!" She raised her eyes to look at Millie who stared at her with a shocked expression.

"You don't know a thing about Tiffany, do you? Oh for Pit sake, I believed that George told you all!"

"No, he mentioned her when he talked about the children, but he never actually talked about his first marriage. I believe it would be too painful for him to talk about her because… He loved her so much!" Millie cut her short with a cry.

"Painful? You are all mixed up here… Painful,? Maybe, but for different reasons than you think. One of these days the two of us must have a long conversation, but not now. In a couple of hours the guests will start arriving, so go upstairs and take a long bath, make yourself beautiful, and don't worry about anything!" Millie gently pushed her toward the door.

In her room Patricia decided to do exactly as Millie suggested, starting with a long bath. The warm water soothed her nerves, but her mind was preoccupied with Millie's puzzling statements. Is she really wrong about George's first marriage? Why has he never told her anything about his deceased wife?

Patricia dozed into a sort of daydream, while her mind was reminiscing about all the events from the time she first met George. He was a mystery for her then, and he is still a mystery now. I know almost nothing about my husband. I never call him that, not even in my mind. He is not my husband, not in the real sense of the word. Nevertheless, I have a nice family, and maybe Millie is right, I could make some friends tonight.

She stayed too long in the bathtub. Tranquility of the warm water appeased her mind and body. The worst thing would be right now, she concluded, to worry herself with what might or might not happen. She pulled out of her closet a beautiful light blue dress. I forgot how elegant it is, and masterfully made. Just looking at it makes me feel much better. It took her a long time to apply makeup. I should practice more, as Moraine suggested, but old habits are hard to break. She was fussing with her lipstick trying to remember instructions she was given when Lindsay burst into her bedroom.

"Patricia, this is Sally!" Behind a little girl, a plump young woman in her twenties stepped into the room. With a broad smile, she studied Patricia.

"Pardon me, Mrs. Hammond, Lindsay said it'll be just dandy to march in!" Sally was still standing at the door.

"Oh, that's all right, Sally! Please, step in! Lindsay, you look beautiful!" Patricia studied Lindsay's curls scooped up on the top of her head, "Sally, you have done a great job! I just hope you will be able to do something with this scarecrow's nest on my head."

"My dear Mrs. Hammond…"

"Call me Patricia, please!"

"…Patricia!" Sally repeated slowly, "I just adore your name. It's so elegant… It suits you, and your hair is so pretty. It will be my pleasure to fix it for you. Well Lindsay, what do you think your new mom should look like tonight?" Mom? Patricia felt strange. I do feel like her mom, though. She glanced at a little girl, who was obviously to excited to pay attention to that remark.

"Oh, Sally, look at her dress. You fix her hair to look like a movie star, and with this dress nobody will be prettier then she!" Lindsay's eyes were shining. Oh boy, Patricia stared at Lindsay in amazement… She loves me! The heart of this little girl has a spot for me! Something tied her throat into a knot, and she had to push the tears back. Overwhelmed by emotions she could not resist but to hug that adorable girl.

"If she makes me half as gorgeous as you, I'll be the second most beautiful girl tonight!" Lindsay took her compliment blushing, but she could not be happier.

While Sally was working on Patricia's hair, the three girls were chatting about the party, dresses, guests… Time was passing almost unnoticeable. While Sally was giving the final touches to Patricia's hair, Patricia rushed Lindsay.

"Go into your room and put your dress on. On your way, run into the boys rooms and see what they're doing. If Mark has any problems, call me. Millie is too busy to help him!" Lindsay was out before she finished the sentence.

Sally left Patricia staring into her reflection in the mirror. This is not me! I still can't believe how good applied makeup and professional hair can make such a difference. This is my face, and just as it happened in L.A. she could clearly see her features enhanced and outlined.

The loud patter of hasty feet down the gallery reminded Patricia, again, how late she is. Two boys and Lindsay rushed in. Two young *men* in suits looked like a small adults. It was obvious how uncomfortable they were clothed in restrictive clothes, but determined to endure. Especially Mark looked like a miniature businessman. He was an exact image of his father. I noticed the likeness before, but in this outfit and with that serious face nobody could make the mistake whose son he is.

"Patricia!" Mark looked her with his usual seriousness, "You are still in your bathrobe. The first guests are already here, do you know? If we don't get down fast, father will make us squat!" He cocked his head on one side, frowning in concentration, "Nice hairdo, Patricia! You look prettier than usual!" It was a fact not a flattery. Andrew pocked him in the ribs. "She always looks good… But, he's right, Patricia, you look very good… What have you done?" Andrew was studying her closely.

"You moron, her hair is up, and she really knows how to do her make up! Will you teach me, Patricia?" The little girl joined her brothers in scrutinizing Patricia's appearance.

"I can feel dad's going nuclear!" Mark turned toward the door.

"Oh, yes! Patricia, hurry up!" Lindsay cried running after her brothers. The powerful noise penetrated through the open door of her sanctuary, clearly announcing that more than few guests have arrived. I have to rush, or the party will be over before I get down. Flinging her bathrobe on the bed, she stepped into her dress. The reflection from the mirror was of some unearthly creature enveloped in a blue silky dream. I can just go down and pretend this is not me. Definitely does not look like me, so I will be more composed if I keep thinking that some actress is impersonating poor plain Mrs. Hammond.

She exited the room. The house was in full light. Over the banister of the galley, she saw people talking, drinking, laughing… Music, hushed by the noise, was coming from the terrace. Patricia slowly approached the banister and pondered for a moment. Put yourself together, my girl, you have to do this. After all, those people came to see you, at least everybody was trying to convince me of this for a month. So, I will not prolong the inevitable any longer. Her sense of humor found it all very funny, so to put the smile on her lips was not hard. If only Francesca could see me right now. And Moraine! She would be proud of me.

Patricia was slowly advancing down the stairs, hoping that nobody would notice her right away. However, that was just a wish. One by one, guests were turning their heads toward her. The conversation stopped. Mesmerized with an impossible situation, her feet were moving on their own. Scanning discreetly the room, she at last, spotted George. He was standing beside a tall older woman in a black elegant gown. She hoped he will do something to stop this embarrassment, but he was looking at her in disbelief. Some spark in his eyes changed his expression, then with a smile he maneuvered his way between the guests heading for his wife. With relief, she waited for him. George climbed the remaining several steps, then reached for her hand. The expression in his eyes was different, which confused her even more. Now was not the time to ponder over it, feeling his arm circling around her shoulders turning toward his guests with an enormous smile.

"My dear guests, neighbors and friends! I have been accused, from most of you, that I'm hiding my bride!" He turned his eyes to a petrified Patricia.… "Which is the truth, but now when you see her, who can blame me?" Everybody laughed in agreement.

"In your place, my dear George, I would have kept her hidden, too! You'll have more visitors now than ever before, but nobody will come to see your ugly mug!" Laughter grew louder along with warm good wishes and clapping. George's hug hardened, but he kept smiling.

"Too late guys. Do not even think about it. If you knew what I had to do to make her fall in love with me, you would lose all respect for your old friend? So guys, keep your hands to yourself!" George glances toward Patricia again. She looked totally composed, with sweet smiles, returning stares from the crowed. She cannot stop to amaze me, he thought.

"Well, this is my wife Patricia, folks!" He simply said releasing her from his grip. Patricia bravely stepped forward, receiving congratulations, good wishes and compliments on her appearance. She just smiled right and left not understanding the real meaning of the words.

"Isn't our Patricia like a princess?" Millie's voice snapped George out of his deep thoughts, "George, my boy, you made the right choice this time. I thought a women like her didn't exist anymore. Isn't it interesting how love can make a woman blossom. She was pretty when you brought her here, but now she is exquisite, don't you think so?" George watched Patricia as she moved about the room.

"You think it's love?

"Men are so brainless. It's so obvious that she loves you more than you deserve, but my boy I think it's not half as much as you are smitten with her!" George jerked his head to look closely at Millie, "You may be fooling everybody around here - not me, ha, ha, ha... If I was in your place I would go over there, Chuck is starting his little games with your wife. He's a handsome devil. There's not many women who can resist him!" Before she finished George was half way across the room.

"Patricia!" He approached placing his hand around her waist, "We have to lead our guests to the buffet!" He said pretending that Chuck was not there.

"Boss, you can't be so possessive!" Chuck's lazy slow manner of speaking raised George's blood pressure. "This is after all, a party for Patricia, so you have to let her mingle with the guests and not make her your little shadow!" Chuck's crocked smile made George clenched his jaw, but replied calmly.

"You are absolutely right, but mingling means to devote yourself to everybody equally, not just to one bad mannered cow puncher!" He gently pushed Patricia toward the long tables overfilled with food.

"Dear friends, I would suggest that we start with refreshments. Any hesitations could leave you hungry. I just saw my cowboys eyeing the food, which means only one thing - it won't last long! So, folks, enjoy!" He took a plate turning to his wife, "Well we have to start, so what's your preference.

"Oh, I don't know, George! I'm not sure I could eat!. The lunch was so generous…"Patricia was overwhelmed by the number of people, everybody's politeness, piles of…

"You have to, Patricia!" He said gently, ""You are being observed closely, although it does not appear that way, but … trust me, they are watching your every move. If you don't eat… It won't look good!"

"George…" She whispered, "You know them… Do they approve of me, or…" He saw a fear in her eyes. He took her hand, and squeezed it in reassurance.

"Don't worry, Patricia, they love you. Can't you see it? They are simple, honest people who don't know how to pretend. If they did not approve, believe me, you would see it clearly. Just be yourself, and you'll end up this evening with a bunch of friends who would do anything for you!" She felt a little easier. George placed some light food on her plate. People were crowded around the tables making jokes and laughing while loading their plates. The atmosphere was so easy and relaxed that Patricia finally started to understand what was being said around her.

Mark appeared beside her, "Patricia would make me a plate, please?"

"Of course, my dear! What would you like?"

"Nothing fancy, please! Some hot dogs, fries, chips, Jell-O and piece of that cake with chocolate cream and that white stuff on the top!" He was precise, just as she expected.

"Would you like coke or lemonade?" She asked equally serious.

"Beer!" he said casually.

"In about ten years, maybe, but for now coke or lemonade!" She responded as if they had this kind of conversation every day since he was born.

"Beer? For you?" Andrew looked at him as if he was a stupid monkey, "Patricia, Millie bragged about some chicken thighs in the cushions, whatever that means. Problem is I don't know how that's supposed to look!" He stood there with a plate in his hands looking straight into her eyes.

"Well, let's see!" She scrutinized the table, "I think these are most likely chicken thighs in the cushions!" Patricia trust a fork into a piece of dough in the shape of a chicken thigh. It looked nicely baked to a golden brown color. She was holding it in the air, looking at Andrew with raise eyebrows.

"Three, please!"

"Is that all you going to eat, Andrew?" A cold voice makes them turn as one. The tall older woman, who stood with George when she was coming down the stairs, looked at them with an icy stare. Lindsay was beside her, held by a wrinkled claw like hand, with long red painted fingernails.

"Yes, grandma!" Andrew flat answer surprised Patricia.

"Of course, because nobody spent any time raising you. All three of you look like orphans. I knew that this woman wouldn't be able to take care of you!" She looked directly into Patricia's eyes. She hates me! Patricia was shocked, looking back mesmerized by those cold eyes. Lindsay looked up at the woman with a frown, shook woman's hand off and protectively stood in front of Patricia.

"My new mother is taking such good care of us, and we think there is no better mom in the world!" Lindsay raised her little chin to the woman in a challenge. Patricia wanted to say something and stop this hostility, but the icy voice cut her off.

"Mother? You children *have* a mother. She is dead, thanks to your father, and no other woman can ever be your mother. Is that clear?" Piercing eyes were jumping from child to child, demanding confirmation of her statement.

"Well, grandma, you'll change your opinion when you try her chocolate chips cookies. She tells stories better than on TV, and writes them, too. She is beautiful, smells great, and never yells or commands. So, as you see, we couldn't get a better mother!" Mark hit the core with his usual efficiency.

"Mark, you are too young to talk like that. Is this what she is teaching you, or is this coming from that servant Millie?" Her face became colder, if that was possible, "I was talking with your father about you coming to live with me when, we were rudely interrupted by the spectacle of an entrance which this woman, no doubt planned to do, to make an impact on these empty-heads!"

"We don't want to live with you, grandma!" Mark said politely, "It's very boring at your house. Nothing to do and you always have a migraine!"

"Nobody asked you for your opinion, young man, you'll do what I tell you to do!" She snapped.

"No, they do whatever their father tells them to do!" Patricia interrupted without thinking. She could not stand any more awful manners and insults from this woman. Who does she think she is?

"And, the manners go with the package!" The older woman spit it out with disgust, eyeing Patricia through squeezed eyelids, "Decent young woman never speak with someone who has not been properly introduced, remember that Lindsay!"

"Grandma, this is our mother - Patricia Hammond. Patricia, this is grandma Laura!" Andrew finally said, Patricia and Laura looked at each other for a long moment, and then Patricia's good upbringing overcame her frustration.

"Glad to meet you Laure…"

"Mrs. Branson, to you Missy. I have one advice for you. Go back from wherever my son-in-law dug you up, because you'll never take my daughter's place in this house, and especially not in George's heart. He loved my daughter more than anything in the world, and when he killed her I saw in his eyes that he died with her, too. Whatever he's doing now is out of guilt that he deprived my grandchildren of a mother. You are nothing but an unwanted surrogate, but sooner or later he'll realize what a mistake you are. You'll be out of here before…"

"That's enough, Mrs. Branson!" Patricia, probably for the first time in her life, lost her patience, thinking that she'll just strangle this awful creature, "How dare you to speak like that in front of the children about their father. Whatever motives George had in marrying me are none of your business. He is the father of these children, and now I'm their mother. If you can't accept that, I feel sorry for you. I'm sorry that they lost their mother, but life goes on. George is their father, and his decisions about the children are valid, not yours. So, I insist that you stop harassing them, or I'll go and speak with… my husband!" Patricia was more determined to protect these children whom she had learned to love so much. Laura opened her mouth, but then closed it firmly, looking above Patricia's head.

"Laura, I told you once tonight and hundreds of times before – I will never allow you to raise my children. I would not let you raise a snake, you might spoil it. And, don't you ever be rude to my wife. If you don't like what I have here, you are free to leave at any time now!" The eyes of the old woman were shooting poisonous arrows through both of them. With an expression of disgust, she turned on her heel and marched out of the house.

"Patricia, and you guys, forget all about what grandma said. She is a very unhappy woman, but we have a party to take care of and a full house of friends, so let's have some fun!" He picked up Mark, and started for the terrace. Lindsay placed her little hand in Patricia's pulling her in the same direction.

"He's right, the best thing is to forget everything that grandma said, Millie always saying that, and we usually do!" Lindsay whispered to Patricia.

The terrace was crowded with couples dancing, not minding the lack of the space, being pushed and kicked too often. Nevertheless it seemed that everybody was having a great time. The band leader suddenly stopped the music. Couples looked around to see what was happening.

"Ladies and gentlemen, make some space… make some space! The next song is only for our beloved newlyweds. They cheated us by having their wedding in some cold place back East, so now is the time for a little pay back. George and you Patricia step forward!" He waved to the men in the band. Soft and beautiful music filled the air. Patricia was scooped up in George's arms, and she found herself gliding over the floor. The first jilt of embarrassment passed and was forgotten when she felt his strong arms on her body. He held her close, so her forehead touched his cheek. In that moment he pulled her closer. Patricia knew that this is no good for her, but some pleasant numbness made her limbs weak and she leaned on him refusing to think. She'll just enjoy this moment. Being in his arms was beyond comparison with anything she ever experienced. Her encounters with men was never successful. Patricia never cared for male companionship very much. Romantic notions of a young girl concerning love and a wonderful relationship changed after several clumsy attempts of lovemaking. After that, she made the decision that she will wait for someone who will love her, or nothing. As she was getting older the realization that probably nobody will ever feel so deeply for her to make her resolution fulfilled. But now she…. Oh no, I cannot be in love. I have known for a long time that I will not inspire love, but it never crossed my mind that I would fall in love. Is it possible that l love him?

The music stopped. Their friends were applauding and cheering. George was still holding her close, and that felt wonderful. Some younger man swept her out of George's arms, and for a moment she felt devastation, but the music and all these pleasant people made her feel light and happy. She did not skip a single dance. The men were waiting for a chance to dance with her. They were nice, fun and unpretentious. Openly showing their admiration for her with respect and acceptance, exactly as Millie assured her would happen.

Her nerves calmed as she started to feel less of a stranger. She would catch a glimpse of George here and there. Every time his eyes were on her. He was watching me too closely and she wondered if he approved or if he was mad .Well, I'll find out sooner than I wish, but for now I'll enjoy myself.

The next song began, and she found herself in the arms of another partner. She looked up. It was Chuck. His handsome face was closer than she liked, his grip on her back was more intimate than decency prescribes. She tried to loosen his hold, but he grabbed her harder. Patricia was in a good mood, and she did not want to make a scene, so she smiled trying to talk him out of it.

"Chuck, please don't squeeze me so hard! I'll have bruises tomorrow!"

"That's exactly what you need honey. A good squeeze! That cold fish George can't satisfy a woman. He never could, and I know that for a fact!" His smile was so self-righteous, that she wanted to smack him across those curved lips. And, what does he mean by knowing it for a fact?"

"When I first laid eyes on you, I knew that you were something special. But, until tonight I didn't realized what a beauty you are. Seeing you coming down those damned stairs, made my blood boil. I'll handle you differently than my other girls. You deserve royal treatment!" His grip was stronger with every word, but Patricia didn't notice it any more. She was for the second time tonight enraged out of her mind. How dare he speak to her like that, and presume she will just go with whatever he wants. Is he crazy? She was trying to free herself, and did not care if others saw it. Fortunately, the music stopped, and she broke free of his hold looking into his eyes with disgust.

"Patricia, I think you promised me a dance! Shall we?" In surprise she looked at Andrew, who was standing next to her. She automatically turned to him placing her hands on his shoulders. He was tall for his age. His eyes were at the level of her chin. Patricia was still shaking with anger, but tried to take control of herself. She looked at the boy, who intensely studied her face.

"I don't remember promising you a dance. Probably because you never asked?" She smiled at him.

"Well I saw that macho jerk trying his dirty tricks on you, so I thought you will need some help!" He said simply.

"Thank you, Andrew. I was in need of some clever man to help me. Is Chuck usually like this?"

"Oh, yes! He always bragging in front of the "Boys" about his conquests. He said that the man is measured but the number of broken hearts left behind. Lindsay said that he is sick. After tonight I think I agree with her." Patricia listened to the boy with admiration. He will be a great man one day... just like his father. She glanced over his shoulder, her heart skip the beat – George was dancing with a gorgeous brunet in gold dress, hugging her beautiful body too tight. He was smiling, and then laughing with delight on the girls remark.

"Andrew, the girl dancing with your father... Who is she?" She breathed out impulsively. Andrew followed her stare, "Oh, damn! What she doing here? Who invited her?" Andrew stopped dancing frowning with detest, "Morgan! I wonder if Lindsay know about this?' He finally remembered petrified Patricia beside him, "Oh, she is just an insignificant toad, who wanted to marry my father for a long time. She lives in New York, and we... hoped she'll never come back!" Patricia felt sick in her stomach, watching this beautiful girl smiling in her husband's face, with ease and familiarity, so much so, that she forgot to scold Andrew for swearing and calling people names.

Music stopped, Morgan reluctantly let go of George. He scanned the room, located Patricia with Andrew , then pulled the girl in their direction.

"Darling, meet my old friend Morgan! We used to play as a kids!

Morgan, this is Patricia, my wife!" The young girl studied her for a long moment, then smiled, "Glad to meet you, Patricia. You are the second woman who stole the love of my life from me!" She meekly laughed, touching George's arm. "I wish you all the best... Take care of my... George, he deserves it. I noticed over their some of my old friends, so... I have to go and say hi!" She slowly departed to greet some young people standing beside the bar.

"Did you invite this... ! Did you, Dad?" Andrew's voice snapped Patricia's frozen mind to reality.

"Andrew, what did I tell you hundred times?" George's voice was sharp and unyielding.

Andrew pressed his lips tight and stormed toward his sister, who watched with a worried expression Morgan standing among her friends.

"George... what was all this about?" She at last found her voice.

"My children never managed to warm up to Morgan. I guess, she lacking your golden touch with them. She has no talent, neither affinity for kids. I did contemplate for a time of marrying her, but my children threatened they'll run away from home, if I do!" He laughed at that thought.

"You loved her. Of course... she is so beautiful!" Patricia asked with knot in her throat. He looked at her surprised.

"Yes, maybe as a childhood friend, but... If I did my kids would not be able to stop me to make her my wife. She fancies to being in love with me. Don't take it serious, she is an actress, and likes to exaggerate!"

"It was nice of you to... invite her to the party..."

"Me? Oh, God no! We can thank Laura for that. She hoped that Morgan would came between us, and... I don't know what is going on in Laura's head, neither do I want to know! Let's have another dance before some other smitten admirer takes you away!" He pulled her toward dancing floor, taking her in his arms.

Soon the guests started to leave, and finally the party was over. Tired, but very happy, Patricia reminisce on the success of the party. Put all together – it was much better that she anticipated, and definitely more pleasant. If it had not been for Laura and Chuck… and even Morgan, it would have turned perfect.

"Millie, shall we start with the cleaning now or wait until tomorrow?" Patricia approached the older woman putting her arm around her shoulders.

"You kidding me, Hun'?" Millie rolled her eyes

"We won't do a thing now or tomorrow!" George's deep voice came from behind. "Do you think that I'll let my two best girls do such a job after all you did to make this party a big success? I contracted a cleaning business, and they are sending their crew to clean up this mess in a couple of hours. You two will stay in bed until everything it is spick and span as usual!"

"I didn't do a thing! Millie would not let me. Now you will not let me help with cleaning. I'm afraid everybody here thinks I'm not capable of doing anything!" She smiled, "Millie I must tell you how great of a job you've done in organizing this party. Everything was perfect. The guests enjoyed themselves, especially the food. Thank you very much for all of it. In addition, thanks to you too, George. You were right about your friends. They are special and very nice people. I think I'll try to make them my friends, too… in time!"

"What are you talking about, girl?" Millie cried, "You won them all over tonight. There is not a thing any of them won't do for you. The compliments I got on your account, made me giddy. Just ask George! Half of those guys wanted information where the girls like you could be found. And, what do you think was his answer?" Millie was in her element, but George suddenly was not in the mood to listen any more.

"Millie, it's late! All of us are tired. Look at poor Peter!" His motionless body stretched out on sofa in the great room pool all eyes toward him and only his snoring in full strength announced that he is still alive. "Millie, I'll help you take him home, and don't you dare come tomorrow before everything is clean again. Patricia go to bed, you barely can stand on your feet!"

"Don't you give me any instruction here, young man!" Millie started to fuss, "Do you think I could sleep while a bunch of strangers are roaming through the house. I'll won't be able to find a thing for a month!" While she was telling George off, they tried to awake Peter. Patricia suddenly felt the effect of her nervousness, and all the dancing and pressure of this evening. Millie and George were arguing, while they, more dragged then helped Peter walk. Patricia slowly climbed the stairs. Her brain was absorbed with the events from the past hours, which began with her walk down these same stairs.

She was too tired to think clearly, but the feeling of George's arms, while they were dancing to the beautiful music was so vivid that she could still feel his hands through the thin fabric or her dress.

While taking a shower she heard George entering his bedroom. As the thousands of little droplets were drumming over her skin, her drowsy mind and the soothing action of the water tingled her nerves. It would be nice if he would, for once, come into my... Oh, Lord! If I don't put myself on guard I'm most likely to make a fool of myself. There is nothing more pathetic than a woman in love flunking herself on a disinterested man. Why did this have to happen to me? She finally had to admit it to herself. I am totally and deeply in love with my husband. But, he is not my husband, neither will he ever be. What am I going to do? I'm to woozy. Climbing in her bed, she knew that a serious decision has to be made.

CHAPTER 10

It looked as if life undertook its usual course. Not quite! Patricia's epiphany about her love for George, put their everyday encounters in a different perspective for her. She was dying out of fear that her feelings for him will betray her, and he will guess her secret. That would be humiliation she could not afford, so she tried to be in his company as little as possible, and never alone.

He would look at her, from time to time, in a very peculiar way, which made her shiver from a terrifying thought that he knew. Next, he would act as usual, and she would console herself that there is no way he could know. Sometimes she wished that he would grew to like her a little, and then her love would be enough for both of them. After daydreaming like this, she despised herself. Half of my life I was so sure I will never fall for someone who would not love me back, but now I am ready to settle for just crumbs.

There were so many unanswered questions, confusing her and complicating things even more. George's first wife was the biggest mystery. Although, Millie offered to clear out that part of George's life, unfortunately the two of them never came back to the subject. Patricia was uncomfortable to start first, or…. Maybe she did not want to hear about George's first big love.

The rest did not change very much. The only difference was that she did not ride with George any more. A week after the party, she exclaimed that the lessons are not necessary any more - she knew how to ride now. She made it sound like a joke, so George who looked like he would protest just pressed his lips together and turned away. Since then, she went riding with the children. The cowboys offered their services, but all three children in union declined – they too, did not need any babysitters. Chuck was the most persistent, distressing Patricia to the point of not going to stables alone any more.

A couple days after the party, she read to kids the last chapter she finished, listening with amusement to their comments.

"I love how they outsmarted evil Moomomba, and saved little lion!" Andrew was caught up in story, jumping around, swinging his arms in some sort of fight with an invisible villain.

"Moomomba is just like Morgan!" Mark stated it as a fact.

"True!" Lindsay cried, "I can't believe that she showed up! I helped Millie with the invitations, and there was not one for her, I'm sure!"

"Grandma invited her!" Another fact stated with complete assurance by the tiny serious voice.

"How do you know, Mark?" Andrew was suspicious.

"She told me!" Mark calmly replied. Three pair of eyes looked at him expectantly, "I asked her!" He informed them calmly.

"I wouldn't talk to her for… nothing!" Lindsay ruffled her nose in distaste.

"Okay guys! That's enough! I met Morgan at the party, and she seemed very nice. So, I won't have any of this any longer!" Patricia stopped this unusual behavior for them.

"You don't know her, Patricia!" Mark sounded even more serious than usual. "She wanted to marry Dad and send us to boarding school!"

"No!" Patricia was genuinely shocked.

"Oh, yes!" Lindsay exclaimed esuriently, "Andrew and I listened her trying to convince father, first to marry her, and second, how their lives will be perfect after we are locked up in a boarding school!"

"She didn't!" Patricia looked at them flabbergasted.

"Oh, I hate her…"Little girl cut herself short under Patricia's warning glare.

"Well, Dad put her in her place, ha, ha, ha…" Andrew threw himself on the sofa laughing.

"Yeah! He told her there is no woman in the world who would come between him and his kids. He was great!" Lindsay smiled happily.

"She left for New York! She calls from time to time, though, but Millie always say that Dad is on a business trip and we don't know when he will be back. Millie also said that this is not a lie, because dad is none of Morgan's business!" Laura probably invited her in hopes to steer some trouble, Patricia concluded unhappily.

"Patricia, I think it's time for a snack!" Mark decided that the conversation about Morgan was over.

The first cold winds were sweeping through the countryside announcing the changing of the seasons. Millie was talking about winter, and the beauty of the mountains under six feet of snow.

"Six feet!" Patricia cried, "You must be kidding me, Millie! How do you walk around…? How do the kids go to school?" Patricia was shocked.

"Ha, ha, ha… My dear girl, I was talking about higher elevations. Here we can get up to three feet, but nothing what regular plowing cannot fix. George attaches a snowplow to his big four wheeler when he drives the kids in the mornings to school. It is very rare that overnight fall of snow is more than that. George's snowplow would easily get stuck. In that case we have to wait for the big machine from Sheridan!" The entrance door slammed. George and the children were home from town. Patricia's heart jumped.

"Wow, girls, I'm sure this winter will be long and cold. I had to take over the driving from Andrew…. "Patricia and Millie yelled at the same time.

"From Andrew?" Millie just turned toward the stove rolling her eyes.

"…Because the wind was so strong…"

"You are telling me that you are letting a small boy drive that… that huge thing?" Patricia looked at him with wide opened mouth.

"It's not like I let him drive in the midst of L.A. traffic. It is our private road. Nobody ever drives on it, this time of day… Besides, I started to drive when I was ten!" He helplessly looked at Millie for help, "Millie tell her that kids here have to drive sooner than kids in the East. On the farm or ranch no job would ever be done if older folks drive kids around all day long!"

"Well, Patricia, that's right!" Millie had to confirm against her will.

"Patricia, don't worry! I'm a good driver!" Andrew tried to smooth over the situation. Patricia helplessly shifted her eyes from one person to the other. Unable to resist she pulled Andrew into her embrace to shield him from whatever is out there to harm him. Oh goodness, she thought, this is not just other state, it is more like another planet. Whoever heard of such a thing? Andrew pulled himself out of her arms, surprised how pleasant that was and that he was not sickened by it. But, George did not give her more time to brood over it.

"Our little vacation on Lake Tahoe is coming up next weekend. This time of year there is very pleasant. We'll start out on Friday morning, so be finished with your packing the night before!" While talking he did not look directly at her, not noticing the distress on her face. She wanted to speak, but whatever she would say it would lead to a discussion, and that was the last thing she wanted. How can she possibly explain that she does not want to be alone with him…? They will not be exactly alone, she comforted herself. There will be other people, and probably lots of activities. So, she just nodded and hoped she could be cool, and her secret would stay preserved.

The cold Friday morning matched the coldness around Patricia's heart. Her feelings were of some sweet anticipation, next, the panic would paralyze her of what might happen... However, she obediently packed her suitcases promising herself that she will try to be reasonable as much as possible.

They arrived in Lake Tahoe around noon. George called his partner, Martin for the exact address so the taxi driver could find their house. Martin offered to come and fetch them from the airport. While they were waiting, George was telling her who will be there and how he was connected with them.

"I neglected to acquaint you with my business and people I'm dealing with. All the wives you will meet know about their husbands dealings as much as they know, so from now on I'll plan to do the same... That is, if you don't mind?" Patricia was surprised with the offer. She never heard Mr. Bathes or Tim discuss business with Mrs. Bathes or Francesca.. For the next half an hour George tried to explain the nature and extent of his connection with Martin and the rest of the party.

Martin was a short plump man, with an infectious smile and twinkling small eyes, which would completely disappear when he laughed. He shook her hand with both of his, scolding George for hiding his beautiful wife for so long.

During the drive he endlessly talked about the beauty of the lake, the countryside, and his sailing boat, which they were going to enjoy as much as possible.

"I just hope, my dear, that you don't suffer from motion sickness! My wife needed a couple of years to get used to it. I was sure she'll divorce me if I didn't sink that thing, but now she likes it... I believe, ha, ha, ha...!" Patricia liked his easy way of talking about himself with humor. She hoped that the rest of the party would not be much different.

"Come on, join us!" Peggy, Martin's wife invited when they arrived, "It's just a light luncheon, it won't spoil dinner. Believe me, it's necessary when you go sailing! I must warn you, with my husband, the-Great-Pirate-of-Tahoe, you never know when we will be back! Come dear, let me introduce the rest of the victims!" Peggy was as friendly as her husband, which put Patricia at ease, "This is my old friend Silvia and her husband James from Portland. Here are our friends from Texas, Catherine and Garry!" The two couples shook her hand and expressed a warm welcome. The conversation was jumping from business to private matters about kids, houses, hobbies and things Patricia would never believe these people would be interested in.

Everybody was ready for sailing. Martin was studying the sky from the big window for a while. Turning toward his guests with the frown asked:

"Patricia, you did not answer me: do you get seasick on boats?"

"Well, I don't know!" She said shyly, "I never sailed before, but… I get a little nauseated on the bumpy rides and in airplanes, so … I believe I'll have a little problem on…"

"Oh, my dear, that is the worst thing!" Peggy made a suffering face, "It took me forever to get used to that floating tub. Martin was close to being murdered by me more times than he thinks!"

"George, I would suggest that you stay behind with you wife. I don't like the look of those clouds out to the west. Everybody approached the window to look at the sky.

"You are right, Martin!" James said with a frown, "They are too thick and dark, This can turn into a storm!"

"Storm?" Catherine cried, "Maybe it would be wise that all of us stay in today?

"Nonsense, my love!" Answered her husband, "A little wind will make it more fun!"

"I agree!" exclaimed Silvia, "We came here to sail, didn't we? So, let's do it, although, I agree that Patricia shouldn't go. The first time has to be a pleasurable one. It's hard to like something after a bad experience!"

"We'll stay behind!" George decided, "We have to unpack, and afterward I'll show Patricia the town, We need to buy some gifts for the kids, anyway! You guys go and have fun!"

"Come Patricia, I'll show you your room!" Peggy put her hand under Patricia's arm, leading her to the stairs, "Martin bring their suitcases, please! I gave you a room on the west side. It has the most beautiful view of the lake. I hope tomorrow's weather will be more pleasant, so we can spend time together and get to know you better!" Peggy was studying her face, "We imagined you different. Don't take me wrong, we knew you'd be beautiful, but… Oh, I'm so glad he didn't marry one of those cold bitches, who use to chase him!"

Martin and George were following them with the suitcases discussing some business matters.

When Peggy opened the door of the big beautifully decorated room, Patricia's eyes fell on the oversized bed. For the first time it struck her that everybody would find it natural to put them in the same bedroom. She looked at George, not to be able to resist, but his expression stayed the same. He was lifting suitcases onto the bed listening to Martin's opinion on taking over the water-pump manufacturing factory in Kansas. Peggy was saying something about the bathroom and how to turn the hot tub on if they want to use it.

"Peggy, let's go, honey!" Martin yelled, "If we don't start now, we'll be sailing under moon light"

"You mean, under the clouds in pitch dark!" Peggy laughed taking her husband's hand, "Have a nice time in town guys!" She slammed the door behind them teasing Martin all the way down. Patricia was still standing in the same spot.

"Let's first put our things in the closet. I think I'll be able to find that great Mexican restaurant where Martin took us last time. The food was really good!" He was in the closet hanging up his pants and shirts. Patricia moved on her stiff legs toward the bed. Her fingers were trembling, and she could not open the clasp on her suitcase. Suddenly a hand came from behind, the clasp clicked and suitcase snapped open. His body was lightly leaning on her back while he was investigating the contents.

"Moraine is really good at her job. These clothes are a very good choice. I like this color!" He pulled out a lime green silky sweater, "Would you wear it tonight, please?" He sounded like it was an everyday occurrence between them talking casually in the bedroom about what she will wear.

"Of course!" She muttered. George took another piece of clothing from her suitcase, and started to hang it in the closet.

"What do you think about my partners and their wives?" George did not wait for an answer, "Martin and Peggy are fun, aren't they? Catherine is a little stuffy, but James is a real Texan – loud voice, big heart and very straight forward. He is pleasant to do business with. Silvia and Garry have six kids! Did you know that? The youngest is in high school now, so they are, more or less, done with parenting. She had a wild strike in her, while Garry is very composed and down to earth. I'll see which car we'll use while you change!" He was out of the bedroom before she could say a word. I would never guess that George is the type to know all those small details about anybody, but then as a businessman he has to know the people with whom he make deals. "This man is an endless source of surprises for me. Made me wonder what is next?"

She looked at her image in the mirror. The lime green sweater went well with her white slacks. A white scarf and a hair band kept he long hair back. She looked fresh and much younger. I'm changing somehow, she was puzzled. My family will not recognize me. Is it love, or motherhood? People always point out how motherhood changes a woman. I am a mother to those kids. I love them like they are my own flesh and blood. Patricia did not have an answer, neither the time to brood over this dilemma, so she hurriedly ran out of the bedroom to join George.

Patricia found him on the terrace. The sky was covered with clouds, and the wind was strong.

"I don't like this!" He said when she stepped on the terrace, "It looks as a storm is coming after all. Peggy was right, and I'm worried about those sailing enthusiasts!" Patricia stared at the sky for a while.

"It's awfully dark in the west. The wind is blowing from that direction as well. You are right, but Martin seemed like an experienced sailor and knows this lake very well. They are probably on their way back by now!" She did not sound as sure as she tried to be.

"I think we should postpone our outing, Patricia. A big storm is no fun on the land ether. We should be here in case our friends need some help. They can reach us here easier than on the cell phone.

"Of course, but I'm so hungry…? She felt that riding through the storm would be less devastating then an evening with George alone.

"Don't worry about that, my dear!" George smiled mockingly. 'This is my chance to show you that you actually married a chef disguised as a cold businessman." He put his hand lightly on the small of her back, leading her to the kitchen "Let's see what Peggy has in her refrigerator. If I remember correctly when they come here, she usually buys out half the grocery store. So, I'm positive we won't go hungry." In the kitchen George opened the overstuffed refrigerator examining its contents.

"Well what do you say about grilled chicken and a salad with some wine?" He was pulling out what he needed, "You sit over there and entertain the chef!" George sent her a smile, searching for a cutting board and knife.

"I'll help with something!" It was better to do anything then sit here watching him.

"Oh no, you won't!" He was determined, "Tonight…" Loud thunder following lightning, made them turn toward the windows, "Now, I'm seriously worried. I'll call the marina! Someone over there might know what's happening." Patricia was standing at the open door to the terrace watching the pouring rain. There was utter darkness outside, and the curtain of rain made it even more weighty and reticent. She heard George talking on the phone but couldn't catch what the person on the other end of the line was saying.

"Well Patricia, they are in trouble, as far as anybody knows!" George put the telephone receiver down, "Several boats are still out, and there's no way to be located. We just have to hope they'll find their own way to safety!" He approached a terrified Patricia, and pulled her into his arms. "Don't worry dear, the officials are sure that the worst thing that could happen is that our friends will have very rough night!" She wanted to believe him, but with every passing moment she became more frightened.

"Someone will call the minute they have any news, so we have to be patient and calm!" He looked into her eyes full of fear, "Let's finish our dinner!"

"I'm not hungry, George!" Patricia whispered.

"But, you will be when we hear the word from our friends, so we'll prepare it!" He led her back into the kitchen talking constantly about small unimportant things, funny things, and she could not help but laugh. Then the telephone rang. George rushed to answer. First he smiled, then turned to Patricia, "It's Martin, they are safe!" She felt such a relief, that she ran to George and hugged his arm with both of hers. Lots of "a-has", "Yeses", "I understands" was all she heard.

"Everything is okay!" He said after putting the receiver on the base, "But, they can't come back tonight. The roads are not safe. Falling rocks and flash floods could be dangerous. So, Peggy sends her apology.

They'll stay in the hotel and be back tomorrow... maybe!"

"What do you mean – maybe?"

"The forecast is not very promising. It looks like the storm will last at least 42 hours, if not longer. So, Martin is sorry that they won't have a chance to spend more time in our company. He insists that we take advantage of being away from the kids and everyday obligations, and enjoy ourselves," Patricia just sighed, she'll, after all, have to spend time alone with George this weekend, and she can't do a thing about it. George was finishing the dinner, suddenly quiet and in deep thought. Exiting the kitchen, Patricia commanded herself to calm down, and accept the situation. I will just let go of my worries and enjoy the time I'll have with my husband. This is probably the one and only opportunity to be alone with him. We are practically cut off from the world, in this house so far from other dwellings, and in the middle of the violent storm.

As this circumstance cannot be changed, I will make it as pleasurable as possible. She entered the dining room looking for some flatware. For several minutes she was occupied with arranging the table. While she was lighting the candles, George's voice announced that dinner was ready.

"Bring it into the dining room, please!" She cheerfully called back. George stuck his head through the door.

"That's one great idea, Patricia! We can pretend we're eating in some expensive restaurant!" He placed the food on the table, "Pull out the glasses, I'll open a wine bottle!"

During the dinner, George was entertaining Patricia with stories about Peggy and Martin. He'd known them for a long time. Martin, as a young man started his business with George's father, and he couldn't remember when he first met him.

"But I remember how I met Peggy! My father had one of his usual 4th of July picnics. Funny thing is that it was everything else but a picnic. He would invite his close friends and business partners to spend the whole holiday on the ranch. I can't remember him enjoying anything so much, but my mother was not so enthusiastic. She used to call it "The Invasion on Independence Day." My father would not give it up for anything in the world. The guests who would stay in the house were invited to go on all day riding trips up the mountains. That was torture for them, but ultimate pleasure for the old bull. My father's 4'th of July parties were famous, people from far and wide would come. Veal, lamb and pork were roasted out on the open fire. Kegs of beer, wine and champagne kept everybody in a good mood. But, the fireworks was a *piece of resistance*. I was thirteen when Martin brought Peggy to one of father's gathering. She was tiny, very slim and beautiful. I developed a huge crush on her, but I supposed nobody could blame me. She was so pleasant, and spend a great deal of time with me while Martin and my father were discussing business. During the party she danced with me. Being so small, she was the only one my size. I never danced before, but she made it so easy. My mother was surprised when I asked for dancing lessons, which had been her desire for a long time, to my horror… Well I did not see Peggy for two years. In the mean time I stretched into an oversized teenager, and she was pregnant with her first child. Everything was different. You can imagine how I hated Martin!" George was speaking slowly like a man remembering the most precious part of his life. "She was, again, so gracious, and handled me like a pro. The rest of the guests were riding with my father, the two of us took long walks. We talked about women and men, marriage, and a lot about love. I believe that was the day I stopped being a child and became a young man. Since then we have been special friends." He poured more wine, "Let's find some music!" George searched through the stack of CD's.

Slow dance music filled the room. Patricia was a little woozy from the wine, but more from the prospect of being in George's arms.

He did not give her time to think about it for very long. They were slowly circling the room.

Patricia was giggling that his mother got her money's worth with his dancing lessons. Playfully he was showing off, and she had to take a good grip on him in order not to fall. The longer they danced the conversation became more scarce, just as the space between them. It was so natural to be here, close to him as it was her place to be. He was holding her too close, she thought, but instead of backing away she nestled even closer. It seemed as they were of one body and one mind, moving so harmoniously to the rhythm of the music, His chin was resting on the side of her head. She felt his breath on her hair deepen and became more rapid. Sometime during the dance, he placed her right hand over his chest. His heartbeat under her palm strong. Beating of his heart was the same as hers. Exquisite lightheadiness released her from inhibition she harbored for so long, along with a fear that he will figure out how much she loves him.

Through fogginess of wine, George's closeness and romantic music, she realized that being in his arms was no longer a dancer's embrace, but the embrace of a lover. Her first impulse was to pull back. His hold tightened. It seemed that all of her rationale floated somewhere far behind her reach. Instinct won - to nestle closer was natural as breathing. She felt a light kiss on her hair, but she must be imagining it... No, another one, a little closer to her forehead, was too real to be imagination. Million tiny butterflies rushed down her spine. She trembled. Out of their own will her arms tightened around his neck. One of her hands lost itself in his tick dark hair. George reacted by pulling her so close to him that she had a hard time breathing. Embracing her small body he melted it into his own. He moved his head away from her, looked it her dim eyes searchingly, then lowered his lips to hers. The first touch of his lips was light, like he was testing her response. She was motionless. Encouraged, he kissed her again, this time harder. Her lips parted, which produced an electric shock throughout him.

They stood there in the middle of the dining room in a passionate embrace, with locked lips and clenched arms. Suddenly he pushed her away from him, but still holding her arms. His probing eyes were studying her flashed face. She was helplessly overtaken by emotions suppressed for so long. It seemed he stood there for an eternity, then he bent down, put his arm under her knees and scooped her up into his arms. Patricia instinctively circled his neck, hiding her face in the hollow on the side of his chin.

She did not doubt for a moment that he was heading for their bedroom, but contrary to her fears of that possibility, she felt only pleasant anticipation. George put her down beside the bed pulling her sweater off. She looked into his dark eyes. They were much darker with some strange vulnerability flooding her heart with love. She passionately kissed him, circling her arms around his body. The storm outside was in full strength. The violent wind along with lightning and thunder matched the storm of passion which overtook two people in a protective cocoon of the house.

Patricia woke up just before dawn. At first she wondered what had happened, then she realized that her head was laying on George's shoulder. Everything came back like a tide. She blushed remembering last night. George's love making was the most ascending and beautiful experience of her life. Only if he would love me, she thought, everything would be perfect. *But nothing is ever perfect, so I will take from life what I can get. My marriage, kids, ranch and all the people in my life, are much more than I ever hoped to have.*

George moved. She shut her eyes tight pretending to be asleep. Unwilling to face him just yet, she motionlessly waited. He was awake now, and she sensed that he was looking at her. Patricia desperately wanted to open her eyes and tell him how much she loves him. What stopped her was the knowledge that he did not want her love. He is a young and healthy man in the prime of his life. It is better for all concerned that he get at home what every man needs, instead of fooling around with women like Alicia. George gently pulled his arm from under her head. She heard him enter the bathroom, then the sound of water. What I am going to say to him? How am I going to act?

Almost soundlessly, he exited the bedroom, so she finally exhaled and moved her tense muscles. The wind was still strong, swishing the rain droplets against the windows. The darkness of the sky did not promise for the storm to ease soon. The sounds of wind and rain reminded her of last night. The flame and hunger for each other was like embodiment of the most romantic and passionate love stories she read as a young girl. The storm will never be just a rage of nature for her any more, but will represent the awakening of a fire hidden deep within her.

She showered and dressed. If I do not show my face downstairs, he will probably come up, and that would be more embarrassing.

Descending the stairs, she heard him talking with someone on the phone. Before she stepped in the kitchen, the smell of coffee and fried eggs told her what he had been up to till now.

"Good morning, Patricia!" He placed the receiver back on the base of the telephone, "I hope you get to sleep a little. The storm is still loud. I just spoke with Martin. He believes that the roads will be cleared up in a matter of hours, so they will be able to return sometime this morning. What do you say we make lunch for them?" He smiled at her, acting as everything is as usual. So, let it be, she thought, excepting his attitude.

"I see you made breakfast! I'm starving!" Patricia placed plates on the kitchen table, "What do you suggest we cook?" She asked calmly. For a moment he looked at her as he would say something that has nothing to do with cooking, then he turned and reached for the orange juice. The morning was passing in preparing a lunch. They talked about ordinary things. She wanted to know more about his friends, their children, how he met them and so on. The anecdotes about Silvia's and James' differences made her laugh until her stomach ached. He repeated Garry's accounts how Catherine would handle the kids making them believe that what she wanted them to do was actually their own idea.

Lunch was almost done! Their friends were still somewhere out in the storm. Patricia was standing beside the window, trying to see through the rain for approaching cars. The silence descended. She sensed more than felt that George was standing very close behind her.

"Patricia?" He started. The long pause told her that what he wants to ask has nothing to do with lunch or their friends. Is he going to talk about last night? About hers obvious lack of experience? Oh Lord, please anything but that!"

"Patricia!" George started again, "Why didn't you tell me that... you never before ..." She raised her hand to stop him. In this moment all what she wanted was to end this uneasy conversation with the shortest possible explanation, when her eye caught a streak of light through the rain.

"George, I think they are here!" She cried, running to the entrance door. They rushed out onto the front porch at the same time as Martin's big Cadillac stopped. Screams, laughter, hugs and talking in one voice went on for some time.

"Patricia, my dear!" Peggy pushed her arm under Patricia's leading he through the door into the house, "I feel so miserable that you had to spend your first time on this beautiful lake indoors. But, believe me, in the seventeen years we have had this house, I never saw anything like this!" Patricia squeezed her hand, "Don't worry about us. We were secure in this fortress, but for you it must have been terrible, out in the boat on a violent lake!"

"Well, I have to admit, for a while I thought that's it. My final hour in this world, but Martin is very good at handling that blasted boat of his, so we got into the marina before anything bad happened! But the roads were a different story. Police would not let us drive home, and for good reason! The trees were plucked out of the ground, mudslides blacked a number of spots on the roads and I don't know what else yet. We'll see it all on the news later on "

The four people were endlessly talking about their adventure, remembering the smallest details, especially about their night in the hotel. The other water lovers were ambushed by the storm, so the hotel was overcrowded. Most of them could not get the room, including two couples, so they spend the night dancing, singing and having a marvelous time.

The afternoon was passing fast. Rain was still falling, but the wind slackened showing that the storm was losing its power. By seven o'clock, it was already dark outside, and everybody showed traces of a sleepless night and the strain of battling the storm. James was the first to bluntly express the desire for nothing but his bed. Everybody laughed and started for their bedrooms. George put his hand lightly on Patricia's back following the others upstairs.

"See you all in the morning, if I'll be able to wake up, or get up, or do anything remotely physical, that is!" Peggy smiled, but it was obvious how tired she was. "I'm bushed, too." George said after he closed the door of their bedroom behind them, "Yesterday was a harsh day. All that worrying and anticipation... and, we didn't have much sleep last night, either!" He glanced at her continuing quickly, "storms can keep a deaf man awake. Why don't you use the bathroom first? I'll go and check through the house and see that everything is secure."

Patricia was in turmoil. Is he going to insist on the conversation he started just before their friends arrived, or... I do not want to think about a thing. George is unpredictable in his actions, I am afraid that he will do something I cannot guess, as usual. With resignations, Patricia took a deep breath knowing she will have to handle whatever comes.

She heard a knock on the bathroom door. He is back, she panicked a little. "Come in, George, I'm finished!" She called. They passed each other. Their bodied brushed in the narrow doorway. The electric shock charged through her body. George stopped for a moment, touching the skin of her bare arm, then he mattered huskily, "It'll take just a minute!", closing the door behind him.

When he reentered the room, Patricia was standing beside the balcony door looking at the weakening storm. She did not hear him approaching, but the warmth of his body behind her penetrated through the thin fabric of the nightgown. Then she felt his hands on her waist, moving slowly to meet each other on the stomach. He lightly pulled her to him. The sensation of his strong hard body down the whole length of hers weakened every muscle from her heels to the very top of her confused head. She just leaned against him, and his grip tightened. They stood like that for awhile. Millions of goose bumps were roaming all over her skin.

"I really need to know… How it happened that at your age, you never…"Oh God, I just cannot talk about this now, she thought panicking again. Patricia swiftly turned toward him placing her hands around his neck.

"Just kiss me!" she whispered, and standing on the toes she feverishly pressed her lips on his, hushing him. George instantly tightened his grip, melting her against him.

Several times that night he reached for her, between woozy naps. All the time she was too aware of his body so close to hers, which make her feel protected, secure, and never happier in her life.

The next morning, their last day on Lake Tahoe, the whole beauty of the lake and countryside exploded under the strength of the desert sun and the clear blue sky. Patricia opened her eyes only to be blinded by brilliant light spilling generously through the windows.

"We'll have one nice day after all!" George's voice woke her up completely. He was already dressed. The cup of coffee in his hand indicated that he had been up for a while. "I'll made breakfast just for us. The rest of the house is in total silence. They must be more exhausted then they looked. So, let's have some food here, and then I'd like to show you Peggy's garden, or what is left of it after the storm!" She was aware of her nakedness under the sheets. It was foolish to be shy, after their intimacy, but she just looked at him with wide opened eyes, not willing to move. They looked at each other wondering what the other was thinking, then George turned back to look out the window. Patricia jumped and run into the bathroom After the door slammed behind her, he looked at it for a long time with a strange expression of puzzlement on his face.

CHAPTER 11

The whole countryside was dressed in white. December came unnoticed until the snow unmistakably confirmed arrival of winter. After their return from the Lake Tahoe, every day routine on the Hammond estate did not change very much. The book was almost finished, and Patricia worked on it all the time. She would still spend time with the children every spare moment they had, besides school and homework.

The swimming shifted from the outside pool to the inside one. Now Patricia did not need to pretend so much about her fear of water, and they had a fun time rollicking in and around the pool. The same with riding. She learned much about the horses, and started to enjoy it more than she ever hoped for.

The only real difference was in her relationship with George. On their way back from Martin's house she wondered if he was going to pursue their intimacy or take it as just a holiday fling, acting at home as before. What would she rather have happen? She was not sure. Her love overwhelmed her and she was not able to deny him anything. To be completely honest with herself, she had to admit that she wanted him with her whole heart and newly discovered passion. Nevertheless, she dreaded his inquiries about her previous sexual experience, or rather lack of any. If he would only love her, he would be able to better understand her desire to be intimate with someone she loves, which had never transpired before. How can she explain her motivations and not admit her love for him?

Fortunately, he never returned to that subject. Maybe he sensed her unwillingness to talk about it or he simply lost interest. One thing did changed, though, George quit sleeping in the dressing room. That first night after their return, George worked longer in the library, to catch up on business that had accumulated over their vacation. Patricia dozed off, refusing to torture herself guessing what her husband would do next.

Patricia did not know how long she had been asleep when the movement of the bed woke her. Next, she felt George's arms around her and being pulled close to him. She, still half asleep, nestled lovingly closer to him. To spend a night like this is as being in paradise. But, George obviously had different ideas on his mind. First, light kisses on the lobe of her ear, then more demanding over her face were shutting hundreds of small tremors up and down her body, which awakened her completely.

The same repeated itself every night. Otherwise, in their everyday life he did not act differently than before. Their nightly lovemaking seemed not to have anything to do with the rest of the world.

It appeared as life neatly fell into a steady routine. Patricia was content, convincing herself that it could not be better. Although, a small voice was crying from the depths of her heart that her life was incomplete without real love. But, her rational side refused to listen out of fear that if she starts thinking this way, it would hurt too much, and she would not be able to go on pretending. Her love for George grew stronger with the passing of every day. Just to think about the possibility of living without him was unbearable. So, she hushed her heart, thinking that her present life is much less painful then life away from all of this – which she had learned to love and cherish.

Life could be better, though, without two people, who made some of her days a living hell. Number one troublemaker was Laura. After they met at her party, the old woman made a habit and enjoyment to torment Patricia much as possible. She would call her on the telephone giving her orders, and criticize every little thing she was doing. Subsequently, Millie noticed Patricia's great distress following some phone calls. She made it her goal to find out who the caller was. It did not take her long to realize that Laura was harassing her newest protégée. She did not say a word to Patricia, but George got a full report.

The next day he visited his ex-mother-in-law. What he told her, Millie could not pull out of him, but Laura never called again. Millie was sure, though, that nothing would stop Laura from pursuing George's new wife, so she tried to subtly trick Patricia into telling her if it happens that "by accident" she meet Laura anywhere else. That puzzled Patricia a great deal. How Millie knew that every time she went to Sheridan, Laura happened to be there. On her riding escapades with the kids, Laura would ride, too. Although, the kids tried to convince her that grandma have not ridden for years. Patricia decided not to let the old woman provoke her, so she always calmly endured every possible insult and command, and tried to put all of it out of her mind the second Laura would depart.

The other one was Chuck. He stalked her every chance he got. She still thought of him as charming in some irresponsible way, but she wished from the bottom of her heat that he would stop. Because of him, she stopped going down to the stable alone, but he just as Laure, found a way to meet her everywhere. Even Millie noticed that he was coming up to the house more than was necessary.

"Patricia, do you know why Chuck would be coming here so often?" She asked bluntly one day. Patricia's answer surprised her.

"Yeah, to see me!"

"Is anything going on that… shouldn't be?" Millie could not resist

"Well, if it would be as Chuck wants, everything would go where should not! "Patricia started to laugh, "Is he like this with every woman?"

"I think so! He is like a little boy who has to have everything or he'll scream and throw a tantrum. I would suggest that you stay as far away from him as possible. Maybe he'll just give up eventually. Although, I've never heard that he did. As handsome devil as he is, there is not many women who can resist him. What do you think?" Millie played it cool.

"About what? Oh, Chuck! I think he is charming, but I have met many charming men in my life. If you really want to know, I wish he would find another subject to practice his charms on, and leave me in peace!" She laughed at the expression and relief on Millie's face.

That evening George did not go into the library or the dressing room to work. He went upstairs with Patricia, chatting about the delicious dinner on their way up. She did not know what was the matter but she decided to wait for him to say what was on his mind. He was pacing the room in deep thought, so she entered the bathroom.

The water was running down her skin making her aware of her body. She wished that George was here with her, next the sliding door on the shower slid open, and she found herself in his arms. We even think the same, she was amazed. Is this what my mother use to say about herself and her father, that after a while married people do not need to talk very much, one knows what the other thinks.

Love making in the shower was new for Patricia, but with George, everything was exciting and new for her. Although, in these past several months she got to know his body very well, and it seemed that he knew about hers what even she did not know.

Afterwards, while cuddled beside him in the bed, she knew that he have a hard time to tell her something, so she decided to help him.

"What is it George? Is everything okay?"

"Francisca called yesterday..." Patricia jumped in anticipation. "Is something wrong?" George scooped her closer, answering fast as possible.

"Oh, nothing is wrong! Everybody's just fine. Do you remember at our wedding how Tim and I planned for our families to spend Christmas together? Well Francesca called to ask when we were coming, so she can prepare everything for us!"

"And what is the problem? You don't want to go?" Patricia still sensed that something was troubling him.

"I don't know how you feel about it… You know, the situation with Tim. I never told you but he calls often and always asks about you. I'm afraid that he didn't get you out of his mind… Not completely!" George sounded worried.

"So, you think we should stay at home? He might reconsider when he sees us with our children! Our marriage *looks* very happy!" His body tensed, so she hurried to explain, "Everybody thinks so… except your ex mother-in-law, that is. People tell me all the time how great marriage we have. Well, if Tim comes to the same conclusion, he may stop thinking about me differently, but as a sister-in-law!"

"You might be right!" George finally agreed, "We must go Christmas shopping in L.A., one of these days. Next week most likely." She cuddled closer to him, then drowsily slipped off thinking about Christmas in Church Hill, her family, Timmy and Puppet, her friends…

Trip to L.A. will be a treat, too! Prospect of seeing Moraine again so soon after their visit to the ranch over the Thanksgiving holiday was exciting. Remembering the fun time they spent together talking, exploring the property, Moraine's endless flirtations with cowboys, and Slim's obsession with purebred horses. The dresses Patricia ordered for Lindsay enchanted the little girl so much so that Patricia believed that a tomboy, she found at her arrival, is gone forever, and newborn fashion diva was born.

Frantic preparations for their departure for Church Hill turned the house upside down.

"Why do we have to go there, tell me one more time?" Mark questioned

"Because, they are our family, Mark!" Patricia explained.

"Family? How come I never heard about them?"

"Because they were not your family before!"

"Somebody is family all the time, not just from time to time!"

"You are philosopher, my dear, and I agree with you, but somebody can acquire a family which he did not have before!"

"Family is not like a club you join in!" Mark was persistent.

"And what about me?" Patricia was amused.

"What about you?" Mark became cautious. From experience he knew that Patricia can be tricky.

"What am I? Am I family or a club?" Oh, she got me.

"Family, of course!" Wow, she joined our family when she married dad.

"Of course!" She repeated, "But you never heard about me before your dad married me, did you?"

"I heard about you before he married you!" Mark was taking control over the situation. Patricia looked at the smirk on his face. He is way too good at arguing for such a little boy.

"You did?"

"Yes, father informed us before he went to fetch you, that he found the perfect wife and mother, so I heard about you before!" He concluded. Patricia watched Mark carefully- did George really use those words - perfect wife and mother?

"Isn't this the same? You heard about your new family from me, and now you going to meet them, just as you met me!" Patricia imitated his way of speaking. She set beside him, and put her arm around his small shoulders, "Mark, they are my family. First, there is my sister, just as Lindsay is yours, then her Husband Tim. They have two children – Timmy and Puppet, then the grandma and grandpa Bathes. I left them when I married your father. One day Lindsay will marry, and she'll go to live with her husband and his family. Andrew and you will marry and bring more people to be part of our family. This is how this thing works. So, we wait until we get there and see if you like them or not. Okay?" He looked at her, for the first time as a little boy, and just nodded.

She couldn't resist, so she bent down and lightly kissed his forehead. Mark blinked, looked at her for a moment, leaned and kissed her cheek.

"We'll see! I will never marry, don't count on that!" Was his comment, before he calmly exited the kitchen. Tears in her eyes blinded her. Mark had started to melt and she knew that she finally has reached him.

Church Hill was the same. Patricia's heart raced when Tim's limo drove through the familiar streets.

"It is much bigger than Sheridan!" Lindsay's little nose was pressed to the window of the car.

"Not as big as Denver or L.A.!" Andrew contradicted his sister as usual.

Patricia's whole family was waiting on the stairs of the Bathe's mansion. She almost cried looking at Timmy and Puppet. How big they were, and I missed it. A clash of people created a mass of bodies, voices, luggage… Patricia tried to introduce her two families, but the confusion was too big, so she gave up. They will get to know each other on their own, she thought philosophically. Patricia's plan was to stay in her own house, but Tim did not want to hear of it. He protested that her house had been empty too long, and it wouldn't be comfortable for five people, besides he invited them to spend Christmas with his family, period.

Francisca seemed to be the same – beautiful, perfectly dressed and not very happy looking.

"Patricia come, let's put the luggage in your rooms!" She waved to the servants to follow them with the suitcases, "The kids seemed to be very nice, how are you handling them… I mean, do you have any problems?"

"Not really! They are like any kids their age. Loud, impossible, sometimes rude, but very sweet and I love them all so very much. George is a good father, and the rest of the people on the ranch are very helpful, too." The sisters entered Patricia's old bedroom.

"I think, you and George will be comfortable here. The kids are in the other wing with mine. I looked forward to see you again! You didn't call very often… I know, there's never enough time. I never realized how much I depended on you. It took me months to take over where you left off. Timmy and Puppet were lost for a long time. They depended on you, too. Tim, mom and dad were nagging all the time how you should have never married and gone away… Well for a bit, I thought that, too. It was so selfish from my side, but … Then, Tim changed a lot!" Francesca sounded like weary old woman. Patricia would glance in her sister's direction, while putting clothes in the closet. She had instantly noticed Francesca's tired look, that she is not satisfied… even worse – Francisca is unhappy.

"Changed? In what way?"

"Oh, I don't know! It's not something you can put your finger on… He is more serious, almost never laughs any more, talks very little… He plays with the kids, mainly reading your books, or they are teaching him the games they played with you. My father-in-law misses your cooking, mother cries that nobody can do anything right with her charity projects, and everybody in town has something they cannot do without you. So, as you see, turned out that you were the most important person around!" Francesca meekly laughed at her attempt to make a joke.

"Well, I may assure you that I miss all of you tremendously. I know I should call more, but everything was so new for me. I was determined to get acquainted with the house, the grounds and people on the ranch as soon as possible. In the beginning, I spent most of my time with the kids. They are special little souls, and I have grown to love them very much!"

"What about them? Do they love you, or at least like you…. How silly of me, or course they love you. You have that ability to make people love you regardless who they are.

"I flatter myself that they do!" Patricia smiled happily, "I believe more and more every day. They are a big inspiration for my writing, you know! A big chunk of my day, when the kids are in school, is dedicated to my book. I travel with George, from time to time, and … you'll never believe this – I ride almost every day!"

"Ride? A horse? You?" Francesca was stunned, starring at her sister not believing a word.

"Yes, me!" Patricia laughed aloud looking at Francesca's frozen face. "And, it's fun, too!"

"But, horses… they are so big and…. dangerous. I'm so happy Tim gave up riding, and I'll never let my kids take lessons, although they are begging for it all the time!" Francesca finally stopped pacing up and down the room. She smiled at Patricia, clapped her hands like a little girl, "Now, I want you to describe everything to me!" She set on the bed crossing her legs under her.

"What do you want to know?" Patricia teased, knowing her sister was dying to hear about the house, the ranch and how her life turned out in that far place.

"Oh Patricia, you can be such a pain…" Francesca was annoyed.

"But, you'll see everything during spring break. Believe me it's not so easy to describe. The countryside is more beautiful than you can imagine. The mountains, meadows with horses and cows... Then, there's the house. A real English manor! You'll love the gardens and conservatory!"

"Conservatory? Like those in old movies?" Francesca was impressed.

"Yes! But, the best thing is that it's connected to an indoor swimming pool. I think you should wait and see for yourself. Millie and Peter help with the housekeeping. She is the best cook, and a real general in ruling the household. I know you'll be disappointed that she is nothing like your housekeeper – proper and stiff. Her husband, Peter, is a peach... Then, we have a bunch of cowboys!"

"Real cowboys? Gorgeous like Jimmy Stewart and John Wayne?"

"No! They are handsome more like Paul Newman and Robert Redford!" Patricia watched the amazement mixed with amusement on Francesca's beautiful face.

"They are that gorgeous?"

"And very nice... at least the most of them!" Patricia added thinking of Chuck.

"Oh, I know! You have made some conquests! Oh, Patricia, that is so romantic!" The young high school girl awakened within Francesca.

"My dear, that is not the case! But, I'm sure they will all go gaga over you!" Patricia teased.

Flora knocked on the door opening it at the same time.

"You are needed downstairs. Lunch is ready, and the rest of the party is quite hungry. Patricia, I cooked all your favorites. I just hope that your family will like it, too. If I may say so, they are a handsome group. And, clever! I just got a full report about Millie's cooking schedule from Mark. Very interesting young man. I am sure that you do not have a single boring moment!" That was a long and very informal speech for an ordinarily reserved and strait housekeeper.

The first evening passed with pleasant and loud conversation, where everybody was speaking at the same time —almost everybody, that is. Tim was quiet most of the time, but he closely watched Patricia and George, who were very entertaining, making everyone laugh hysterically. This side of George, Patricia had never had a chance to see before now, which made her look at him with surprise. What she did not know was that her love for him was plainly written all over her face. All the time George would hold her hand, or casually throw his arm around her shoulders.

Interestingly enough, Francesca studied them, too. She, who never showed any interest in other people, suddenly found herself wanting to know more about the relationship between her sister and George. She never doubted for a moment that Patricia fell in love with George. After all, he was very handsome and rich. The only other man who showed interest in Patricia, so far as she knew, was that impossible blowfish Michael. To even think to compare those two for Francesca was preposterous. She could never understand what possessed George to marry her sister. Of course, both of them tried very hard to prove their love before they got married. Anyway, she was not able to believe that her plain little sister inspired love in such a man as George.

It seemed that they did love each other. After long scrutiny, Francesca concluded that Patricia did look like a content young bride. In her self-centered world the value of beauty was the most precious asset in the game of life. The fact that most of the world was not blessed with the same gift, she considered it a lucky thing for her. To feel remorse or compassion for the less fortunate was not in her character. After all, the rest of the universe was not important. However, since Patricia married, she started to notice other couples around her, especially happy ones. She suddenly remembered the couple she studied the other day in Nick's Café. The man was good looking by Francesca's standards, but the woman was anything but pretty. She wondered then, just as she did now, *what did this man see in her?* He treated the woman as the most valuable jewel, which amazed her greatly. Abruptly, Francesca asked herself, *maybe there is something else a man wants in a woman besides beauty.* A little twinge in her heart accompanied the realization that she never shared such a moment with anybody, including her husband. The only important thing for her was to be admired and worshiped by every man around her. Nevertheless, since the clamor around her sister started, first with Michael and then finished in an unexpected marriage to George, Francesca popped out from her lifelong bubble. The biggest surprise, though, was the fact that Patricia looked different. Pretty? No, her sister was beautiful! Was it love or the whole circumstance – marriage, children and a man who obviously adored her.

Watching them now it was clear that her sister and George were happy. *That is much more than I can say for myself and Tim,* she concluded miserably.

"Francesca! Hey girl, are you okay?" Tim shook her lightly, "We have been trying to get your attention for a century!"

Francesca smiled, and replied casually to hide her real state of mind, "Oh, I'm just little tired. All the preparation this past week started to show! It's late and the children are beat, so are most of us!" She looked at George with a funny grin, who looked like he just started to party.

"Okay, my dear sister, I can take a hint!" George laughed, helping Patricia up, then picked up asleep Mark in his arms. Lindsay tried to make Andrew and Timmy race to their bedrooms, but they ignored her. Patricia put her arm around Puppet's shoulders thinking how the girl had grown at least two inches. Her throat tightens. It is never easy to let something you love go, and these kids she loved so much were now out of her life. Oh, they see each other a couple a times a year, and every time she will be surprised how much bigger they are, how much they have changed, and how farther apart they have become.

After they escorted the kids to their rooms, two couples wished each other a good night and headed for their bedrooms. Patricia looked over her shoulder, Francesca and Tim slowly walked beside each other, but they could have been miles apart as well.

"Do you think?" Patricia started, after George closed the door behind them.

"No, it's obvious that he is still in love with you!" George entertained the same thoughts as she did. Patricia nervously walked to the window.

"Do you think that Francesca -" But George interrupted again.

"No, I don't think she knows, but She's not happy. They are not happy. She probably sees that something's wrong, but still doesn't know what." He approached Patricia at the window. The darkness outside was impenetrable, making their reflection on the glass clear. George slid his arms around her waist, pulling her back to himself.

Patricia leaned on him helplessly. "What if she.... I don't want to hurt her. What are we going to do?"

He pulled her closer, placing feather light kisses over her head "Well, we have to convince him how much we are in love. That's the only thing that might sober him. Maybe Francesca will never figure out what is the reason for their problems. If he doesn't snap out of this infatuation, they will slowly drift apart, I am afraid. So, starting tomorrow morning you will have to be a woman deeply in love, and I, totally adoring husband!" Patricia stiffened a little along his body.

He took it as her resistance, "You have to try, Patricia. These are not simple people on the ranch, who believed, before you came, that you must love me very much. Tim and Francesca were never completely convinced of our love. Each of them for different reasons, but nevertheless, they had their suspicions. This is our only chance to change that. Will you try?"

Patricia turned around to look at him, placing her hands on his broad chest. "Yes, George, we just have to succeed!" desperation in her voice assured him she is serious.

"My good girl!" George whispered, bending his head to her lips. He lightly brushed them with his. She trembled with shock waves of tingling sensations shooting throughout her. George felt her reaction, feathery touches of his lips turned into hungry kisses, leaving her completely powerless. His hands, burning her skin through the silky fabric of her dress. He drew her closer, her arms, on their own will, rose and tightly wound around his neck. What a great opportunity she faces. The possibility to be able to touch him every time she felt like it, to sit beside him holding his hand, feel his arm around her shoulders or waist, to laugh with him in front of everybody, freely and unrestrained, filled her heart with warm anticipation. Pressed so close to his chest, she felt his heart beat as her own.

"We will worry about other people tomorrow!" His voice trembled as he lifted her small body, closing the short distance to the bed with just a few strides.

Sometime during the night Patricia awakened. With a smile she remembered their lovemaking. It could not be more perfect. *It could. If he would only love me*! That thought had haunted her for a long time, although she tried all that time, to stifle it and push it aside. Her love for him flourished, knowing that he would never return her feelings. With this aching thought, she slipped back into sleep.

The next morning, the two sisters send their families out on the town. Every child should see Santa Claus, what a great excuse to get them out of their hair, and of course, Santa was exactly where he was supposed to be, in the mall. The house immersed into silence, which Patricia and Francisca embraced with gratitude. The unparalleled rampage which the kids brandished bright and early, jerking the rest of the household out of their beds, made everybody eager to do whatever was necessary to keep them in a more manageable condition.

"I still have to wrap presents!" Patricia collapsed on the sofa with a meek smile, "But, first I need some time to recuperate. Believe me, those three usually behave much better or their dad would have a fit. I'm surprised how George seemed not to notice any of that silliness!" "Patricia was aware that her sister observing her closely, more like scrutinizing her, but I have to play it cool. So, she sprang up and with a funny face waved at Francesca, "Come with me, my dear! That big suitcase, for which everybody things contains my wardrobe, is full of presents. I wanted to wrap them all nicely at home, but I would need three suitcases to bring it here, which was out of the question. So, we'll do it now!" Patricia decided to play total ignorance over Francesca's curiosity. From the experience she knew that excessive talking would eventually snap Francesca's mind out of this inquisitive state, and she'll stop searching for answers.

All the fuss around Christmas dinner paid off. Patricia could not remember better food or a nicer atmosphere, since she was a child. Even Tim loosened up a bit, allowing Patricia and George to relax at last. Somehow, calm Patricia and George were more convincing in showing their affection.

Kids were allowed, as a result of the whole day's pestering, to each open one present. Tired of the excitement and too much activity during the day and now opening presents showed their toll. As a result, everybody willingly agreed to early retirement to their bedrooms, especially with the prospect of early rising to charge through the rest of the nicely wrapped boxes.

Patricia woke up early in the morning. Outside was still dark, which accounted for the silence throughout the house. George's deep even breathing showed that he, too, like the rest of the household, slept a sleep of the righteous. Her head rested on his shoulder, while her left hand lay across his chest. She contentedly sighed, snuggling closer to him, deciding to sleep a little longer. In half an hour it was obvious that is easier to decide than to do.

After all, I have to put the rest of the presents under the tree, including those which George bought yesterday and acted so secretive about. So very slowly Patricia slipped out of George's embrace, and even more carefully crept out of bed. To wake up her husband was the last thing she wanted. He deserves it after yesterday's bravery, when he almost singlehandedly managed these wild Neandertals, and kept his sanity.

With an armful of packages, Patricia carefully advanced down the stairs, remembering her first encounter with George on the bottom of them. *Tim*, her heart skipped a beat. He was standing below, watching her. Patricia smiled.

"Good morning Tim! You too have some unfinished business?" When she reached the last stair, he took several packages from her.

'Well, I couldn't sleep any longer, and I thought I'd make some coffee before the staff invade the kitchen." He smiled looking at the packages in his hands, "Wait until those ungrateful pirates see all the presents. Hahaha. George will have to split himself in half to be able to keep them sound." Tim was scratching his chin, puzzled. "I never realized how much patience George has with children. Miracles never cease, I guess it's you. I'm sure. He is a changed man. Love for you, no doubt, bent the old stick. If I hadn't seen it firsthand, I wouldn't believe it."

Patricia was placing gifts under the beautifully decorated tree, thinking how George and she managed to convince her family of their love. *If Tim knew the truth, what would he do*, she wondered.

"Tell me Patricia, are you really happy? Sorry. Sorry! I can see that you are happy, more than happy!" Tim stuttered, trying not to look directly into her face, "You know what I mean, Patricia!" He smiled.

"Tim, that's okay. I know. I'm good, very good! My new life is more than good. George is a good husband, and we are exceptionally happy. Then, the kids! They are a handful, but I do love them like they were my own, and the ranch is more than you described. People accepted me as one of their own. I know I sound like a commercial, but it's the truth!" Patricia was smiling convincingly, feeling weird. She tried to paint for Tim a picture of her good fortune, but she did not exaggerate a bit. *I do feel happy, and I do think that my life is more than good. If George loved me just a little, I am afraid my life would be perfect, and such a thing does not exist.*

Tim lowered himself onto the sofa, watching her closely "I'm glad for you, my dear!" He finally said, "You deserve the best!"

"All is in the desire to overcome the obstacles. You think it was easy for me to leave my life here and go to some far and strange place, full of unknown people. To marry a man with three children and make them accept me as their mother? It was equally hard for Francesca in your house. Did you forget how much your parents were displeased with your choice of a wife? I watched her everyday fight to be the best wife, the best daughter-in-law, and afterward the best mother. Try to remember how much *you* had to invest in your marriage! I'm not saying that you love my sister less then she loves you, but for you everything was easier!" As she casually spoke, she noticed the change on Tim's face. He frowned sinking deeper into his memories. Patricia continued to rearrange gifts under the tree, giving him time to reflect.

"Hey, you two! You look as though the cat ate you tongues!" George's voice yanked both of them back to reality, "The morning is perfect, don't you think so? How is my beloved wife?"

He approached Patricia, pulled her up, and not so gently squeezed her arm. Patricia stared at him with surprise, feverishly trying to understand what came over him to act like this. She twisted a little in an attempt to free herself, but George's grip was too strong for her. She looked up at his face. He was smiling but his eyes were icicles boring through the soul. He had never acted like this before. What is wrong? What did she do to make him mad like this? George searchingly stared into her eyes , keeping her hypnotized like a snake its prey. Tim's voice broke the spell.

"George, my boy, you have one clever little wife!" He did not notice the tension between George and Patricia.

"Oh really?" George fought with all his power not to sound sarcastic, "Can you elaborate on that a little?" His grip on Patricia's arm did not loosen a bit.

"Ah-ha!" Is seemed that Tim was still pondering inside his mind, "She just gave me the tongue lashing of my life in the most unceremonious but gentle way. Now I know, old boy, how she twists you around her finger!" He looked at them with the smile of a man who just discovered a whole new world, then got up not noticing the couple's surprised stares, "I'm going to see what that sleepy head of my wife is doing. Oh, coffee is ready. Help yourselves!" He strode upstairs skipping every other step.

George and Patricia were standing motionless for a long moment after he vanished.

"What is all this about?" George asked with a frown of a man who is accustomed of being on a top of the things, and now has no idea what hit him.

"I have no idea. But we made it. I mean, he is sure of our love. We convinced him! Isn't that great? And, if you ask me, he is right now making up with Francesca!"

"How do you know that?" He studied her, searching for any sign of deception.

"I don't know how I know, George! Don't you ever have a feeling about something? Just wait and you'll see!" Patricia finally freed herself, taking advantage of George's confusion. "Let's see about that coffee! Tim is right. When Flora and the staff barge into the kitchen, we won't stand a chance!" She took his hand giving him a slight tug to follow her.

Christmas morning was wilder then the days past, if that was possible. Kids were squealing and opening presents, decidedly tearing them up in haste. Adults were laughing and talking at the same time, all but one. This time George was the quiet one, closely observing Francesca, Patricia and Tim, who, by the way, looked as a different man. Even Francesca was puzzled as to what had happened to her husband. He overtook George's role from last few days, acting silly, while opening packages with the children.

"What got into him" Francesca whispered in her sister's ear.

"I have no idea!" Patricia played ignorance, although she suspected, but could not be sure, that her little speech made a big impression on her brother–in–law.

"Bull. He woke me up with some muddled prophesies about life commitments, difficulties of adjustments, lifetime struggles, and I cannot recall it all, but he didn't sound like himself at all. When I asked from where all that coming, he just said something about how clever my sister is! So?"

Francesca tried not to laugh at Tim's attempts to put Timmy's ski pants on over his trousers. He was on his back pushing his foot with seriousness, which made kids scream and roll with him around.

"I just talked about my difficulties in leaving everything behind me, and go so far away to live amongst strangers. I'm positive my complaints have nothing to do with this clown rolling over your carpet!" Patricia thought if she humored her sister, maybe this change in Tim will be taken as something he did on his own.

On their way home, Patricia reminisced about the past holiday. She did not want to admit to herself her fear of what might happen when she faces her sister and her husband again. She hoped that Tim would overcome his weakness toward her, if he ever had one. Especially, she wished with her whole heart, that her sister would not figure out what was going on with her husband. The telephone conversations all those months were not encouraging. Francesca sounded edgy and frustrated, just as she looked when they arrived several short days ago, although Francesca tried to act as if things could not be better. But the first glance at her sister proved to Patricia what she suspected. Now it seemed that Tim had snapped out of his gloominess. She hoped he realized that there were way too many things at stake, including seeing that Patricia and George had created a life together. On the other hand, Patricia hoped that her self-centered sister through this entire bad ordeal learned a valuable lesson. She never saw Francesca to worry about anyone except herself. With a smile, she remembered the change in her attitude these past few days. It was clear that Francesca was surprised, then amazed by Tim's transformation. Genuine happiness made her more beautiful than ever. The future will prove if those two can overcome their problems. Patricia was inclined to believe so.

CHAPTER 12

March almost passed. The snow did not came in abundance this winter. A blanket, two feet deep, covered the countryside in crisp whiteness. Cold and much deeper snow on the mountains did not promise an early arrival of spring, though. Usual peaceful and slow pace on the ranch turned almost into hibernation. George and the kids were leaving for Sheridan as usual, cowboys would ride horses around in idleness, Peter without yard work would snooze beside the fireplace between breakfast and lunch, and then between lunch and dinner. When Patricia would descend down from her sanctuary for a cup of coffee or a sandwich, Millie would shake her head. "I don't understand that man! He sleeps the whole day, and a normal man wouldn't be able to shut his eyes at night. Guess what? I'm the one who can't sleep! My dear husband snores so loud that I'm afraid he'll wake up the spirits of our ancestors!"

Patricia finished her book before the deadline, so she took advantage of the extra time, fixing and making changes. Today she read it from beginning to the end. The feeling of satisfaction was more than rewarding. *I'll call Paula with the news,* Patricia decided.

"Paula, the book is finished!" She announced, "I'm sending it tomorrow. Hope you'll like it! It's nothing like the stories about Patty, it's better, I believe. The best new is I don't need the illustrator!" She laughed, but Paula did not respond on that insinuation. She was thrilled that the book was finished, and she could not wait to read it.

"Send it priority. No, better send it overnight. And Patricia, I expect a synopsis of your next book. The board would like it to take place in Egypt. I'm sending you a bunch of books on Egyptian culture, history and geography. Okay, doll?" Her editor and dear friend did not change a bit.

Patricia was smiling in amusement. *Always three steps ahead of everybody.*

"Paula, do you ever slow down? Not a word how you are doing, and how life is in New York? Now, that I don't have to go there any more, you have to fill me in with all the gossip and news!" Patricia tried to sound serious.

"Okay! But, remember, you asked for it! First, I got a promotion, although, my job did not change that much! I got a bigger office, more money and more power in making decisions. Second, my secretary Sandra, got married, and naturally, I got a new one. You would never guess – my new secretary's name is Patrick! The cutest thing you ever saw! I think, I'm in trouble! But, the biggest news is that our adoring big baby Michael got married!" Paula stopped awaiting Patricia's response.

"Well, all splendid news! Congratulation on your promotion! I feel sorry for poor Patrick already! He doesn't have a chance, you barracuda you! You'll eat him for breakfast. I hope that Michael is half as happy as he ought to be. Did he choose wisely, or -?"

"Of course not! It was on rebound, I'm sure. She is a spoiled little thing. Her daddy owns some electronics business. Lots of money, but no substance. Two years, that's all I give them!"

"You are terrible, do you know that! If she is more spoiled that he is , it could help him to grow up. It could turn out to be the best solution for him! Why can't you see things from the bright side?"

"Get real, Patricia! Two years is seeing things on the bright side. Way too optimistic prediction! Ihave to go, my dear! Busy, busy, busy! Send me your book tomorrow. After I read it, I'll call you immediately! Bye!" In a second, Paula was gone.

The relationship between Patricia and her husband slipped into a comfortable routine. Weekdays he would come home with the kids late in the afternoon, usually in a good mood. They would rush in the house noisy, laughing and horsing around. All of them would in one breath tell Patricia what happened in school, during the recess, on the way home. She would listen amused, remembering her childhood and the quiet dinners in her parents' house. The children were allowed after homework was done to watch television for a while, or play cards with Patricia and their dad. Sometimes, which they liked the most, they begged Patricia to tell them stories. Seating in front of the fire place, with only flickering firelight, she would narrate adventurous accounts of pirates with chests full of gold and jewels, kidnaped princess and brave young men ready to do anything to save them.

After the kids were tucked into their beds, George would circle his arm around Patricia's shoulders or waist, walking her slowly to their bedroom. He got into the habit of sleeping regularly in her bed. In the beginning of their intimate relationship, he would leave her in bed before she woke up. If he worked late, he would retreat in the dressing room, not to disturb her. That happened less and less.

On the occasions when late work was over, and she was long asleep, George would climb next to her taking her gently into his arms and contentedly falling asleep. In the morning, they would get up together, talking about simple everyday things, like they were a normal ordinary married couple. Many times, Patricia would think, *even I forget what kind of an agreement is between us.* Often after her family would leave for Sheridan, Millie would busy herself in the kitchen, Patricia wondered how her life would be different if George never appeared . Thought of a meaningless existence without those dear kids and this man and the love for him, which grow greater every minute. She will love him forever, regardless of what happens in the future. If they stay married or not, she will never be able to love anyone in her life in the way she loves George. The children will grow up one day, leave the house, and then what? George will not need her any longer. The painful conclusion that the best thing would be to quietly leave on her own seemed to be the best solution. In her most optimistic state she hoped that George might get used to having her around, and they could just continue as it is now.

His passion and her love for him awoke some primitive response in her. She could never, in her wildest dreams, believe that she had it in her. Her passionate response surprised him, but not as much as her. In the beginning she was confused and a little embarrassed, but as time passed his masterful lovemaking and knowledge of a woman's body freed her from all inhibitions, and she returned every passionate kiss, touch, caress back with equal strength.

What Patricia *knew* about men was not encouraging. How long will George be interested in her was the question often passing through her mind. So many times, she heard that men eventually lose interest in a woman. *It all depends on how much he cares for her, and George does not really care for me,* she had to admit with distress. A couple of months was her first prediction. But, time was passing and their hunger for each other did not lose its intensity. It seemed as they got to know each other better, their need for one another grew.

Patricia stopped wondering about it. Philosophically concluded that she has to take each day as it comes. Inevitably, some Alicia will take him away one of these days, but nobody can take what they have now, nor the memories which will have to last her a lifetime. Patricia was sure of one thing – she will never regret the decision to marry him. Otherwise, she would not have a chance to know what real love and passion was.

The next several weeks were very busy. Paula was thrilled with the book, and all kinds of things were sent from New York and back. Several short changes in the story did not take a lot of time. Four different sketches for the book cover were discussed, and finally one was chosen to everybody's satisfaction. Finally, the contract was signed, and Patricia felt the anticipation as her latest baby went out into the world to live its own life.

Spring was not far from changing the countryside again. Warmer weather seemed to inject fresh energy into the peaceful existence of the ranch dwellers. Cowboys were outside from dawn to dusk, checking on how the cattle survived the winter, how many were with calves, how much of the fence was down. The horses, which got fat and lazy, now were happily running around and enjoying every opportunity to be ridden. The same was with the children. So, just like the horses, they could hardly wait to kick up their heels outdoors. For the kids who are very active, confinement bored them to the point they became restless and fought too much and too serious. Patricia was taken by all that buzz sensing some other changes in the air beside the change of seasons.

The kids were eager to start horseback riding again. Reluctantly Patricia agreed to ride with them. She goofed that her liking of snow is not such to make her trilled to be thrown by the horse into it. Anyway, every Saturday and Sunday the four of them would go down to the stables and saddle the horses. Once away from the stables, Patricia would relax. Not even wanting to admit to herself, she dreaded to linger for too long around the stables and the "Boys'" quarters. The cowboys were servile and useful, and she liked them, all but one. Chuck would, every time, try to talk to her, touch her hand, or the worse help her to mount the horse. Every excuse was taken in order to put his hands on her. Patricia pretended that she was not aware of Chuck's sleazy attentions, but she could hardly wait to be far from the stables and her tormentor.

May brought an abundance of rain, dressing everything in crisp, reach green. Patricia started to work on her new book, lacking her usual patience and drive for work. Everything made her edgy, feeling restless. In the air was this feeling that something was bound to happen, something significant, and she could not wait to see what. Puzzled by feelings like that, she became more irritable, knowing that nothing was in store to happen. Her life was nearly perfect, both private and professional. George could not be a better father and husband, kids were their usual handful but delightful, and she felt they started to love her. But, something was lurking on the horizon.

"Tell me Patricia, is something wrong?" Millie asked, while they prepared dinner plan for the 4th of July celebration.

"No, no! What do you mean wrong?" Patricia turned toward Millie defensively, *is it that obvious that I am completely wacko.*

"You seemed, if you excuse me to say so, tired, impatient. You've lost some weight, not that you have any to spare. And, if that does not scream wrong, I don't know what does?"

"You have a point here, Millie, but nothing is wrong.! I just don't know what's with me? I am a little bit on the edgy side. Don't you worry, I'll be okay. " *Will I*, she wondered. Millie just looked at her with raised eyebrows. "Tell me, Millie, do you know why George didn't invite guests this year for the 4th of July, fireworks as usual?" Patricia wanted to change the subject, but was puzzled about George's decision not to honor his father's legacy.

"I don't know, although, I asked him the same question . He just mysteriously smiled. Do you want to know what I think? He is so content and happy with his family, that he wants to spend more time with you guys!" Millie checked the apple pie in the oven, "But, for consolation, George is preparing big fireworks in the court yard. The kids would never forgive him if there wasn't any!"

"I am looking forward to that, just as kids do! My father thought it silly, and Francesca was afraid to handle it, so my mom and I would have a blast with fireworks every year!" Lately she often thought about her parents and her childhood. Noise and loud conversation stopped the two women in what they were doing. Andrew and Lindsay stomped in, yelling at the same time.

"Girls are like that, and I don't know why I have to have one."

"Being a boy doesn't make you cleverer, it makes you stupid, you moron you."

"I'll show you a moron, you silly goose!" Andrew grabbed the sleeve of Lindsay's tee shirt, pulling it roughly. She screamed, clasping his ears violently.

"Stop this instant!" A shocked Patricia and Millie exclaimed together.

The children did not seem to hear anything. Patricia being so tense for weeks, finally exploded. She grabbed the arm of each child, pulling them, not so gently, apart, "Will you two start to act your age? I want silence for the rest of the day. One more outburst and the two of you will spend a 4th of July in your bedrooms cleaning!"

Everybody stopped in surprise. She had never acted like this, so they aborted their fight watching her closely.

"Grandma said the other day, that we'll give you a nervous breakdown, and if that means you'll start to yell, she was right!" Mark, in all the commotion, unobserved perched his little tosh on a kitchen chair, then helped himself to a freshly baked chocolate chip cookie. Everyone hushed as one. Patricia felt nauseous. It had never happened before for her to lose temper so completely and for no reason.

"Oh, I'm sorry, my darlings! I don't know what's came over me," She started.

"Don't worry Patricia, they deserved it!" Mark was licking chocolate off his fingers, "I would yell at them if I thought it would stop them. I have to say you did it better than I would.!" He helped himself to another cookie, taking advantage that nobody was objecting to him eating sweets before lunch.

"Hey guys, are you ready?" George barged into the kitchen with several oversized plastic bags full of fireworks, "Andrew. I found it!" He triumphantly pulled out the big box with a flashy sign "Grand Finale". Andrew cried out with delight, snatching the box out of his father's hands. Lindsay ransacked through the other bags, shouting excitedly.

Patricia felt even worse. She looked at these people around her. They accepted her into their home and hearts. She was never happier, nor had more to live for. The question was, what was she doing? Brooding over her little romantic frustration? She married him knowing what the reality was, and she accepted this marriage to be of convenience, which turned out to be much more than she expected. So, why is she so nervous and upset now? *Maybe because I did not expect to fall in love! I thought I would have a relationship with purpose. The purpose was to put my sister's marriage in order, give George's children a chance to have a mother, and make my life complete by becoming a mother myself. The universe knows those reasons were significant enough to made up my mind and settle for half of something I always felt strong I will not, loveless relationship.* It looks as the plan works! According to Francesca, the relationship between her and Tim is much better since Christmas. Andrew, Lindsay and Mark excepted her with much less rebellion then was a reasonable to expect. The best part was, turning herself into a mother was one of the most invigorating experiences of her life, which she could not have predicted.

"Will you stop this unbecoming behavior! The dinner will spoil if you wild cowboys don't leave those fireworks alone, it will be no food for you!" Millie pretended to be serious, although nobody bought it. Reluctance in the postures of "Wild Cowboys" amused her which she hid. "The sun is still strong! Who, in their right mind, will have fireworks in the middle of the day?"

The rummaging through a variety of packages and boxes with intriguing contents were abandoned in favor to get over with dinner as soon as possible and start the preparations for the biggest fun of the year.

Peter enthusiastically marched in, announcing that the "Boys" had cleared the yard as instructed, "So folks, the only thing we have to wait for is night, night, night." He was tapping some old Irish dance while approaching the frowning Millie.

"You old fool, nobody moves an inch until the plates are cleaned to high shine, and that includes you too!" Peter stopped, making goofy faces while turning away from Mille, obediently sliding behind the table.

The kids tried to stifle their giggles behind the hands covering their mouths. George was having a hard time keeping a straight face, which made Patricia laugh. Millie turned swiftly toward the table with raised eyebrows, still pretending to be mad. In the same time all of them pointed the finger at a roaring Patricia. She could not stop once she started, releasing the months of overloaded frustration. Everybody looked at her for several seconds, then burst into equally frantic laughter, including Millie.

The kids could not wait for night to fall. They sat in the great room eating Millie's delicious pie, making fun of every possible thing they could come up with, not forgetting to keep an eye on the window.

Summer days are fortunately long, but that was not appreciated today. Finally, twilight propelled the them out of their seats. George got up smiling, "Wild horses could not drag them out of that yard! Well girls, you can finish cleaning the kitchen in peace. I will send someone to fetch you before we start!" And he marched out in haste.

"Men never grow up, Patricia, remember that! Doesn't matter how important and serious people they pretend they are, the little boy sleeps underneath, just waiting for the right time to claim that oversized zombie. Hahaha." Patricia could not erase the wide grin from her face. Picking up the dishes from the coffee table, she was making the decision not to worry about her unreturned love. *Life cannot get any better than tonight, and for what it is worth, living for moments like this.* Lindsay stuck her head through the barely opened door just enough to yell, "We are starting!" and disappeared at light speed.

Patricia and Millie were comfortably seated on the cushions of the patio chairs. The fireworks were breathtaking, but the two women were more amused watching a bunch of grown men competing with three excited children.

"I'm afraid that George buys more fireworks every year. It's a frightening thought! I'm sure in twenty years from now we'll sit here the whole darn night watching big boys playing!" Millie chuckled.

"All but Mark!" Patricia interrupted, "This boy doesn't know how to be a boy! When I listen to him, and not look straight into his face, I have the feeling I'm talking to an adult. I've tried everything, but he just refuses to be a child. Do you see him? He was here a minute ago!

You see, this is what I'm talking about! Even Peter gets a kick out of this, but not Mark!" Patricia set up in her chair searching with her eyes for a small figure.

"He'll do this from time to time!" Millie tried to calm her down.

"I know, I know. But not when it's pitch dark. There is not a single light on the whole ranch, and the lights from the fireworks are so short. He can fall and break a bone, or something." Patricia got up, "I'll just…" and she disappeared in the darkness.

While walking through the impenetrable blackness of the garden, Patricia tried to think as Mark, and guess where he would go alone when everybody else was having fun.

Suddenly it hit her - the new colt! He was expressing "his concern" as he put it, that the fireworks with all the noise and the light would frighten the new baby horse. The way to the stable never seemed so long. *Damn*, she swore, I know that George meant well by not wanting light to spoil his blasted fireworks, but not a single light?

Footsteps? She turned around seeing nothing. These are not little boy's steps. *George, it must be George!* She opened her mouth to call him, then she realized that the approaching person was wearing cowboy boots. An uncomfortable twitch in the stomach warned her. *Chuck!*

And there he was! When he saw her, his hurried walk turned into his normal lazy stroll.

"I noticed you left! Is there something wrong? It looks like I'm the only one who notices you anymore. What are you doing? Where are you going?"

Like a rabbit trapped by a rattlesnake, she stood there watching him coming closer. He placed his hands ever so lightly on her arms just above the elbows. She trembled, foreshadowing an unpleasant encounter, like several similar ones recently. The voice in her head was screaming *Danger*. She tried to pull her arms away from his hands.

Being alert for such move, his grip tightened, pulling her closer to him. His lazy, seductive voice was brushing her horsehead.

"Don't fight me, Patricia. Don't fight yourself! I can feel you are attracted to me, just as I'm to you. I can understand, my pet, old man George was never a big lover!" He huskily laughed, "And, I know that from reliable source, if you catch my drift!"

Patricia, on mentioning George's name snapped out of her numbness, and started to twist her arms in an attempt to free herself, hissing through the clenched teeth, "Let go of me! I don't know what you're talking about but believe me I'm not attracted to you at all. If George finds out about this, I'm sure he'll fire you, Chuck, just stop now, and I promise I'll never mention it to anybody."

Chuck tightened his hold on her, then lowering his head and harshly pressed his lips on hers. Convolutions of disgust and panic paralyzed her for a moment. Suddenly she was free, struggling to regain her balance. At the same time, the sound of a hard punch made her look in that direction. Short flashes of light from fireworks penetrated heavy darkness. She saw George, big as a mountain, towering over Chuck spread out on the ground, moaning and shaking his head.

"I could break every bone in your miserable body, but you are not worth it. You... You... Tomorrow pack your things and don't let me see you anywhere near here ever again!" George abruptly turned to face Patricia, giving her an icy look, grabbed her hand, and with no fuss dragged her toward the main house.

"Thanks, George. It was terrible. George, you're hurting me. Slow down little, please!" But, he yanked her even harder, spitting, "Spare me, You little cheating slut!"

What does he mean "cheating slut"? Patricia felt even more sick. *Does he... No, he can't think that I let Chuck...* They approached the house, where the fireworks were in full blaze, George stopped for several minutes, and it was obvious he was trying to compose himself. He glanced at Patricia, "Straighten your hair. It's not necessary that everybody see the results of your extracurricular activity. Your lover will spread the news faster than prairie fire!" He snapped.

"But, George, you can't ... "She tried once more to explain, but he looked at her with a murderous expression. Millie was still sitting on the porch. When she noticed Patricia and George, she waved. "You were right, my dear, that little monster went to stables to see that blasted colt!"

Patricia turned to see if George had heard this, but he had already disappeared into the house. She made herself sit down, and pretended to enjoy the rest of the fireworks

The children were so feverish that Patricia and Millie had a difficult time putting them to bed. Closing the door of Mark's room Millie smiled at Patricia, "You look tired, my dear. My advice is – go to bed, tomorrow you'll feel better. Good night!"

"Good night, Millie! I'm okay!" She whispered, turning to her bedroom. *Feel better tomorrow? I do not think so, my dear Millie,* she helplessly thought. *How am I going to make George listen to me and see what really happened? He thinks that Chuck and I... Oh God, even the thought is repulsive.*

Entering the bedroom, Patricia half hoped that she would not need to face George tonight, but he was standing, erect and stiff beside the big French door. His hands were clenched tightly behind his back, tension in his shoulders showed that he would not be open to rational explanations. She hesitated at the door.

"Get in and close the door!" His voice was low and sounded calm, but this did not fool Patricia for a second.

After she silently closed the door, George turned on his heels watching her with contempt.

"George, listen -"

"You listen! I have no patience, nor nerves to be entertained by your lying talents. I should know that all the women are the same. For a while, I was fooling myself that you could be different. You hoaxed my better judgment by acting so innocent and righteous!" Patricia's bewildered face made him turn away, "You should see yourself! How a woman can be instinctively deceiving, I'll never be able to understand. I caught you with your lover, and you still think you can play your way out of it!" He swung furiously toward her again.

Patricia realized that he had no intention of letting her explain. She must make him listen. In desperation she stepped toward him with raised hands pleading.

"George, I think I deserve at least the courtesy of letting me speak. You are wrong -" She started determined to make him listen, but he mercilessly cut her off.

"Yes, I agree! I was wrong thinking that you might be a real woman, if such a thing exists. I don't want to continue this discussion any longer. I waited here to tell you that I should never have broken our first arrangement. It was my mistake, and I apologize for it. If I could turn time back, I would. Doesn't matter. I will never come to your room, but I will have to stay in my bedroom… dressing room, for appearance's sake. Don't you dare talk about what happened tonight with anybody. I had enough of it the first time around?"

He started to pace up and down the room, and it seemed he sank deeper into his thoughts. Patricia heard the words, but her heart refused to accept them. Her mind expected from the very beginning that the time would come when George would abandon her bed and her. She was sure the reason would be some beautiful young girl, but it never crossed her mind that her nonexistent love affair would be the reason.

Patricia shrugged her shoulders in indignation. The reason is not important, the result is the end of her happiness, *And What does he mean by he had it enough the first time around? He can't be talking about his wife! Maybe Alicia? Or some other woman like her.*

"The children have grown to love you very much, and they depend on you. I just hope you won't disappoint them one day, too. We will continue to pretend that we have a marriage. I'm sure you realized until now that Tim is trying hard to put his life with your sister back on track. Only they believe in our love and happiness induced that effort. So, we are on square one. We have to go on!" He sighed, pushing his fists deep into the pockets of his trousers, "One thing more!" He looked straight into her eyes, showing all the strength of his iron will, "Don't ever try to humiliate me by flinging yourself on my workers, or any other man around, for that matter! If you have to satisfy your urges, take a trip to New York or L.A. Nobody would question that, but I demand discretion!" With heavy and tired steps he exited the room.

Patricia was numb. She still felt Chuck's creepy hands on her body, but George's unjust accusations froze her heart. Why he would not let her explain? All he saw was her in other man's arms, and that was enough to proclaim her guilty. What made him so bitter that few seconds were enough to forgot all the love, passion, closeness, and all the beautiful memories they shared? Somebody must have hurt him very much! But who? Certainly not his perfect wife!

Patricia shuddered violently, realizing the consequences of this evening. She will probably live the rest of her life beside the man she loves more than life itself, the man who despises her and does not want to have anything ever to do with her.

Hysteric sobs, like huge waves were coming from deep inside of her, started to shake her small body. She curled up on the top of the bed spread, burying her face in the pillow. The more she tried to stop, the more intense tremors shook the whole bed. In all that distress she dreaded the possibility that George might hear her cries interpreting them, no doubt, as another deception. How long she cried she could never recall. Sense of time disappeared. Finally, she did drift into a feverish, disturbing slumber.

The next morning she awoke by an attack of unbearable pain. In a flash last night's events came back in the whole it's ugliness. Every atom of her body ached. All she wanted was to curl under the covers of her bed, and never to crawl out again.

The faces of the children vividly beamed in her brain, then Millie and Peter, her family in Church Hill, all the people who knew her very well, and, of course, George.

Patricia forced herself to get up, and dragged her painful body into the bathroom. Another shock made her sick. Her reflection in the mirror frightened her. She would be able to act calmly in front of everybody, but her physical appearance was screaming the truth of the state of her soul and body. Puffy eyes, red nose, feverish glaze, and shaky movements will betray her instantly. Desperate to hide her terrible appearance, she took a cold shower, brushed her hair until her scalp hurt. Applying make-up was an excruciating job, partly because her hands trembled, and partly because any amount of make-up could not hide her looks.

She glanced at the clock. Fortunately, George and the kids left an hour ago, so, this morning she will have to face only Millie. She put on wide slacks, long shirt, big straw hat and dark glasses. This will take some explanation to Millie, but anything is better than letting the old woman suspect the truth.

Patricia hesitated to leave the solitude of her bedroom. *If I am not down for breakfast soon, Millie will come up personally to check on me.* Reluctantly descending down, she stopped in front of the kitchen collecting all the energy left in her and put on a wide smile and marched in.

"Morning Millie, Mmmm, I can small fresh biscuits!" She strolled to the cupboard, pulling out a plate and a big coffee mug, "I'm bursting with ideas today, so if you will excuse me, I'll go straight into the conservatory and start writing." She was almost at the door when an expected question stopped her.

"Well young lady, what are we pretending to be today? A Hollywood movie star?"

"Oh Mille, you know how sensitive my eyes are. All that light from the fireworks made them red and painful. And the hat, well, I'm afraid that the sun in conservatory will hurt my eyes more, so -" She slid through the door, listening to Millie shouting after her.

"I never heard of such a thing… Fireworks don't hurt the eyes! Even cowboys take their hats off in the house!" Millie was standing in the middle of the kitchen, thinking. *What happened with these people?* First, George acted this morning as somebody had performed a root canal on his wisdom tooth the whole night long, then Peter came with the stupid idea that George fired Chuck. Heavens knows that Chuck has been asking for it for a long time, but why would George do it in the middle of the 4th of July celebration? And, now Patricia acting as she lost all the marbles she ever had.

Patricia sat behind her computer, which George moved into the conservatory when he realized that was her favorite place. *I have to calm down, not move until the effect of last night's disaster vanishes, at least from the outside.* She knew her insides will stay wounded without the chance of healing for the rest of her life.

By evening the puffiness and redness of her eyes were gone, and with extreme willpower she managed to steady her quivering body and trembling voice. When George and the kids appeared for dinner, she looked more-less as usual. She asked the children the usual questions about school, and if they had any fun? They were very chatty, as usual, so Patricia did not need to speak very much. A couple of glances in George's direction confirmed her fears – he was still mad as hell.

"I have a truck load of work to attend to!" George said as soon as he was done with dinner, and abruptly got up and left the dining room. Millie raised her eyebrows observing Patricia.

"Is he having some problems with the business? I haven't seen him like that since Tiffany created all that trouble." She stopped noticing the rising interest in Patricia's eyes. "Well guys if you are done, move into the entertainment room and play a little before I chase you to bed!" She busied herself with the dirty dishes, "And you, my dear, look tired. It would be the best if you went directly to bed. This is not a suggestion!" Millie tried to look serious. Patricia smiled and obeyed.

This evening repeated itself for a whole week. Patricia waited to see if George would loosen up a bit, but he looked equally gloomy and untouchable. Millie observed them closely, so Patricia tried to behave as casual as possible. In a couple of days she assimilated the new roll so well that even George glanced from time to time in her direction wondering.

The days were different all together. When she was alone, numberless questions tormented her mind. No man without bad experience would act as George does. More and more she was sure that some trauma from the past prohibited him to think rationally.

She could not go like this any longer. Torturing herself with impossible questions and guessing could not be healthy. Patricia decided to find out what was behind his behavior. Remembering that Millie once volunteered to tell her about George's first marriage, she decided that now was the time to find out the truth. Many times, she wanted to ask Millie about it, but the fear of hearing the story of their great relationship and love George shared with Tiffany, stopped her. Desperately clinging to what she had with her husband, she was not in any mood to listen about the woman he loved.

Patricia energetically dashed down the stairs to the kitchen. There was nothing to lose anymore - she already lost a big part what was important to her life. Bravely entering the kitchen and before she had time to change her mind, asked.

"Millie, I want to know everything about George and his first wife?" Millie looked at her for a long time, at least it felt as such too impatient Patricia.

"Please, Millie! It's important for me to know. I *need* to know!"

"Well, it's about a time! I wondered many times if George had ever told you about Tiffany before he married you, but soon after your arrival I suspected he didn't. Now I know it. I can't imagine why. I think you have the right to know, more now than ever, and don't think for a moment that you and that foolish husband of yours managed to fool me for a minute! Don't look at me with those blue eyes as you don't know what I'm talking about. Something is very wrong between the two of you. Don't worry, I won't ask you to tell me what it is. I just hope you'll resolve it soon so all of us can get on with a normal life. Hopefully before your family comes to visit next month!"

Oh Lord, Millie is right. Tim and Francesca are bringing the kids for their summer vacation. I have to do everything in my power to keep up an appearance of a happy marriage.

"Yes Millie, I know, please tell me!" Millie took a deep breath, put the bowl with peas in her lap to shell them.

"Everything started long before George and Tiffany were born. George's father, Samuel and Tiffany's father Brandon were friends from early childhood. In these parts, as you know, there aren't too many people, but at that time were even less. Everybody knew everybody, and it was normal that the only two sons of the richest ranchers would be friends. And, they were! Almost like brothers! I remember those times as the most easygoing and relaxed on my life. Things started to go downhill when George turned twelve. His mother was not from this area, Samuel met Diana in England, where he was attending a college. Her parents were some impoverished nobility, so the little princess agreed to marry the rich American. Samuel was very much in love with her, and as you know when man are in love his brain stops to function. From the moment she came, all of us saw that she didn't care for him at all, and on top of that, she didn't realize what a ranch was before she came. She imagined some big English estate two hours from downtown New York. In a couple of months she was ready to pack her things and go back to England, or *civilization* as she called it, but she was already pregnant with George.

Pregnancy was hard on her, and she took total advantage of it, managing to manipulate her doctor to send her to Palm Beach, as it would help her with her problems. After George was born, she was hardly ever here at the ranch, but when she was she made great effort to be a good mother and adorable wife. George adored her beyond understanding, regardless of her constant absences. Samuel knew that she fooled around with other men but he pretended he didn't.

Several months after George was born Brendon married Laure. Well, you saw her, and let me tell you, with age she got better. But, she was beautiful. In the early stage of her life she decided to cash in with that only asset she had. When I said only, you better believe it. Her family was what we call – white trash. Her father was an alcoholic and her mother a sickly woman without any ambitions. Daughter, though, had it for both of them. She decided to marry the richest man around, and that was Samuel. Her plan did not go exactly as she plotted. In her schemes, love didn't exist, but in high school she did fell in love with Samuel. Being so beautiful and all, she was confident that wouldn't be a problem to make him fall for her, like every other boy. Unfortunately for her, he didn't, but Brandon did. Normally, that should satisfied her ambition, but she fell too hard for Samuel to let go. For her wining him, became the most important thing in her life.

Samuel's decision to go in England to college enraged her. It was a setback, but she was determined. Patiently, she waited for him to come back, thinking that it was wiser to let him kick his heels off while he was young, and not after they are married. But, as I said he came home with a wife. That was the shock of Laura's life, and I think then and there she lost any human fillings she ever had. Three days after Samuel announced, during a big party, that he and his wife were expecting a child, Laura eloped with Brandon. Well, she was rich now and had a husband who adored her, but her fixation on Samuel didn't lessen a bit.

A year after George was born she gave birth to Tiffany. Brandon was so proud and happy, poor man. Laura never loved her daughter very much, I think mainly because Tiffany was the spiting replica of her- beautiful, but cold and unfeeling. Laura turned into the biggest snob in the country, and that was the only thing she ever taught Tiffany. To Laura's horror, Tiffany , I think more out of rebellion than of conviction, socialized with everybody.

Samuel and Brandon, from the very moment their children were born, entertained the idea of their marriage. In the beginning, I'm sure, it was only a joke, but in time everybody took it as a matter of fact, including George and Tiffany. They were a couple during school. Every birthday party, rodeo, dance, they were together. George loved her, there was no doubt about that, and Tiffany considered him her personal property. As the most beautiful girls, she grew up believing that her looks entitled her to have things her way. She loved to be admired, to be watched all the time, and make every boy and girl crazy. Boys' crazy with love, last and rejection and girls of jealousy, envy and quite frankly hatred."

"Her biggest enjoyment was to break up couples, and then throw away the poor confused boy."

"Laura, in the meantime, still brooded over her unfulfilled dreams about Samuel. With Diana being almost all the time somewhere else, Laura had an ideal situation for her little schemes. She used to spend hours every day here helping Samuel, although he didn't need it at all. She tried every trick in the book, but Samuel didn't notice or didn't want to notice her attempts. I believe it partly because he never liked her and partly because of Brandon. The two men despite the situation remained best friends.

The year George left for college, Laura put her daughter in some private school with the excuse that her grades were not good enough to be accepted into any decent college. According to the rumors, Tiffany became wil, and only a huge checks signed by her father kept her from expulsion. Brandon managed to put her into some girls' college in Florida, in hopes she'll calm down. But again, rumors were disturbing. She was the toast of social life. Brandon went to Florida way too often, just to pull her out of some problem with the dean of the college, parents of other girls, or even the law. It cost him a pretty penny to keep her there, but after two years no amount of money could do it any longer. The options were not encouraging. No other similar school would accept her. I guess that *good reputation* travels far and fast, but she refused to go to school anyway. She wanted Brandon to buy her a flat in New York, with the excuse she wanted to study art, but Brandon for once, firmly said no! He brought her back home just to behave worse than ever. She liked to party and drive men wild, as always. Sadly, she was not a high school girl any more. Her encounters with men were not so innocent as before.

Brandon was desolated, while his wife couldn't care less. At that time, she finally realized that she'll never have Samuel. So, she put all her energy into preparing a marriage between George and Tiffany. Why, I could never understand. Maybe as a twisted revenge, or maybe she wanted to at last, have Samuel's property in her family."

"After graduating George came back. He accepted the idea of an immediate wedding without questions. Only Diana tried to make him aware what he was getting himself into. Laura almost murdered her, and even Samuel chose to put her in her proper place, reminding her that it was too late for her to start being a mother to his son."

"The wedding was big and a distasteful show. Laura wanted to announce loud and clear that the two richest families and neighbors were becoming one. Tiffany and George went along with it, like two puppets on a string. It was obvious that they were not in love, but in Tiffany's vocabulary love was not included anyhow. On the other hand, George was determined to make his marriage work. In short period of time it was clear that good intentions were not sufficient.

"Tiffany got pregnant almost instantly, and she made a huge issue of it. For days she rampaged through the house accusing George of tricking her and getting her pregnant without her consent. Well, I never bought that! As an experienced girl she knew very well how to avoid pregnancy. It was just the weapon to keep George where she wanted him."

"George endured it all patiently, thinking about the child. After Andrew was born, Tiffany went back to her old lifestyle of parties, men and drinking, while George completely dedicated himself to the boy. Unfortunately, Tiffany was in quest to destroy herself and anybody else in her path. Her regular routine was partying deep into the night, sleeping until noon, snapping at everybody in the meantime. She would come every day into the nursery, but only during the time when Andrew would be asleep."

"As a rule, when George would come home in the evening, Tiffany would already be somewhere else. If they did cross paths, it was anything but a pleasant encounter. Her habit was to start drinking as soon as she woke up, which would make her way under the influence when George would show up. So, to prevent him from scolding her, she would start with shouting, yelling and accusations. In the beginning, he tried to calm her explaining the dangers of drinking, reminding her that she was now a mother and so on. Nothing would touch her. She would curse him, slam the door, and off she would go to another night of who knows what?"

"A little time before we celebrated Andrew's first birthday, she collapsed at some rodeo party. Her no-good friends dumped her unconscious body on the pavement in front of the hospital. Three months in some detox institution restored her health. After all, she was young, and seemed that she wised up a bit."

"The first several months after her return were the only peaceful time in their marriage. George was going out of his way to make her feel good, and everything was to be as she wanted. When she got pregnant with Lindsay, it appeared she was happy about it."

"Then Dave and Chuck Malloy drifted our way as a plague. From where they came, it was never found out, but from the first moment trouble was written all over them. You know Chuck, and I must admit - he is one handsome devil, but Dave was like a Greek God. Handsome, Charming, easy going, a _ expert on the dancing floor, a wild rider - you can imagine, all the girls near and far fell for him. He knew his power over women, and was taking total advantage of it. Hearts were broken, engagements forgotten, friendships destroyed."

Tiffany was six or seven months pregnant when she first met Dave. She heard of him, of course, she thought all the stories about him were exaggerations. He'd heard about her, too – all about her partying, drinking, loveless marriage and the most important detail for him, her inheritance of the second largest ranch around. For a long time he'd been searching for someone like Tiffany."

"During the dance, after Samuel's big Thanksgiving dinner, he made his move on her, and she fell like a ton of bricks. In spite of her high pregnancy, she managed to snick out of the house every day to meet Dave. We weren't aware at the time what was going on and the change in her attitude was blamed on her state".

"Everything came out after Lindsay was born. First, the rumors about their affair were spreading like forest fires, but we hoped she wouldn't do anything stupid. Yeah, right! Brandon, thrilled by another grandchild, confronted her with the demands to go home and stay there, or he'll disinherit her. She screamed how much she loved Dave, that her life had no meaning without him, and no threats could or would change her mind. Dave wouldn't give her up too, not so eager to dismiss all that money so easily. Maybe everything would finish better, but Tiffany didn't depend on Brandon's money. Her grandmother left her a substantial amount to use as she please. Tiffany almost forgot about the money, but now in desperation she remembered."

"This time was terrible for George. He never loved her as a man should love his wife, but for such a proud and important man this last humiliation was too much. Laura came with accusations that his lack of feelings drove her daughter in search of love elsewhere. She was going on and on, making George the villain and her *poor child* a victim. That was the only time I saw George lose temper. He turned to her, and with cold voice snapped that her lack of feelings and of motherly care had turned her daughter into a selfish brat."

"A week later Tiffany and Dave vanished. Brandon's health worsened, and within a year he died of heart failure. For two years nobody heard a word from the fugitives, nor did anybody know where they were. Even Chuck swore he knew nothing about his brother and Tiffany. But just between us, I never believed him. Then, Laura got a letter in which Tiffany explained that she and Dave spent all the Granny's inheritance. She begged her mother for money or she was afraid Dave would leave her. Laura, in her caustic manner, flatly refused to oblige and suggested that she should find a job to support her lover. After a few weeks, Tiffany showed up at her mother's home, to beg in person, but again, Laura in her ice queen fashion refused."

"Apparently, when Tiffany called Dave to tell him about her unsuccessful mission, he told her that he had no use of her without the money. She pleaded for him to be patient, but he knew Laura all too well. As long as she was alive, he'd have a zero chance of seeing Brandon's money. Tiffany rushed back to wherever he was, but he vanished without a trace. Next day Laura got a call informing her of Tiffany's suicide attempt. Instead of going to see her own child, she marched here trashing the news into George's face, coldly informing him that his wife was still his problem."

"Again, George had to pick up and put together the broken pieces of Tiffany's life. For months she lingered throughout the house like a ghost. The liquor was taken away, and she was all the time under someone's supervision".

"Laura stayed away, but the gossip went wild about Tiffany's condition, so one day Laura showed up after dinner with an announcement. We gathered in the great room to hear the ultimatum put to Tiffany. If she didn't pull herself together, forget all about that "pig", and became a normal wife and mother, Laura would change the will leaving everything to Andrew and Lindsay. In other words, Tiffany will never see a dime of Brandon's wealth. After her mother left, Tiffany cried and let hysterics make her sick again. I couldn't believe, she still hoped to get that cold bastard back when she inherits the ranch!"

"I think that was the moment when George gave up. Several days of thinking about the consequences of her mother's threats, Tiffany decided the best thing for her would be to go with the flow. I have to admit, she tried. Most of her time she spent with the children which gave George hope that things could change for the better in time, and they could be a real family."

"Tiffany always needed a lot of attention and admiration, and in lack of any other admirer she spread her web over George. That's how she became pregnant with Mark. Several months later Laura had an almost fatal fall from the horse. For weeks she lingered between life and death. Nobody believed she'll ever recover. That was the precise time Dave "The Leach" chose to show up again. What I always suspected was true – Chuck was regularly informing him about everything. His black, calculating heart figured that Laura was as good as dead, and Tiffany is again a rich woman, therefore very desirable.

"He needed less than half an hour to twist her brain and convince her that he left because he couldn't take care of her as she deserves and give her what she was accustomed to. That same day she asked George for a divorce. I thought at the time that was the best idea she ever had in her life, but George refused. First, she had to promise to stay in the house without meeting Dave until the child was born, then she had to sign, before filing for divorce custody of the children to him without any visitation rights, and second, she will sell the Brandon's ranch to him, and finally she'll live somewhere far away and never come back."

"But, once more, destiny dealt the cards against Dave. Although George instructed people who cared for Laura not to tell her any of this, some Good Samaritan always finds the way to do the opposite. When Laura realized that her daughter and Dave were just waiting for her to die, take everything she fought her whole life for, she promptly got better. Doctors couldn't believe her miraculous recovery, neither could Dave. Tiffany went to visit her mother to see for herself if the rumors about her restored health was true. When she got there, Laura was in the process of changing her will with two lawyers, a psychiatrist and her three doctors as witnesses of her mental and physical well-being. Tiffany collapsed right then and there of stress. Fortunately for her it happened in the hospital. Mark was prematurely delivered, but Tiffany lost all will for life. She realized that her mother would never let her have Brando's wealth, and Dave would never have her without it. I think she knew what a beast that man was, but she was totally obsessed with him.

George stepped in again. He explained to her that she was too young and strong to die just lying there, and that he had a solution for all of them. The suggestion was that they will get divorced, and he'll give her enough alimony to make Dave happy, but she has to go and never come back. She accepted and Dave knew that it would be all he'll ever get, so he agreed too."

"Tiffany recovered enough in two weeks to leave the hospital, and divorce proceedings will soon be finalized. But, Dave just couldn't let go. His greed was not under his control any more. Knowing that nothing will work with George, he turned to Samuel. While working on the ranch, Dave often rode with Samuel, and he knew the paths the old man frequented. One morning he followed him up the mountain in hopes he'll be more compliant, but he was wrong. Samuel suffered his whole marriage because of the wrong choice he made, his friend Brandon lived with a woman who could and would never love him, and now his son living a nightmare. He decided it was time that somebody said no! When Dave started with threats that if he didn't came up with some serious money, he'd convince Tiffany to sue George for custody of the children. That was pulled out of Chuck afterwards, because nobody know for sure what had happened. The police reconstructed the event according to the tracks. Samuel probably got mad and refused. Who started the fight we'll never know, but we know who did win. Dave threw the older man over the cliff. When Samuel was found it was too late."

"Dave, in the meantime, rushed back to Tiffany, hoping that nobody would figure that he was with Samuel. But, unfortunately for him, some cowboys were fishing that day, and after Samuel was found dead, they reported they saw two of them riding together."

"Not knowing if Samuel was found by someone, Dave was nervous and on the lookout the whole day. When the police car pulled up in front of the hotel where he and Tiffany were staying, he ordered her in the car and they took off. That was one of the most dramatic chases of Sheridan police department, not that they ever had one before. That unfortunate madness finished on the bottom of the Minor's Canyon. It was awful! The car exploded, like in the movies. Both of them were killed on impact, and then burned beyond recognition."

"Well, that is the ugly story, I'm not surprised that George never wanted to talk about it. Since he married you, he is a changed man. I haven't seen him so relaxed and happy since he was a little boy. That is until recently. What happened Patricia? Something must have happened during the Fourth of July fireworks. I know it is none of my business, but…" As Millie finished, she wondered what Patricia was thinking. She just listened without interruption, and without exhibiting any emotions. Millie wasn't sure what to think. Was Patricia shocked? Disappointed? And, for providence sakes, what is going on between those two?

It looked as though Millie would not get her answers today after all. Patricia got up and left.

CHAPTER 13

Patricia finally understand! Now she knows why he would not let himself fall in love, why he did not want to listen to her explanation about Chuck, why he will not ever let himself trust anybody, especially not her. She was practically running down to the stables, and for the first time she rode by herself. The confinement of one place was unbearable, made her jittery and nervous. She needed to think, think, think. *Millie was upset enough as it is, and if she sees me going to pieces like this, the poor woman will become a crackpot like me.*

Ferocious shudders of cry could not stop for eons. Vivid pictures of George's life were creating a chaotic mess inside her mind. She always thought about his perfect first marriage, irreplaceable love, loving mother of his children. And now, this haunting image which she blamed for George's incapability to love again, turned into the worst nightmare. Patricia always hoped he would put his great marriage and love for his wife in the past, where they belong and find some feelings for her. He would never allow his feeling to be involved. She could picture a little George watching his parents and their unusual loveless relationship. His college experiences, according Tim, were probably disastrous. Selfish self-centered women like Alicia confirmed his childhood experience.

Most likely this indignation led to the wrong choice of a wife. He probably thought that any woman would do as a wife and a mother, so he married one his family wanted. Patricia's heart shriveled in pain. Her tremendous love for George developed a new dimension. Now she understands his decision not to marry until he met her, a not-so-attractive, uncomplicated spinster, who did not have many prospects in her life, neither a natural inclination toward flirtation and men.

His anger finding her in another man's arms was understandable now, under the different light. The horrid thought stricken her – that man was none else but Dave's brother. Her heart quivered with new waves of pain, regret and sorrow. What could she do now? He began to relax in her company, the children accepted her as a mother, which George acknowledged several times with pleasure. She became accustomed to country life beyond her wildest dreams. *I'll never have that again! There is no way to recover that fragile trust he started to develop in her. I'll just die!*

To make things even more complicated, her sister was coming! Elongated evening shadows warned her that it was time for going back. If George and the kids came home before her, who knows what he will make of it. Unfortunately, her fears were not without the reason. When she hastily ran into the kitchen, six pairs of eyes were fixed on her. George's frown projected disgust and impatience, but he did not say a word.

"You went riding?" Lindsay asked Patricia, she nodded sliding in her place at the table. "I never knew that you ride alone!"

"I do sometimes!" She stuttered. To avoid further uncomfortable questions she asked about their day in school. The conversations turned into a normal everyday routine, and glimmer of her eye, from time to time in George's direction, confirmed her fear that he was even gloomier then she expected.

That evening George chose, instead of his usual fast retreat through the room to the bathroom door, to remain beside the closed door thinking for a moment.

"I thought, I was perfectly clear the other night that I don't want you to go around meeting your lover. I think you can show that much respect…"

"Damn you George!" Patricia almost screamed, which caused his head to jerk in surprise, "Respect? You don't know the meaning of the word! You accused me of being a slut, never giving me a chance to tell the truth. But I know now that you would never believe me, so I'll have to live with that. But I won't stand by passively while you take the liberty of insulting me. I would never insult *myself* by sneaking around with your hired help. Therefore, I won't let you insinuate such a thing. You may go ahead and think whatever you like, but keep it to yourself!" She was so upset that her voice was shaking, just like her whole body did. She furiously stared into his eyes challenging him, and then turned on her heels and marched out onto the balcony.

If I stay with him a minute longer, I will lose it and tell him how much I love him, and that would be the worst scenario. He will just have one more thing to accuse me of - being a manipulative bitch. The delicate smell of the climbing roses calmed her a little bit, and she felt the pangs of a bad conscience. Knowing his first wife's habits, she could hardly blame him for thinking that history repeats itself, but the pain of the realization that he did not know her at all, that he never took the time to get to know her, triggered the flow of tears. If he ever even tried, he would know she had nothing in common with Tiffany, or any woman from his past. The tears were rolling down her cheeks unnoticed. She did not know any more who was to be pitied more, she or that damn man. And her sister was coming! Oh, *Holly caw!*

And, there they were. Tim – tall, smiling, Francesca, beautiful as ever, looking around in an attempt to see it all at once, Timmy and Puppet, frantically running to their aunt's embrace. The whole staff were on their toes, including three new girls hired as reinforcement for Mille, who was determined to show those pompous easterners what western hospitality was. The food was so fabulous that Tim shamelessly flirted with Millie, exaggerating immensely. Millie was taken in by his charms, made her cooking for him dishes she forgot she knew. He would listen with an open mouth to her stories about her mother and grandmother's recipes created out of almost nothing, such treats as their seventeen ways of preparing jack rabbit, which in many occasions was the only accessible meat, potato pie, corn bread.

Francesca was bustling around from the moment she arrived. Wanting to see everything and meet everybody was understatement. The second after they arrived, she made Patricia give her a detailed tour of the house and gardens. Francesca was enchanted with an outdoor pool, indoor pool, conservatory and especially cowboys.

The children were in a frenzy having so much fun. They were running up and down the property with Peter the whole day, who took it upon himself to teach those "city slickers" something about real life.

George tried his best to act like nothing had changed between Patricia and himself, not that anybody paid any attention to them anyway. Their guests enjoyed themselves so much that they would not have noticed if they openly fought, which put Patricia a little bit at ease.

They had been at the ranch already a week and their stay could not be better. The kids were watching some karate movie for who knows how long, while the two couples occupied themselves in the great room in content, easygoing conversation.

"What do you think Patricia, can I go into the kitchen and beg for another piece of pie?" Tim was lovingly caressing his stomach, sporting a satisfying grimace on his face.

"Tim, for heaven's sake, you'll have to buy a whole new wardrobe if you don't stop stuffing yourself as a pig!" Francesca studied him with a disapproving grin and disgust on her face. Patricia laughed, "Dear sister, let him be! I was the same way when I first got here. Millie's cooking is absolutely irresistible, everybody thinks so! Right George?"

Leisurely stretched beside Patricia, not touching her, his arm laid behind her shoulders on the sofa rest. They looked like a content married couple, even to Patricia, who knew how far that was from the truth.

"Well, I've been on her food since I was born, and for me, there is nothing better in the world than her food. Often people try to steal her from us, which she takes as a compliment, but many times I didn't take it so casually. Tim, my boy, I urge you to get some more of that pie, if not for any other reason than the next several days you'll be feasting on my diet in the confines of the mountains. And let me warn you, I never took a single lesson from Millie. Hahaha!"

Oh, damnation, I almost forgot about that, Patricia quivered inside. Three days in a small cabin, without the children and the rest of the household, they will be more visible. *I simply must speak with George and warn him.*

But she fell asleep before George passed through her room. In the morning things were so frantic that she found herself in the saddle before being aware that she was awake. Francesca was excited and nervous. She recently, in the light of coming to cowboy country, took riding lessons, which was a miracle of its own.

"George, I am warning you, I won't have another wild horse like you served me with last time!" Tim has been shouting from the moment he first opened his eyes, "First, I'm much older! My poor bones won't survive your pranks this time. Second, you have to take under consideration that I'm now a married man with two small children, and I would like to have more of them too. And third, one bruise, scratch or tender muscle, I'll kill you, George!" He suspiciously walked around the saddled horse, staring at the stable boys searching for the smallest hint or sign of some conspiracy. If he had been a little less apprehensive he would see that the young men were engrossed in helping his beautiful wife mount her horse, giving her endless advises and suggestions, not paying the slightest attention to him.

Half an hour later, the little group headed for their destination. Four riders and two overloaded llamas disappeared behind the hill. The day was brilliant, and riding through the woods saturated with the enchanting smell of sage, pine needles and freshly disturbed dirt under the horses' hoofs was more than pleasant.

Conversation was scarce. The rarely used path allowed only one rider at a time. Besides that, George was taking care of two llamas, while Tim was still worried that his horse would suddenly show his true nature and turn into a wild stallion.

"Tim, I never knew that my big handsome brother-in-law was such a chicken!" Patricia could not restrain herself any more – she burst into laughter.

"Oh yeah, you disappointed me too, Patricia! That demon you married turned, the nicest and most generous girl that ever existed, into an unfeeling desperado!" Everybody were suppressing their chuckles, but Tim did not care what they thought, continuing to scrutinize his horse.

"Tim, that is an old mare, not a stallion. And, if I remember well, the "Boys" told me she was the mellowest horse we ever had, even when she was young. So, you have nothing to worry about!"

"Look at her Tim! She is a girl and you hurting her feelings." Patricia could not resist.

The noon sun, peeking through the branches of the tall pine trees, enhanced the discomfort of the long ride, George mercilessly refused to let them rest, although they begged for it. He insisted if they dismount they would not be able to get back in the saddle again, and sleeping under the cold mountain sky is not an adventure they were ready for.

In the late afternoon, the group finally caught a glimpse of a small cabin situated on the bank of the shimmering creek. George was right about aching muscles and sore bones. Francesca, after practically falling off the saddle, walked on stiff legs, holding her bottom, bewailing, "I'll never sit on that damn horse, or any horse for as long as I live, If I ever survive this. Tim's right, Patricia, you are one unfeeling ruthless woman. Is this some sort of revenge for whatever I did to you in the past. Oh-h-h-h, my poor sore legs! I'm not able to use my hips."

She drugs herself to the stairs in front of the cabin and then stopped there, thinking what would be more excruciating, to sit or to stand?

Tim felt the same, but being so happy that the ride was over for now and still being in one piece, did not complain too much. The other two were unloading the llamas, worriedly watching their guests.

"Don't worry, Francesca, it will pass in no time. Just walk around a little." Patricia tried to comfort her sister.

"Walk? What do you mean walk? I can't move. I can't sit. I can't stand. But, damnation, if you don't stop trying to patronize me, I'll find that much energy to strangle you. Oh-h-h!" Her voice showed that she did have enough strength, and will recuperate in no time. Francesca debated for a moment, then decided that it would be easier to do what Patricia suggested, then to sit on the most painful part of her body.

When the last of the sun light disappeared in full glory of deep reds and oranges, everything was unpacked, sorted, and dinner was ready. Francesca and Tim felt much better, discovering that hunger is as unpleasant as long rides.

"Oh, what is it, George? Smells heavenly!" Tim poked his nose into the kettle.

"I swear he doesn't think about anything else on the side of his stomach?" Francesca looked at her husband as he was some alien from outer space, "If I ever file for divorce, that will be the reason. I can picture him twenty years from now, one big sloppy walrus, blubber and all!"

"Oh woman, be quiet! I'm in great shape, and you know it, which by the way, I'll prove it tonight!" He looked at her with a comical expression of lusty seducer, which made both sisters burst in laughter.

Tim acted as if his feelings were hurt, so he turned to George.

|"Old boy, tell me how much that small bed up there can endure. I'm afraid you'll need to haul a new one after I'm finished with that insulting girl tonight!" The girls' hysterical laughter made George laugh too, although he tried to keep a straight face.

"Those are serious promises Tim, are you sure you are up to it?" Francesca provocatively blinked at her husband, "Maybe I'll hold you to that, so stop fussing and save your energy to avoid any possible disaster!"

After dinner, George built a fire in the cabin's fireplace. It was summertime, but being so high in the mountains, the nights could be fresh and even cold. The fire generated the only light in the room. Warm dreamy shadows on the walls enhanced the coziness and contentment of the small group.

"Are you sure that you and Patricia will be comfortable here? I didn't even think about the size of this dwelling. You always refer to it as a 'small cabin', but -" Tim started.

"Oh, don't worry about us!" George smiled, "We'll stretch out our sleeping bags in front of the fire place. I've taken Patricia several times camping. We've slept on the ground beside the fire. And it was, if I remember well, a great experience!" His voice gave the description of a double meaning. Tim looked at Patricia with an uplifted eyebrows, which made her blush.

"That reminds me that I have some unfinished business with my wife. The sooner I start the sooner she'll have to apologize!" Tim got up, pulling tired Francesca onto her feet.

"George feel free to be naughty as it suits you, this big pompous Casanova will fall asleep faster that he talks!" Francesca chuckled, but it was clear she'd be asleep just as fast, "And tomorrow morning don't try to show me the sunrise, I would rather be awakened in the blissful light of noon!" Her significant stare at George make him nod.

"Okay, okay! I'll be silent as a mouse!" He looked after the couple until their door closed, "Let's move this coffee table, so we can spread out our sleeping bags!" He started to collect knick-knacks from the table top.

"George, both of us don't need to sleep beside the fire, so why move everything. I can spread my bag beside that wall."

"Don't be silly, Patricia! What would your family think if either of them gets in here during the night and find us in that loving distance? Just come over here and help me!" He sounded impatient, and Patricia a little bit tired of the physical strain of the day and extreme exhaustion of constantly pretending that things were what they were not, so she grabbed the table on the other end and lifted. They worked in silence. Some brief instruction broke the reticence of the space. Although they assumed the impression of calmness, the tension was building. Patricia glanced around. *I knew that the cabin was small, but I didn't notice, until now, how small. The space between the fireplace, sofa, armoire, and that stupid stand with a falling-apart saddle, was barely enough for two sleeping bags closely put together.*

I dreamed about something like this, but George would never… Why does he have to be so stubborn? How am I going to survive this, I wonder.

"Well, I think there is some warm water left in that barrel. Go ahead and use it, I'll walk to check on the animals and go down to the creek. Cold water always soothes my nerves!"

Patricia studied the most primitive shower on the planet. A big barrel was affixed on the roof of the porch. From the side protruded an old rusty showerhead. *This rope must have some purpose,* she thought, so she yanked it. The splash of lukewarm water startled her for a moment. She chuckled. The shower did not last long, but refreshed her. She pulled a long tee shirt over her head. *Very sexy Patricia,* she chuckled again. *Who cares? My husband made it very plain he's not interested, so I'll just go squeeze myself into my cozy sleeping bag, and the hell with everything.*

Both of them entered the cabin at the same time. She in her oversized tee, he bare chested in wet jeans. Patricia frowned. *Damn, he looks gorgeous and sexy, and I like an old farm madden.*

"You look -"

"Ridiculous!" She looked down at her *gown.*

"Great!" He finished, walking toward her. *Great? Is he losing his marbles?* With a fascination of a trapped animal, Patricia watched him approaching. *If he does not stop I will, against my better judgment run into his arms.*

The next moment she *was* in his arms, being almost sure that she did not run into them. He crushed her chest against his, and she was lost. His kiss was not gentle, neither did she want it to be. Long repressed passion erupted beyond their comprehension. She knew it will bring regrets tomorrow, but for now, all she wanted was to be near him, feel his arms, lips, his body close to her. *Closer.*

The flames in the fire place slackened, but not the fire between the rumpled sleeping bags. Sometime during the night she half awakened just enough to realize she was still in George's arms, tightly pressed to his long hard body. She snuggled closer like a cat and fell asleep again.

Francesca was right - she and Tim did not creep out of their bedroom until noon. Of course, George was up first, taking care of the horses and llamas, and then peacefully worked on the fishing poles, having fun in advance picturing Francesca fly fishing. When Patricia poked her head out of the door, he was still smiling.

"What do you think will be the best time to start breakfast?" That was good reason to get out and check in what kind of the mood George was in.

"What I think is that those two won't get out of their bed at least for a couple of hours, or more. So, we can have some snack if you are hungry, and then - don't sweat over it. We are on vacation after all. Breakfast at noon, lunch at six, and dinner under the stars at midnight – sounds very good to a man on a tight schedule all the time!" *Thanks, dear stars, he sounded lighthearted and content.* The heavy load dropped off her heart. He, obviously, did not regret last night nor blamed everything on her as she fearfully expected.

Time flew. Experiencing all sorts of activities, they never tried before which make time go fast while having ultimate fun. On their way home, the predicted discomfort was taken on the fun side. Tim forgot about wild horses, endlessly bragging about the "huge" trout he caught.

That last week, her family had a great time, and Patricia enjoyed it much more. Although, George did continue to treat her in a friendly manner, he did not come back to her bed once they were home.

The night they got back, he accompanied her upstairs, and by the way he held her elbow she knew that there was something on his mind. He slowly closed the door, scratching his forehead.

"Patricia, I must apologize for… for my behavior up at the cabin. I never came around to tell you about my first marriage mainly because it's not a very nice story. I should…"

For a moment Patricia entertained the idea of letting him tell it, but she knew she would break down in tears, running to him and professing her undying love, before he would really start the narrative. And, she could not bear the thought to put him through those painful memories, although he would deserve it.

"I know!" she interrupted. His whole body stiffened. Motionless, he stared into her eyes for a long time. Patricia saw all the pain and frustration he buried deep within himself, "I asked Millie after the Fourth of July party, after you found me with… You did not even want to hear what I had to say. I knew then, there had to be a bigger reason than just finding me being pawed by some - So, I had to know what it was?" He still did not move. She just waited to see what happened next.

"You know. Good! Than you understand why I can't go through that all over again. Please let me finish!" George raised his hand, to stop Patricia from interrupting again," Since that damn party, I was positive that I had made a mistake in marrying you. I mean marrying again, in general. But, seeing Francesca and Tim so happy, my kids adore you, not to mention all the cowboys and stuff. Millie thinks you are a package from God. What I want to say, it was not a mistake from that point of view, but I can't put myself in a situation, you understand"

Patricia listened, getting more upset with every word.

"Now, you listen to me George!" She hardly restrain herself from exploding, "I know what your wife did to you, and I'm thrilled you think that marrying me is not *complete* mistake. All that I'm hearing here is what *you* can, what *you* can't, what is it that *you* want or do not want. Everything is about you, you, you! You never had that much decency to let me explain, putting me in the same bucket with Tiffany. If you don't want me, I can live with that, but I will not allow you or anybody else to insult me like you just did. I'm not in the habit of going around flinging myself on strange men! You go and think whatever makes you feel good and justify your bad behavior. According to you, the rest of the people here love me, so all of them are wrong? They do not see the sinister side of me, as you do. Do what you want, but you will never insult me again with your unsupported accusations!" His expression snagged from determination to bewilderment, "And now, George, will you be so nice as to leave my room. I'm tired! Thank You!" She slowly turned and entered the bathroom.

The next morning, her sister took back her family back East, leaving Patricia almost in the same situation as she was before her guests came. One thing was different though - she equaled the score with George. Not that anything changed in their intimate life, but he stopped frowning and acting like a bore. She finally made peace with George's decision about their relationship, concentrating on her book, kids and taking more time for herself.

Taking some time for herself was a novelty in Patricia's life. She had always been involved in other people lives, pulled or pushed in all kinds of activities which had nothing to do with her own desires or interests. She decided to pay attention to what she wanted. Writing was one of those things. She started her second African adventure book, which she did with more enthusiasm, viewing it as fun and fulfillment, and not an obligation as what others wanted her to do. The result was Paula's overwhelming praise after she read the first three chapters.

"My dear, never better. Never better. You were always good, but this is something else. I don't know what is the reason, but my guess would be that marriage agrees with you!" You would, Patricia thought, wondering what Paula would think if she knew that my marital disaster is that great catalyst for my improvement. "And, when I'm on the subject on marriage, you'll never guess – our wonder boy got a boot. Yes, Michael was abandoned by his spoiled wife. She could not endure his foolishness any longer. He is now in the state of hating every female in the world. Professionally, though, he is as good as ever. We are just preparing the book he illustrated. The author is happy with his work, but the poor woman almost went berserk working with him. He makes me loony, too. I'm puzzled how you managed to work with him without problems?" *Old same Paula, completely engrossed in her work.*

Patricia changed her ways with the children, too. With the two older kids, she stopped being so protective, but with Mark she did the opposite. His habit of acting as he is way older than was excepted by everybody as a matter of fact, not knowing how to change it - she decided that was unnatural, and it was high time for him to be a small child. Consequently, every time she had an urge to hug him, or kiss him, or pamper him as a little boy should be, she did just that. For a while he, just as everybody else, was surprised, a little annoyed, but then he got used to it. He got used to it so much that in time he would climb into her lap, snuggle comfortably, letting her kiss him and squeeze him as much as she wanted.

The biggest change in her life was indulging in every little thing that crossed her mind. Riding was one of them. She knew that George did not like her going alone, but she could care less. He thinks of her the worst anyway, so what more damaging can come out of it. In August she went twice in L.A. More to spend some time with Moraine than to shop. When she did shop, it was not so much for clothes, but she browsed through antique shops, art galleries, ending up having coffee in some pleasant little coffee shop. Moraine was fun companion, easygoing and engaging. All of that made her feel that her life is not a complete flop. *I have my kids, my friends and my career. I never expected to have any of that, so I have a better and a fuller life than I ever expected. That has to be enough for me.*

Every time she came back, George would look at her in that strange way of his. She could not decide is it reproach or apprehension. She knew very well that he entertained the thought she took his suggestion to go somewhere else in search of a love affair, or was it just to visit a good friend as she claimed? He did not know her, not really. He never tried to get to know her, and the best way to make him do that was to intrigue his imagination. After long soul searching, Patricia perceived that the only way she will ever have her husband back would be if he fell in love with her. Men usually fall in love with woman who intrigue them, and recently, she was sure he was intrigued. Good! Idea was not so farfetched! Michael believed he was in love with her. Then Tim; she even married to stop that stillness. To be mysterious and patient was her strategy.

CHAPTER 14

It was hot for the end of September. *My birthday is in two weeks! I will be thirty-three. Not young anymore, but far from being old.* She halted the horse on the top of the hill. The view of the mountains was still taking her breath away. Ancient in their beauty, huge, endless, wild. They crept into her heart, filling her chest with some primal tide of grandeur of nature's creation. It was a strange unknown country when she first came, but now it felt like she belongs here. This was her home.

She smiled. As a matter of fact, since this morning a smile had been a permanently chiseled on her lips. Patricia could not remember when she was happier in her whole life. For a whole week she suspected, but this morning it was clear – she is pregnant. With George's baby! He would doubt it, she was sure, but it could not lessen her delight. The baby was a result of the mountain excursion with Francesca and Tim. For as long as she could remember she wanted a baby, and for the same duration she was sure it would never happen. Then she got three wonderful kids, but the baby of her own! In the beginning of her intimacy with George, she hoped, but when she asked her gynecologist why she did not conceive yet, his answer was discouraging. In a very polite way he told her that a woman of her age, being sexually inactive for so long, would need some time to awaken her body's natural purpose. The suggestion was to be patient, which she translated it as a nice way of telling her to forget all about being a mother. She did just that, until a couple a weeks ago. Her first morning sickness was taken with surprise. Ordinarily she was hardly ever sick, and the food in Millis kitchen almost walked by itself into the pot, so the next morning, during violent vomiting, Patricia knew in her heart of a hearts, she was going to have a baby. In the beginning her rational side did not dare to hope, but now there was not a shred of doubt. Question was how and when she will tell the news to George and the rest of her family? She will tell him first alone, and then together announce the good news? That would be wise, because she expected a wild reaction from him, definitely not a pleasant one. To spare the rest of people she loves of that undesirable scene was a priority. But maybe it would be wise to share her delicious secret in front of everybody, he will not be inclined to strangle her, at least not immediately.

Something made her turn around. She could not pinpoint what. Was it a sound, or movement, or just intuition? Nothing was to be seen. *Maybe some animal,* she thought, and turned back to admire the countryside, visualizing her body swelling in time, definitely becoming ugly, but she did not mind.

Patricia turned again. This time it was a noise for sure coming from a small clump of pine trees. *A movement. It is a horse. A horseman, but who?* All the cowboys were miles away rounding up the cattle on the most eastern part of the ranch, George and the kids are in Sheridan, and Peter did not ride any more, complaining about rheumatism.

The rider slowly entered the open hilltop. *Chuck!* It looked like him. Gossip flourished that George had fired him, and everybody was burning to know why. He disappeared without a trace.

The horseman advanced slowly. It *was Chuck! What on the earth was he doing here,* she wanted to know, but some sick feeling in her stomach screamed a warning. Whatever it is, it could not be anything good.

He halted his horse several yards from her.

"Hey, Patricia!" He said with a grin, "You look exceptionally beautiful today. I see, you knew I'd find a way for us to be together!" Patricia stared at him not believing her ears. Is it possible that he actually thinks she wanted to see him, to be with him?

"Old man George thought he'd get rid of me just by dismissing me as I'm a bell boy!" He chuckled, looking at her under hooded eyes. Patricia could not move. Her brain worked at lightning speed, trying to figure out if he was joking or is he was completely crazy. Her first impulse to laugh was suppressed. Instinct alerted all her senses. *If this is not a joke, it can be dangerous to provoke him.*

"Why, Chuck, I thought you were long gone!" She tried to sound casual all the time, studying him carefully.

"No way, sweetheart, I couldn't leave you heartbroken!" Leisurely he dismounted, flicking his hat up with forefinger. Smiling, he stretched his arms in a motion to help her off her horse. She hesitated.

"Chuck, it was nice to see you, but I'm expected home soon, so…" Chuck reached higher, placing his hands on her waist, and with no effort pulled her down beside him.

"Why should you worry about them? You are with me now!" He tightened his grip on her waist, pulling her closer.

"I'm not sure what you mean by that!" Fear stopped her impulse to push him away.

"You and I baby are going away to live happily ever after!" When she first met him, his lazy way of talking seemed interesting, but now made her skin crawl.

"Chuck, please, I still don't understand what you're talking about!" Devastating realization flushed through her body as a doomsday wave. *Something terrible is going to happen.*

He laughed with enjoyment, let go of her and in some sort of dancing stapes approached his horse. "Then let me enlighten you, my dear Patricia!" He snatched his saddle bag off, opened it in from of her face. She peeked in.

"Chuck? Where did you get all this money?" She gasped.

"I took it from your husband. He owns is to you, I figured. Wasn't enough that he made one woman miserable? He had to do it all over again! Dave and Tiffany were not fortunate enough. But sweetheart, we will be!" Suddenly he sounded feverish and incoherent.

"How… how did you do it?" She whispered terrified. She shivered, *did he hurt George!*

"Old George is working, making more money! Nobody was at the house. I watched you leave, and I knew you'd be out for a long time, as" - He looked at her significantly -" You've been riding a lot lately, thinking about me no doubt. Oh, how many times I wanted to talk to you, while you were riding, but all those smelly cowboys were everywhere I didn't dare. It could spoil everything for us. I knew that Old George would send a sheriff with all his deputies from five counties to hunt me down. You see." He chuckled sadistically, making her tremble with fear and disgust, "He holds some grudge against the Malloy boys!"

Grudge? You crazy unfeeling brut, but how did he get hold of George's money? Feir shook her soul.

"Chuck, you still didn't explain about the money?" Patricia became acutely aware that Chuck is a seriously disturbed man. If she could only understand what sick plan he masterminded, she'll be in a better position to outsmart him.

"In a moment, my dear. One little kiss, like on the Fourth of July, Hah?"

She pushed him slightly, speaking fast. "I can't think or do a thing until I know everything!" She smiled, trying to look less apprehensive.

"You are so beautiful, I can't refuse you a anything. As I said, you went out riding, and while I watched the house, Millie and Peter headed for their cottage. In that moment the streak of brilliance made me realize this was my, our chance! I snuck into the house. I remembered Tiffany once telling Dave about George's safe stuffed with money. She did blabber about his reasons for having so much money in cash at home, but I didn't listen. Then and there I knew this little bit of information would come in handy one day. Well, when I got into the house, I tried to remember where she said the safe was. Logically and more likely, it would be in the office or library. And, I was right again!" He exclaimed triumphantly. Patricia looked at him in horror. *He is mad!*

"The safe was, as you probably know, behind that ugly painting of old Samuel. How original! I can see on your face, you're thinking, how on earth did I open it? A fast movement and his big gun appeared in his hand, "One precise shot, and that miserable excuse for a safe popped wide open in front of me!" He took a small baw with a self-satisfied smirk on his handsome face, interpreting her stunned expression as approval and admiration. Hundreds of questions ran through her head, but she didn't dare to ask a single one.

"I know what you are thinking! How much? It was no time to count, but by the look of the pile, between two and three hundred thousand!" His raised eyebrows expected a response of delight and esteem.

"But that's robbery!" His frown alerted her wits, "Chuck, they'll put you in jail for a long time."

He laughed maliciously. "Nobody will put *me* in jail! I'm too clever for them. I'm too clever for Old George, too!" He stepped nearer, reaching for her elbows, "You and I baby, we'll first go to Canada and from there on to Hawaii!"

"But, I don't even have my driver license with me! I can't go anywhere without some identification!" Her hopes rose. If she got a chance to convince him of the necessity to let her go for her documents, and maybe some clothes, she'll…

"As I told you before," he interrupted her with satisfying smirk, "I thought of everything! After I snatched the money, I knew that was our chance to be together. In that precise moment the whole plane popped in my head, Canada, Hawaii and then South America! So, I ran upstairs to your bedroom. To find your purse was a snap. The passport took me some time, but while I searched your closet for it, I took some of your warmer clothes!" He waved toward another, heavily loaded horse.

Patricia's heart sunk. Realization hit her that the load contains, besides her clothes, everything for a long outing. Her attempt to outsmart him was pointless, but she just couldn't give up.

"You must be aware that George will alarm the police! Every road will be watched, including airports and bus stations. They will find us, sooner or a latter!" Reasoning seemed a good idea.

"You think I didn't consider that? We won't use no roads! We'll reached Canada through the Rockies. I know these mountains like the back of my hand. It will be like a long camping trip. And we can turn it into a honeymoon!

His significant glance, full of expectation and promise, curled her toes. Hope of a swift resolution faded fast, but the next statement destroyed the last hope she had that George will send some men after them to save her.

"After George reads your message, he would not want to see you ever again. He was willing to pay to get rid of his first wife, after her little pranks with my brother. He will just let you have the money being happy not to see you again!"

"My... My massage?" She whispered with a sinking heart. Like a cold shower it struck her that George already believed in her involvement with Chuck, and seeing this horrid man for what he really was, she didn't doubt for a second that the message was devastating.

"George! I can't stay any longer and pretend. I never loved you, and now that I found my one and only true love, I have to go after it. Kiss the kids and forget about the money. You owe it to me. Don't try to find me, Patricia." He recited the message with upmost pleasure.

Chuck swept her swiftly into his arms again, "I would love nothing more but to ravish you right here and now, but we have to go as far as we can today. Can't take a chance of meeting any of my *old friends*. Hahaha!" He pulled her short coat from the pack horse's backpack. "Hold on to this, it will soon be too cold for this fancy shirt of yours!" He mounted the horse in one swift move.

Patricia's brain searched for any possible chance for escape. She could try to outrun him, but he is a much better rider. To catch up with her would be a joke for him. The result would be - losing his trust, which could be dangerous. Caution with a crazy person is always wise. With all her heart she hoped that George *will* come after her, that he *will* not believe she was capable of writing such a note. But he will, like Chuck predicted, call the police, and they will concentrate on the main roads, airports, bus stations. George will never guess how Chuck's twisted brain works. She will have to rely solely on herself and her wit to outsmart this lunatic, or... Patricia could not even think about the consequences.

While riding, she discreetly scanned the horizon in hopes of seeing somebody, or to be seen, so George would have some leads. She stopped herself knowing that George would not even try to find her after he read the note. It's hopeless to expect help from anyone.

They rode fast until sundown. Chuck had in mind the camp side for that night, and it was far up the mountain. They had to gain time and significant distance as advantage from any possible pursue. While building a fire, Chuck chatted about the benefit of the camp site. Patricia did not catch the meaning of the words. She was devastated, and at this point did not care what he would do if he realizes that all she wanted was to be back home with her family.

"Oh, my poor Patricia! I'm a brut! You look totally exhausted! Of course, you are not used to such a long and hard ride. You are something else, you know that girl? Not a single word of complaint!" He hurriedly approached, "I'll fix your sleeping bag. What you need is a good night rest. Wait, first you have to eat something!"

"Please Chuck, I can't…"

"You have too, my darling! You'll need your strength tomorrow, and for the days to come. This is going to be a long and exhausting ride up to Canada. One thing I didn't take into consideration is that you are a city slicer and started riding not so long ago. You have to be patient and try as hard as you can, for us, my love! This is our only chance!"

A first flicker of hope shed a little light on her impossible situation. If she acted tired, he will at least leave her in peace with his amorous attempts.

"Okay, I'll eat, but I really need my rest even more If we want to get to Canada at all!" She tried to sound sincere.

For three endless hot days and three cold nights Patricia hoped they would be seen, and somebody would help her. Her little plot to pretend exhaustion kept Chuck physically at a distance. His endless blabbering about their blissful happiness made her sick and mad. His arrogance about her compliance with his preposterous plan was so absurd that even a child would laugh.

The fourth evening, after he built a fire and fixed dinner, Chuck handed her a coffee mug, lowering himself beside her.

"We've covered a lot of distance, and fortunately nobody has seen us. I knew which path to take. People come here only during hunting season. We have to be careful, though, which means it will take some time, but we'll reach Canada. Don't worry about that!" His arm crept around her shoulders. That made her twitch in revulsion.

"Chuck, please, I'm so tired, and -"

"Come on Patricia. You can't make me suffer any longer! You have no idea what it's doing to me having you here and not make love to you. Be merciful and give me a little smooch!" His other arm encircled her closer to him. Feverishly she searched for a way out.

"Yes Chuck, I do understand what you mean, but I never expected you to be so unimaginative. You know women way to well!" *Flattery can take you far, as Francesca used to say. To boost his sick ego could be useful,* "I want us to have a great time together, not like this!" She twitched her nose in disapproval, "Besides being tired, I'm dirty, achy, bitten by a million mosquitoes. I want it to be special, romantic. Like you said, Hawaii would be perfect. Imagine the beautiful evening breeze from the ocean, soothing music, good wine." While painting this magical picture, she noticed a self-satisfying smirk on his face.

"Yeah, that would be great. That *will* be great! You are right, I don't feel very affectionate myself, but I've wanted you for so long. Sometimes it feels as I'll explode!" He reluctantly moved away. She sighed with relief, realizing that this round was won, but how long will she be able keep him at a distance?

Four days of this torment passed. Deep down she nursed the flicker of hope that George will come after her. It was clear - that would never happen. This echoed inside of her mind, and she had to accept that at last.

The expression "broken heart" had full meaning for her now. The long-harbored wish that her husband would love her one day was shredded into small pieces, and she did not have the luxury of crying. And to cry was all she wanted, to curl up and cry herself to oblivion until the last conscious thought would leave her tormented mind.

Next morning while Chuck was fixing their breakfast, Patricia decided that nobody would help her but herself. In order to be able to do this, she cannot continue to work herself sick by worrying and fruitlessly hoping for some miracle - unobtainable miracle like George showing up and rescuing her.

Pretending to be still asleep she began developing a strategy.

It would be best to continue pretending exhaustion. That would achieve two purposes. First, Chuck would stop to be amorous, and second, he would not pay close attention to her. Not being under constant scrutiny will give her more of a chance to do something when the situation presents itself. Furthermore, she will lead him to believe that she is here voluntarily. It's better to keep him in a good mood until they reach Canada, and some inhabited place. As long as they are in the mountains there was not very much she could do. After all it seemed he knew a great deal about these mountains, and she absolutely nothing. If he chooses, he can keep her in the wilderness as long as he wanted, and that Is the last thing she can afford.

At that precise moment she opened her eyes startled. Something rushed beside her, scaring her out of her mind. An animal? The next moment she saw two figures rolling on the ground, dangerously close to the fire. *What is happening? Who is that man? Is it possible that somebody did come after her? No!* She could not raise her hopes just to be disappointed again! It might turn out that this one is worse than Chuck, if that is possible. Patricia struggled to see better what is going on. He looks like… Visibility was obstructed by the smoke from disturbed fire and the violent tugging, hitting and pulling.

George?

Is it possible? Her heart paused in desperate yearning for her husband.

The other man worked his way on top of Chuck, hitting his face ferociously with his fist over and over again. His back was exposed to Patricia's view, who urgently needed to see if it was George or just a stupid wish of her heart. She finally managed to get up, hastily rushing to see. The man turned. Her heart stopped.

"George!" She gasped for air. One swift move forward to fling herself into his arms, was cut by sheer fear - he might push her away, and she would die! George, still straddling the unconscious Chuck, was looking at her with some strange countenance. It seemed that both of them did not know what to do.

This awkward situation was broken by a sudden loud noise which whirled her around. The strong rotation of a helicopter propeller, besides the loud noise, produced a strong wind. George pushed her toward the forest, lifting a lifeless Chuck and followed her. The small meadow was just big enough for the powerful machine to land.

The sheriff jumped out, and started to run toward them bent over at his waist, holding his hat.

"George!" He yelled to cover the noise of the helicopter's engine and strong slicing of propeller's blades. "I specifically told you - No, I ordered you not to do anything by yourself, but wait for us! This was stupid, and you know it. Is he dead?"

"No, I just think I hit him one time too many!" George yelled back.

Once? Patricia looked at him mystified. She did not know what puzzled her more – his violent behavior, so atypical for him, or him trying to minimize the fist fight.

"Help me carry him to the helicopter!" The sheriff yelled, waving his hands in dismissal.

George nodded, grabbing Chuck under his arms. Patricia watched the two men carry a limp body. After they tossed him in, shortly exchanged several sentences, then the sheriff climbed in. The helicopter took off immediately after George reached her side.

They still looked skyward long after the noisy machine vanished. Apprehension was thick in the air. Patricia suddenly dropped to her knees. George huffed some horse sound, dropping beside her.

"Patricia, what is it? What's wrong?" His voice was saturated in fear.

"On nothing, George!" She breathed out, "I think it's just momentary release of five days of emotional overload!" She managed to smile.

"Of course! How can I be so stupid! You must have gone through hell, my poor darling!" George scooped her into his arms like a little girl, rocking her gently. *Darling? Did he just call me darling?*

"Unfortunately there was not enough space in the helicopter to take us all, so I suggested that we'll wait for them to return to pick us up. They're bringing a couple of cowboys to ride the horses back to the ranch." He was talking compulsively, stressed to the brink of endurance. "I don't know what I was thinking? I watched you yesterday evening how exhausted you were." His self-reproach would not slacken.

"Yesterday? You were here yesterday?" Patricia cried.

"Yes! We caught up with you yesterday, and -"

"We?"

"Joseph Bear, you know him, that old Indian who used to work for Brandon. He's a good tracker. Without him I would never have found you, Patricia. He looked in her eyes melting her heart and soul. She ached to hug him, tell him how much she loved him, and beg him to take her home and forget all this ever happened. But she did not dare. Her mind was running hundred miles per hour, this sudden dramatic rescue, by no one else than her husband, for what all her hopes were focused on. A million questions bubbled inside of her head

"Where is he now?" She asked looking around.

"Well, I better tell all. As I said, it was around noon when we spotted you. Originally, the sheriff suggested a big search party, but I was against it. Knowing Malloy, I was afraid he'll hurt you if he sensed he'd been tracked down. The sheriff agreed to let me go alone with Joseph, if I promised to call him when we found you, and not try anything alone!"

"You didn't kept your promise, George! Why did you attack that lunatic? People out of control, as he is, are very dangerous!" She started to see the whole reality of his action. He could have been killed. She shivered from a shear horrible thought.

"I couldn't stand it any longer watching you in the clutches of that…" He swore something under his breath, "When Chuck finally decided to stop last evening, I sent Joseph down to the nearest ranch to call the sheriff. I snuck closer to your camp, in case he… he.. Honestly I tried to keep my promise to the sheriff, not to try anything on my own, but when I saw you this morning peeking over your blanket to see what he was doing, the desperation in your eyes was too much. I attacked him, and that is that. The sheriff will give me a good lecture about it in time, but I prefer not to talk about it ever again!" He conclude.

"But why did you go after us?" the shock froze his features, which made her speak faster, "I mean, after you read my note, Chuck's note, I was sure you'll never want to see me again, much less come after us to rescue me?" The tension on her face made George shrug.

"The second I read it, I knew it wasn't you who wrote that note!" He said in disbelieve she would think otherwise.

"How did you know that?" Is it possible that he does know her, that he took time to study her enough to be *sure* in a second she could not write something like that.

"Patricia, you have been my wife long enough that, even me with all of my insecurities when wives are in question, I saw what kind of person you are. If you fell in love with somebody and wanted to leave me, you would have said it out straight into my face loud and clear. Further, you are the last person to break into my safe, and write such a stupid note. And, of course, I know perfectly well that you are financially independent with your inheritance and royalties from your books. Nobody here knows that, so whoever wrote it must have believed that you depend on me financially. So, after I read it, the question was, who did it and why? It was clear that you did not go of your free will. Somebody forced you! Essential thing was to figure out who was it, and what was the plan to do with you!" She calmed a little, so he propped her up, watching her closely.

"I suggest we eat breakfast now. Chuck was just about finished with it. Let's go and check it out!"

Patricia nodded, rising on her feet.

"You are right, I'm starving!" And she was. All the while she was with Chuck she had to force herself to eat, but now she could eat a whole cow.

The fire had been extinguished by the helicopter, but George hurried to make another one, refusing any help from Patricia.

"You just sit over there and don't move. The ordeal you went through would give most women a nervous breakdown. You are a strong woman, Patricia. Every day I discover something new about you, something wonderful!" He added quietly.

"George, I still don't understand how did you knew where to search for us? What made you think we were in the mountains?" She asked while they were eating their breakfast.

"It was not my first thought. After we alarmed the sheriff and police, they did their routine job of searching the airport and bus stations. The highway patrol was alarmed, but we couldn't figure which car you'd taken. All the cars and trucks on the ranch were there, but your horse was missing. That information made me think about mountains. Millie pointed out that you rode a lot lately, but never that long. That was when it hit me that the abductor used the horses and headed for the Rockies. Instantly I sent for Joseph. It didn't take him long to follow your tracks to the top of the hill. Following the other horses tracks to the ravine where somebody was camping for a long time. We were sure that you were stalked and took against your will. I was out of my mind not knowing who took you. Unfortunately, the tracking is not a fast process, and one can't track during the night. I couldn't help but think the worst. But then, I was hoping, knowing how witty you are, that you'll outsmart that creep, whoever he was! Oh Patricia, I went through hell of my own!" His searching gaze told him that what he didn't dare to ask. Patricia hurriedly put him at ease.

"Well, I did outsmart him a little. Can you believe the audacity of that man? He sincerely believed that I was in love with him! I can't imagine why? He was always fresh with me. I didn't want to tell anybody about that, although, I'm sorry for that now. I should have told you about his ridiculous behavior, but then everybody always makes those jokes about cowboys being big flirts, so I thought you'd think me silly. When you found me with him that night, you didn't want to hear what I had to say. You just jumped to the conclusion that I… that I… Oh George, I couldn't understand why you never let me explain." She choked a little, trying to push back tears.

"I know what kind of jerk I was, but I had had a bad experience… I should have told you a long time ago about my first wife." With a troubled heart she watched him struggle to find the words.

"I know!" She interrupted, "As you know, Millie told me the whole story about Tiffany!" He frowned, so she rushed on, "I asked her! As I said, I couldn't comprehend why you wouldn't let me to explain. I knew you well enough to know that you are not unfair. Had to be something else, something that had a strong impact on you. I speculated for a week, and everything pointed toward your first marriage. Don't blame Millie, I made her tell me!" He smiled nodding his head in assurance that he wasn't upset.

"I'm not mad at Millie nor you! But, don't be fooled, nobody can make Millie do what she doesn't want to do. I bet she was burning the whole time to acquaint you with all the details about her least favorite person!"

"Well, I equally burned to hear it, but I was never able to ask her before, to make myself listen how much -" She blabbered out and regretted the same moment.

"How much – what?" George closely observed her embarrassment.

"Oh, nothing!" Patricia lowered her head over the plate of food.

"Patricia, I want to know. I have to know!" The change in his voice rushed tremor through her body.

"How much you loved your wife!" She whispered at last.

"Loved her? Whatever made you think I loved her?" He was astonished.

"You never wanted to talk about her. When a person loses someone he deeply loves, he usually doesn't want to talk about it out of pain, and Tim told us -"

"Tim? He never knew anything about Tiffany and me. When he visited the ranch for the first time, Tiffany was in England, so how could he say something like that?" George shouted in disbelieve.

"It's to be blamed on Francesca and me. When you came to visit us that first time, my sister and I were making fun of you. Well, we were making fun of Tim's exaggerations of you. As he insisted more of making you a prince, we twisted his every word making you a toad. So, I think he wanted to soften our hearts by a sad story about your beloved dead wife, although, I'm positive he believes it's the truth. Did you ever talk to him about your marriage?"

"No, I never did! How foolish of me! In college every time I was in a relationship, I made it clear I was engaged to my childhood sweetheart back home. It was so convenient because I never fell in love before -" He hastily lowered his eyes, collecting dirty dishes.

"Before what?" Her heart jumped into her throat. *Before he met Alicia or some other gorgeous woman.*

An eternity went by, while George silently went after his business of gathering camping equipment. It seemed as he did not hear her question. With her throbbing heart, she dared not to breathe. Just waited. He slowly raised his eyes to meet hers. With a frozen mask of apprehension, wide open eyes in expectation, she looked like a little girl.

"I met you!" The circumstance, exhaustion, concern, and anguish of the last five days had worn out his nerves, and lowered his shield of protection. In any other normal situation he would have never let his guard down, but days of nerve wracking tracking and chase, and now something in her expression, diminished his control.

Those three words petrified Patricia's life force. *What is he saying?* She did not dare to believe. Is something wrong with her hearing? Does she heard what her heart desired or did he really say it? George watched her solemn face and turmoil behind her eyes. He did not mean to shock her like this. How is she accepting his clumsy discourse? His attempt to speak and lessen his declaration, but was stopped by her question.

"What are you saying, Gorge?" The seriousness in her voice, and the realization that he had gone too far to retract his admission.

"I'm saying that I love you, Patricia!" He said softly. He wanted some reaction. Any reaction. Happiness preferably, anger or even ridicule, would be better than this impenetrable façade?

"You love me?" She did hear correctly. "How is that possible? Since when?" She blabbered out unconsciously, she just could not believe it. She did not dare to believe.

"What do you mean since when? Since ever. Since you ran into my arms on those damn stairs. I did think you, at that time, somehow plain and simple, but when I grabbed you to prevent your fall, the molten lava rushed through my veins in place of my blood. That whole damn evening i watched you, comparing you to your glamorous sister other women in my life. I tried to find a single thing against you, something silly that I could despise. Anything. Anything to stop that unknown fire in my stomach!" While talking to her while putting out the fire, glancing in her direction every so often.

"But you did despise me! It was obvious in every word. Glance!" She remembered well the feeling of inferiority under his scrutinizing stare.

"I was jealous!" He breathed out.

"Jealous? Of what? Whom?" She could not believe her ears.

"Everybody! Tim, for one. If I wasn't so smitten with you, I would have probably needed a week to notice his love for you, if ever. Your relationship was somehow too personal. Every time he touched you, or hugged you, which he did way too often, I had the urge to spill his blood. Anger made me insane! Anger, mainly at myself because of how I felt about you, then anger toward Tim, who couldn't stop calling you "my girl" Then that character Michael. He never stopped nagging, but you had ultimate patience with him. Besides, Francesca was sure you'd marry him. Damn, I was in more trouble than ever in my life!" A little laughter on his own account escaped from his throat.

"I can hardly believe it! You looked so anxious to go. I remember explicitly you couldn't wait to get me out of your site!" She cried. For a moment George silently looked down at the ground, then straight into her eyes.

"Yes, I did! I literally ran for my life! Do you think I liked what was happening to me? I never ever in my entire life experienced anything like that. All I wanted in that moment was to get as far away as possible from you or I would do something stupid."

"Like what?"

"Like grab you, carry you up to your bedroom, and make love to you until you couldn't be able to move. Heavens, Patricia, I had only one thought in my mind – if I didn't see you any more, I'd forgot all about you in time!" He drew his hand through his rumpled hair. Her heart skipped a beat. How many times she saw this gesture, and every time wished to trace the path of his hand.

"Well? Did you?" She knew that he most likely did not, but it would be heaven to hear it from his mouth.

"What do you think?" He snapped impatiently, "If I did I wouldn't have been back in a month being determined to do whatever it took to make you marry me, would I?"

"You did that. We did that to help Francesca and Tim and, of course, for your kids!"

"It doesn't matter how much I love and admire Tim, I'm not sure I would put myself in a situation to marry a woman I didn't even know! But, how could I not fall in love with you? You, in your little black dress with mom's pearls and that delicious food you cooked to impress me, or to confirm Tim's bragging about it – I didn't know which. Then, how you were with Timmy and Puppet! Watching you play with them, I felt the emptiness in my kid's lives. You were more mother to your niece and nephew than Francisca. When I got back home to my family, I asked myself, why not my kids? Why not me?" George dived deep into his memories, his face tensed reliving his struggles. Patricia craved to hear more, but was reluctant to disturb him. Then, he was back, turning to her, as he was checking to see if she was still here.

"So, that's how my big scheme was born. First, I prepared the house and people in my household for you. Redecoration of your bedroom and dressing room for me, was an easier task then convincing my children to, at least, wait to meet you before they ran away from home. I never doubted that I would be able to manipulate you into marrying me. My vanity took for granted that you were seeking my attentions, like all the women who saw a dollar sign in my place. Hahaha." He laughed, but it sounded bitter.

"But, you surprised me as always. You can't even imagine my terror when I arrived at Tim's house and found you cozily stretched out in Tim's back yard. It looked as though I came too late. My first impulse was to turn around and run back home. What stopped me was a deep feeling that you wouldn't break your own sister's marriage, no matter what. But, knowing what love can do to a person, was ever so fresh on my mind. There I was acting totally atypical for me, with sweaty palms, knowing that my whole life depended on what you would do. And there you were, sitting under the tree with a children having a nap beside you. The picture of my vision. That should be my tree and my children. Frustration was building."

"George, I remember very well how you acted. Your appearance was everything but of a man who came to woo a woman into marrying him! You treated me as I was some wanton woman. Every second sentence directed to me was an accusation of seducing my brother-in-law!" Her memory selectively popped up all the obnoxious stunts he pulled on her.

"I was hurt and disillusioned!" Her shocked expression amused him, "First, you killed my ego by being genuinely annoyed at seeing me again so soon. My hopes were seriously shook. Second, my proposition to marry me was repulsive to you more than destroying your sister's happiness. At that point you became a challenge. I realized that your standards in life were reputable to the point of no negotiation. That was new for me, and I wasn't sure I could handle it!"

"I did agree to marry you, George! You *did* handle me like a business!"

"Well, that is one other thing I'm not particularly proud of!" His voice was full of regret.

"One?" She stared at the man in front of her more confused with every next admission.

"What I should have done was, when I managed to trick you into this unfair deal was to court you, to make you feel like a woman who is appreciated and loved, but I was afraid!" His voice was oddly unsettled.

"Afraid?" Patricia was taken aback, unable to see him being afraid of anything.

"To control myself beside you was never easy! I desperately wanted to touch you, which I did in front of others as much as I dared. It wasn't enough, I wanted more. I wanted your response. I lost count of how many sleepless nights I spent staring at that blasted door between our bedrooms. Not once did I rush to open it to claim what was mine. Then, I would see your reproaching glare, disgust or even worse hate! I didn't know what to do to make you love me, so I behaved like a jerk!

"No, you didn't! Most of the time you were a perfect gentleman" You remember L.A.? I was drunk, and completely out of decorum! You made me feel like it was not a big deal!"

"Amazing thing is, Patricia, sometimes you are like a little girl who knows nothing: Moraine dressed you in that incredibly sexy dress. Your hair and makeup, everything about you was different, but you were ever so yourself. For a long time I knew that you are beautiful, but never like that night! Every man in that damn restaurant stared. I couldn't take my eyes off you. I never wanted any woman as much as I wanted you that night, and believe me, if you hadn't been drunk, I would probably have made the biggest mistake of my life." Patricia mockingly raised one eyebrow and let out a little loving laugh.

"Until the *mistake* at Lake Tahoe!" George actually blushed. "Oh yes, Lake Tahoe! I dreamed of some chance like that. That storm cut us from the rest of the world. Being so insolated, just you and me. I did want to be fair to you. But it was out of my control, especially since you didn't object. let's say to my advances. We were very seldom alone. Always the kids were around, Millie, and a dozen other people. Suddenly there you were, mine. I held you in my arms while we danced, and I was lost. That morning I wanted to kill myself. What I expected was your hatred, but you… you are not the type who can hate anybody!" The goose bumps prickled the skin down her spine. She never heard him speak in such a soft voice. A stream of pure love flowed through her soul.

"Well George, those are *big* sins!" She mocked again, "I forgive you! After all you were my knight in shining armor today! What damsel in distress can resist such a romantic act!" Seeing him so totally vulnerable, knowing he'll hate himself tomorrow for it, Patricia tried to smooth things over with a little bit of humor. It looked to her that his soul searching through his memories put him into glum and anger.

"That is not all, Patricia! I tried to manipulate you. Something like that can't be forgotten so easily. Maybe my actions in the beginning could be overlooked! My feelings were such a novelty for me that I couldn't think rationally. I didn't have right to use Tim's infatuations as a means of persuasion, but at the time I thought I'd be doing a favor for all of us - save Tim's marriage, spare you the anguish of being the means of your sister's tragedy, giving my children the best possible mother, I could, and me. I knew I'd have to make you mine. You were in my every thought night and day. I always believed that love is the invention of fools, fools without purpose and wits, but when stricken I turned into a manipulating brainless fool myself. That's my only excuse, Patricia, to dragging you in all of this. I just hope you'll be able to forgive me in time. But trying to get you pregnant, just to keep you is beyond me, and I can't blame you if you leave for that reason."

"George, what are you saying?" Patricia knew, she had to finish this torment. He did look like he was on the brink of defeat. Urge to throw herself into his arms proclaiming her love and end his misery was more that she could bear, but she had to know! Is it possible, he wanted a child with her?

"After my stupid pride made me act as an imbecile by casting you out of my life on the Fourth of July, I didn't know what to do? I wanted you more than ever, but the thought that you loved someone else drove me insane. One moment I knew you were too honest not to tell me. I *knew* women all too well. On a top of it, your family arrived. On the outside we were the epitome of a perfect couple. I never wanted more that to be the truth. Tim, the day before we went up the mountain, asked what I was waiting for, pointing out that you are ready for motherhood. I have to admit, it did cross my mind several times before, all that intimacy could result in a baby. I was comfortable with it, but after Tim put that bug into my head, it looked like a solution to my problem."

"I wanted our lives to get back where they were, and more importantly, I wanted you to stay with me forever. At the time, I wasn't sure that you would. A baby seemed like the perfect answer for my predicament. So, I acted abominably up in the cabin, you remember? Don't take me wrong, I would probably have made love to you anyway. It was never easy for me to be alone with you and not want to hold you. Regrettably, the truth is the baby was my main motivation. It didn't last long. On the way back I realized it was for a wrong reason, and that a child is something both of us should want. Back home I stopped. I couldn't trap you like that. For days I wondered what to do? The conclusion was I have to put my cards on the table and plead for your compassion! I had an idea to take you to some romantic place, where we could be alone, and talk things through. I planned a trip to the Virgin Islands that blasted day you were kidnaped." George was exhausted. It seemed as all his energy ran out of him.

"George, what make you think that I wouldn't want a baby?" Patricia knew it was time to finish this torment. "I do, especially your baby! I thought you knew that I love you!" George's head jerked up, disbelief was written in his eyes, but just for a moment. He sprang up, and in two big strides he reached her side. Patricia found herself pressed to his broad chest, more crushed. For a very, very long time he held her tight, not that she minded a bit. Incoherent murmuring was muffled in her hair, where George had buried his face. She happily leaned into the length of his body. Being nested like this was heaven, and the only place in the world where she wanted to be anyway.

George slowly loosened his grasp on her, and looked into her eyes, holding her by the shoulders. "Tell me again, please, my darling! Tell me." His face was glowing, softening his rather sharp features.

"I love you, George. I do!" Patricia's eyes radiated the warmth of her love. She wanted to tell him in thousands of ways how much she loved him, but she'd have the rest of her life to do that. Now, she had a more important thing to tell. One which will make him even happier.

"George, that idea of yours, you know, to make me pregnant!" She started, not knowing how

to tell him, "It worked!" She whispered.

"Worked? What are you talking about?" The next second his face shone with the most exquisite delight, "Do you want to tell me that you are pregnant?" She just nodded.

George scooped her into his arms, then released her in fear he would harm the baby. He laughed and frowned alternately, in one moment kissing her forehead with ultimate gentleness, next passionately crushing her lips.

"Let's sit under that tree over there. The helicopter will come soon to pick us up, we can at least be comfortable!" George happily smiled, lifting her into his arms with no effort. Cozily nestled in his lap, Patricia experienced complete happiness. Words were not necessary, their hearts were beating as one.

*****

A year later, Francesca and her family visited the ranch again. A four month old boy was the center of attention.

"That's not fair, Aunt Francesca, another boy! I wanted a girl, to have someone to play with, but no-o-o she had to have a boy!" Lindsay nagged, although all the time she looked at her youngest brother with adoration.

"Be patient, Lindsay, my dear!" George proudly held the little boy, "The next one will be a girl for sure. Patricia will do the impossible just to make you happy!" Everybody laughed.

"And, if that's goes badly, Aunt Francesca and I are working very seriously on our next child, which has a great chance to be a girl!" Tim smiled at Lindsay, hugging his wife. Millie entered the great room carrying a tray with coffee and lemonade for the children.

"Okay George, all of us are here, as you wished, can we finally know what the boy's name is? I'm tired of calling him a "baby" or a "boy"!" Millie placed the tray on the coffee table, resting her hands on her hips, "Four months without a name is plenty!"

"My dear impatient Millie, it was never up to me! My beautiful wife was the one who wanted her whole family to be present, because the decision is hers! I'm curious as much as you are!" He hugged the older woman, turning to his wife, "Well honey, the ball is in your corner!"

Everybody stared in expectation. Patricia looked down at the sleeping baby in her arms, then up at all those loving faces.

"I knew what I wanted to name him from the moment I knew he was on his way, but, first I waited to see if he was going to be a boy or" - Her loving glance brushed over Lindsay - "this little rascal could succeed with her Voodoo. So, I want my son to be named after his grandfathers, Samuel Robert!"

Content buzz of approval swept the room. George looked at her for a long moment than sat down beside her, circling his arm around his wife and youngest son with loving gentleness.

"This is the best choice, my dear!" He kissed her forehead. She was *his* best choice, being thankful for the opportunity to make that choice.

The End

www.ingramcontent.com/pod-product-compliance
Lightning Source LLC
Chambersburg PA
CBHW060909120626
46553CB00001B/257

9 79 88 93 91 06 74